BASIC
FOR HOME COMPUTERS

MORE THAN A MILLION PEOPLE HAVE LEARNED TO PROGRAM, USE,
AND ENJOY MICROCOMPUTERS WITH WILEY PAPERBACK GUIDES. LOOK
FOR THEM ALL AT YOUR FAVORITE BOOKSHOP OR COMPUTER STORE:

BASIC
FOR HOME COMPUTERS

BOB ALBRECHT
LEROY FINKEL
and
JERALD R. BROWN

Dymax Corporation
Menlo Park, California

JOHN WILEY & SONS

New York • Chichester • Brisbane • Toronto • Singapore

Editors: Judy Wilson and Irene Brownstone
Production Manager: Ken Burke
Editorial Supervisor: Winn Kalmon
Artist: Brenda Tighe

Photograph credits

Page 4. Courtesy of Apple Computer, Inc., Cupertino, California.
Page 6. Courtesy of Radio Shack, A Tandy Company.
Page 7. Courtesy of Processor Technology Corporation, Pleasanton, California.
Page 8. Used by permission, Commodore International Limited, Palo Alto, California.

Library of Congress Cataloging in Publication Data:

Albrecht, Robert L.
    BASIC for home computers.

    (Wiley self-teaching guides)
    Includes index.
    1. BASIC (Computer program language) I. Finkel,
LeRoy, joint author. II. Brown, Jerald, 1940-
joint author. III. Title.
QA76.73.B3A413   001.6'424   78-9010
ISBN 0-471-03204-2

Printed in the United States of America

78 79   14 13 12 11

Acknowledgments

The authors wish to thank MITS Inc. for the loan of a MITS ALTAIR 8800B computer to be used in developing this book.

To The Reader

With the advent of integrated circuits and miniaturization in electronics, suddenly a complete computer, with all the peripherals or attachments needed to use it, can be purchased for as little as $600. Now a computer for your home, club, school or business is in the same price range as the less expensive stereo component systems! Many of these inexpensive computers use the computer language BASIC.

BASIC was developed at Dartmouth College by John Kemeny and Thomas Kurtz who recognized the need for an all-purpose computer language that would be suitable for beginning programmers whose educational backgrounds would be varied and diverse. Beginners All-purpose Symbolic Instruction Code (BASIC) was originally designed as a simple language which could be learned in a few short hours. With improvements over the years, the language now may take a few days to learn, but you will find that you can do nearly anything you want in BASIC. And with this Self-Teaching Guide, you don't even need access to a computer to learn BASIC—you need only this book and a pencil.

The BASIC you learn in this book will apply to any computer that "understands" a similar version of BASIC. To show you how to converse with a computer using BASIC programs, we have used the particular version of BASIC called MICROSOFT™ BASIC, developed by the Microsoft Corporation. MICROSOFT has written the BASIC you will find on personal computers like the Commodore PET, Radio Shack TRS-80, Apple, Ohio Scientific Chullenzer, some HEATH Computers and others. Most BASICs found on personal Computers are similar (interestingly, some of the most advanced and versatile versions of BASIC are those developed by manufacturers of personal computers). In this book we have tried to point out some of the common variations in BASIC that you may encounter, so that you can easily adapt what you learn from this book to other computers that also "speak" BASIC.

If you *do* have a personal computer to use, be certain that BASIC is installed in the computer's memory, so it will understand instructions given in BASIC. We can't help you do that because the procedure is different for each brand of computer. Some of the least expensive computers, such as the Commodore PET computer and Radio Shack's TRS-80 microcomputer, have BASIC built into the electronics as part of the computer system. With these systems, you simply plug the computer into an electrical outlet, turn it on, and use it—no "loading" required. Many other computers are made to use various computer languages, BASIC among them. For such computers, you or someone else may have to "load" or install or otherwise get BASIC into the memory of the computer.

Perhaps the system you will use isn't a personal computer at all. It may be a larger, more expensive computer, such as a Digital Equipment Corporation (DEC) computer using the language DEC BASIC PLUS™. MICRO-SOFT™ BASIC and BASIC PLUS™ are very similar; nearly everything in this book will be applicable to BASIC PLUS™. When using a large computer system, you may never see or be near the computer itself; instead you will use a computer terminal connected to the computer by wires or even by telephone. You see, computers are general purpose machines. Any computer, whether it is a personal computer or a million dollar business computer system, can do the same things—that is, perform the same basic electronic operations.

With the development of low cost computers, literally hundreds of small retail computer stores have appeared in the U.S. and Canada and other countries. These businesses sell ready-to-use small business computer systems such as the Northstar Horizon, Alpha Micro Systems, and Cromemco as well as assemble-it-yourself computer kits. They also sell computers for personal use such as PET, Apple, Compucolor, EXIDY, Texas Instruments, Atari and Radio Shack. All of these computers use a BASIC similar to the language you will learn from this book.

Dozens of publications and magazines for the beginner, intermediate, and advanced nonprofessional computer user have also appeared. They are a good source of information on where to shop for a personal computer system, as well as what to do with it once you have it working. A list of some of the popular periodicals (including one of the oldest as well as one of the most recent, both founded by the authors) can be found in the Appendixes.

Now take a look at How to Use This Book, and then go on to learn BASIC!

How to Use This Book

With this book's self-instructional format, you'll be actively involved in learning BASIC. The material is presented in short numbered sections called frames, each of which teaches you something new about BASIC and gives you a question or asks you to write a program. Correct answers are given following the dashed line. For the most effective learning we urge you to use a thick paper to keep the answers out of sight until you have written your answer.

You will learn best if you take pen or pencil in hand and actually write out the answers or programs. The questions are carefully designed to call your attention to important points in the examples and explanations, and to help you learn to apply what is being explained or demonstrated.

Each chapter begins with a list of objectives—what you will be able to do after completing that chapter. If you have had some previous experience using BASIC and the objectives for that chapter look familiar, take the Self-Test at the end of that chapter first to see where you should start your close reading of the book. If you do well, study only the frames indicated for the questions you missed. If you miss many questions, start work at the beginning of that chapter.

The Self-Test can also be used as a review of the material covered in the chapter. You may test yourself immediately after reading the chapter. Or you may wish to read a chapter, take a break, and save the Self-Test as a review before you begin the next chapter. At the end of the book is a Final Self-Test which will allow you to test your overall understanding of BASIC.

This is a self-contained book for learning the computer language called BASIC. You do not need access to a computer to learn BASIC. However, what you learn will be theoretical until you actually sit down at a computer terminal and apply your knowledge of the computer language and programming techniques. So we strongly recommend that you and this book get together with a computer. BASIC will be easier and clearer if you have even occasional access to a computer so that you can try the examples and exercises, make your own modifications, and invent your own programs for your own purposes. But computer access is *not* essential; all you need is this Self-Teaching Guide. You are now ready to teach yourself how to use BASIC.

Contents

BASIC
FOR HOME COMPUTERS

CHAPTER ONE

Your Personal Computer

This chapter will introduce you to low-cost, personal-size computers for home, school, club, or business use. When you complete this chapter, you will know more about some of the personal computers available. You will also be able to use the following words and phrases from the language of the computer world.

> computer language
> BASIC and, specifically, MICROSOFT™ BASIC
> teletypewriter and TTY
> keyboard
> printer
> terminal
> video terminal and video monitor
> cathode ray tube and CRT
> program and programming
> BASIC statements
> line numbers

1.   We will start slowly and simply, easing you gently into the world of personal computers and BASIC. Just keep in mind that this is intended to be a friendly book about personal computing, and an easy-to-learn, easy-to-use computer language called BASIC. We will do our best to teach you how to read and understand computer programs written in BASIC and to help you get started writing original, never-before-seen-on-earth programs, *your* programs.

A personal computer may be one of many types. We'll discuss some of the most common variations in the next few pages. For this book to be useful to you, only one thing is essential: your computer must speak a version

of the computer language called _____.

— — — — — — — — — — —

BASIC

2.   The personal computer we use speaks a version called MICROSOFT™ BASIC. Most BASICs used on personal computers are very similar to MICROSOFT™ BASIC. The differences that exist are minor, as you will see; even though this book emphasizes MICROSOFT™ BASIC, you should find it useful no matter what particular BASIC you are using. (The reference manual for your version of BASIC will come in handy.)

We don't know just what the computer you use looks like, but ours looks like the one shown below.

The ALTAIR 8800b

Our personal computer system consists of an ALTAIR 8800b computer connected to a *teletypewriter.* Similar to an electric typewriter, the teletypewriter consists of a keyboard and a printer. (See the sketch of a teletypewriter on the next page.)

We use the keyboard to type information into the computer. As we type characters, the information we type is sent to the computer and also is printed on the printer, thus providing a printed record of what we have typed.

The computer also types information on the printer. Thus, the teletypewriter provides (one-way or two-way—choose the correct answer) _____

_____ communication with the computer.

— — — — — — — — — —

two-way

3.   Below is a sketch of the teletypewriter. We have identified the key-board and the printer.

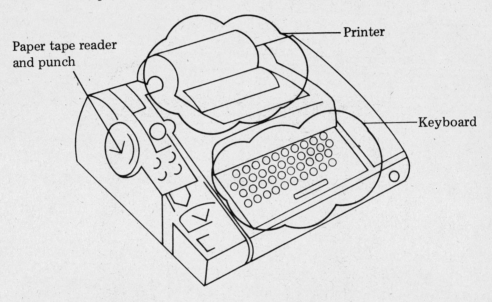

Paper tape reader and punch

Printer

Keyboard

(a)   We use the keyboard to type information into the computer. What happens to the information that we type? _____

_____

(b)   How does the computer communicate with us, the users? _____

_____

— — — — — — — — — — — —

(a)   It is sent to the computer and is also printed on the printer.
(b)   It prints information on the printer.

4.   Since "teletypewriter" is such a long word, people frequently abbreviate it as "TTY" (pronounced "tee tee why"). In this book you will use the information we type into the computer and the information it types back to us. This information is shown as it would be printed on a TTY. The information printed by the TTY on paper is often called "hard copy," because it is something substantial that you can take with you after you have used the computer.

(a)   Whenever we refer to the TTY, what do we mean? _____

_____

(b) What two main parts of the TTY do we use to communicate with the computer? _____

_ _ _ _ _ _ _ _ _ _ _

(a) teletypewriter; (b) the keyboard and the printer

5.   If you have access to a personal computer, it may look more like the one pictured below.

The TRS-80 Color Computer

Instead of a teletypewriter, this personal computer system has a *video terminal*. The video terminal consists of a keyboard and a televisionlike screen.

You would use the keyboard to type information into the computer, just as you would use the TTY keyboard to communicate with the computer. However, as you type on the keyboard, the information is printed on the screen instead of on paper. The computer, in turn, also prints information on the screen.

(a) In the computer system pictured above, how do you send information to the computer? _____

(b) How does the computer communicate with you? _____
_____

(c) What are the two parts of a video terminal?_____

— — — — — — — — — —

(a) You type it on the keyboard.
(b) It prints information on the video screen.
(c) A keyboard and a video screen.

6.   The video terminal is also called a *CRT terminal.* "CRT" is an abbreviation for *C*athode *R*ay *T*ube.
     What is another name for the CRT or the CRT terminal? _____
_____

— — — — — — — — — —

video terminal or cathode ray tube terminal

7.   Perhaps *neither* of the computers described above looks like *your* personal computer. Well, maybe it looks like one of those pictured below.

The APPLE II

The Atari 400 Personal Computer System

The TRS-80 Model III Microcomputer

These personal computer systems consist of a keyboard, a computer, and a television set. The computer is inside the keyboard unit. This kind of system is essentially the same as the video terminal of frame 5; the main difference is that the keyboard and the screen are not combined into one unit. The TV can be a standard television set such as you have at home or a more expensive *video monitor.*

(a)   With this kind of system also, we type information into the computer

on the _____.

(b)   The information we type is displayed or printed on the TV screen, and

the computer displays or prints information on the _____.

— — — — — — — — — — —

(a) keyboard; (b) TV screen or TV set

8.   Some of the least expensive personal computers are now made with the computer, keyboard, CRT, and a cassette recorder all built into one unit. One is shown on the following page.

The IBM Personal Computer

The cassette recorder is a memory storage device which is separate from the computer's own electronic memory. It can be used to store or save your computer programs and information (called data) such as mailing lists, recipes, appointments, and budget or accounting figures. Once you have mastered the BASIC computer language, you will find this kind of storage device quite handy and easy to use. In addition to cassette tapes, there are other ways to store information and programs separate from the computer. All such *external* storage methods are convenient ways to feed or "load" programs and information you often use into the computer without taking all the time needed to type them in from a keyboard. Punched paper tape, magnetic disks, and even phonograph recordings are other external storage methods. However, in this book you need only the three main parts of a

computer system we have discussed earlier, which are _____

_____.

_ _ _ _ _ _ _ _ _ _ _

_____

a computer, a keyboard, and a printer such as a TTY or a CRT

9. Think back over frames 1 through 8. We have described several personal computer systems. For our purposes, the important ingredients are these:

(1) The computer itself. The computer we are using to write this book is an ALTAIR 8800b. However, any computer that can "converse" in a version of BASIC similar to MICROSOFT™ BASIC is suitable for our purposes. It may be close at hand, or, in the case of a larger computer, at the other end of some wires or a telephone line. (If you haven't already read To the Reader on page vii, do so now. Then continue here.)

(2) A keyboard, which we use to type information into our computer.

(3) A device—either a printer or a video screen—which displays information typed on the keyboard or sent by the computer.

(4) BASIC installed in the computer, ready to go.

For most of our discussions, we have used a teletypewriter (TTY). However, if you have a chance to use a video terminal (CRT), you will find it very easy to transfer ideas for use on your system.

In this book, we will show you many *programs* in MICROSOFT™ BASIC, and will help you learn to read, understand, and use these programs for your own enjoyment. We will concentrate on applications that we think will be of interest to users of home/school/personal computers. And so . . . for our appetizer, a computer game.

```
100 REMARK *** THIS IS A SIMPLE COMPUTER GAME
110 LET X = INT(100*RND(1))+1
120 PRINT
130 PRINT "I'M THINKING OF A NUMBER FROM 1 TO 100."
140 PRINT "GUESS MY NUMBER!!!"
150 PRINT : INPUT "YOUR GUESS"; G
160 IF G<X THEN PRINT "TRY A BIGGER NUMBER." : GOTO 150
170 IF G>X THEN PRINT "TRY A SMALLER NUMBER." : GOTO 150
180 IF G=X THEN PRINT "THAT'S IT!!! YOU GUESSED MY NUMBER." : GOTO 110
```

These lines, down to the word RUN, are a computer program.

```
RUN

I'M THINKING OF A NUMBER FROM 1 TO 100.
GUESS MY NUMBER!!!

YOUR GUESS? 50
TRY A BIGGER NUMBER.

YOUR GUESS? 90
TRY A SMALLER NUMBER.

YOUR GUESS? 75
TRY A SMALLER NUMBER.

YOUR GUESS? 65
TRY A SMALLER NUMBER.

YOUR GUESS? 58
TRY A BIGGER NUMBER.

YOUR GUESS? 62
TRY A SMALLER NUMBER.

YOUR GUESS? 60
TRY A BIGGER NUMBER.

YOUR GUESS? 61
THAT'S IT!!! YOU GUESSED MY NUMBER.

I'M THINKING OF A NUMBER FROM 1 TO 100.
GUESS MY NUMBER!!!

YOUR GUESS?
```

And this is what the computer does that appears on the TTY or CRT.

The guesses are typed by the computer user.

This part is called a RUN of the program. The computer generates a random number from 1 to 100. The player types in guesses. After each guess, the computer types a clue to help the player make a better guess.

If this sounds confusing, read on! All will be revealed. And it won't be long before you can read and write programs like this in BASIC.

And so on. Chances are that the computer will have a different number this time.

Look again at the program shown in our computer game. The program consists of nine (9) *lines*, each containing one or more BASIC *statements*. Each line begins with a *line number*.

This is a line number.

130 PRINT "I'M THINKING OF A NUMBER FROM 1 TO 100."

This is a statement.

In our program, each numbered line contains one or more BASIC _____

_____. The numbers, 100 through 180, are called _____.

— — — — — — — — — —

statements; line numbers

10.   The program in frame 9 was typed one line at a time, on the keyboard.
As we typed it, the program was stored in the computer and also printed on
the printer.
      On a video terminal, as we type the program, it will be stored in the

computer and also will appear on the _____.

— — — — — — — — — —

screen (video, TV, or CRT)

Note: Video terminals can typically display from 12 to 25 lines, depending
on the terminal. So, if the screen is filled, new information typed in will
cause old information to be "pushed off" the screen.

11.   First, we typed in the entire program (lines 100 through 180). This
process is called "entering the program." This stored the program in the
computer's memory. Then we typed RUN. This tells the computer to RUN,
or carry out, the program. Computer people also say "to *execute* the program." In other words, after storing the program, we then told the computer
to follow the instructions (statements) of the program, or execute the program.
      If there is a program in the computer's memory, then typing RUN tells

the computer to _____.

— — — — — — — — — —

carry out or execute the instructions in the program.

12.   During the RUN, the computer obeyed the instructions (statements) in
the program, as follows: First, the computer generated a random number
from 1 to 100, inclusive (line 110). This number is an integer—a "whole"
number with no fractional part.

```
110 LET  X  =  INT(100*RND(1))+1
```

Next, the computer typed instructions to the player (lines 120, 130, and
140).

```
120 PRINT
130 PRINT "I'M THINKING OF A NUMBER FROM 1 TO 100."
140 PRINT "GUESS MY NUMBER!!!"
```

Then, the computer asked for a guess (line 150).

```
150 PRINT : INPUT "YOUR GUESS"; G
```

After the player typed a guess, the computer compared the guess with its secret number and gave the player the appropriate response (lines 160, 170, and 180).

```
160 IF G<X THEN PRINT "TRY A BIGGER NUMBER." : GOTO 150
170 IF G>X THEN PRINT "TRY A SMALLER NUMBER." : GOTO 150
180 IF G=X THEN PRINT "THAT'S IT!!! YOU GUESSED MY NUMBER." : GOTO 110
```

If the player did *not* guess the computer's number, the computer went back to line 150 and asked for another guess. But, if the lucky player *did* guess the secret number, the computer acknowledged the correct guess and went back to line 110 to "think" of another number.

```
100 REMARK *** THIS IS A SIMPLE COMPUTER GAME
```

Oh yes, line 100 is a REMARK statement. It doesn't tell the computer to *do* anything. It is simply included to tell something *about* the program to us humans who may read the program itself.

What do we type to instruct the computer to execute or carry out a program? _____

— — — — — — — — — —

RUN

Now, to see how much you've learned from this first chapter, try the Self-Test. Then on to Chapter 2 where you'll start to learn how to actually use the computer.

SELF-TEST

Try this Self-Test, so you can evaluate how much you have learned so far.

1. If your computer does not have an electric typewriter or teletypewriter as a terminal for communicating with the computer, what other kind of terminal would you expect it to have? _____

2. If your computer "speaks" a different BASIC than our computer does, would you expect your computer to "understand" the terminology taught in this book? _____

3. Since a computer doesn't have legs, what do we want a computer to do when we tell it to RUN? _____

Answers to Self-Test

The frame numbers in parentheses refer to the frames in the chapter where the topic is discussed. You may wish to refer to these for quick review.

1. a CRT (or video terminal) (frames 4-7)

2. yes, because most versions of BASIC for personal computers are like the one we use, with only minor differences which will quickly become obvious (frame 1)

3. execute the program (follow the instructions we give it) (frames 11, 12)

CHAPTER TWO

Getting Started

To get you started in computer programming in BASIC, we will now introduce you to some of the statements used to instruct the computer, that is, to tell it what you want accomplished. In this chapter, you will use the *direct*, or immediate, mode of operation. Using direct mode, you tell the computer something to do, and it does it immediately. When you complete this chapter, you will be able to:

- use direct statements to instruct the computer;
- recognize error messages from the computer;
- use the PRINT statement with quotation marks to print strings (messages);
- correct typing errors or delete a statement with errors;
- use direct statements to do arithmetic;
- compute values of simple mathematical expressions using the symbols and rules of BASIC for arithmetic;
- use the short form for PRINT statements (?);
- recognize and convert floating point or E notation to ordinary numbers.

1. Now we begin "talking" with the computer. The computer is plugged in, our terminal is connected to the computer, the system is on, BASIC is resident in the computer. . . . We are ready to begin.

We will start by assuming that we are using a TTY (teletypewriter) to communicate with the computer. On the following page is a typical TTY keyboard diagram.

In the diagram, there is a large black arrow pointing to the key labeled

_____ .

— — — — — — — — — —

RETURN

Other keyboards may have a different RETURN key and it may be in a different place. If *your* keyboard does not have a RETURN key, find out what key is used in place of RETURN.

2.   If you press RETURN (without typing anything else), the computer will space up one line on the printer. This is called a *line feed.* Then the computer prints OK. If you are lucky enough to be sitting in front of a computer, you could try this: Type your name and press RETURN. The computer will probably print an *error message* on the printer.

We type: BOB, LEROY, AND JERRY

It types: SN ERROR
              OK

By "it" we mean the computer. Saves space in writing this book!

Hmmmm . . . we know what ERROR means, but what about SN? Well, SN is an abbreviation for SYNTAX. You see, the computer is of quite limited intelligence. It simply did not understand us.

(a)   If you type something, then press RETURN, and the computer types

SN ERROR, what is the computer trying to tell you? _____

_____

(b)   After typing SN ERROR, what did the computer type? _____

— — — — — — — — — — —

_____

(a)   It does not understand you.
(b)   OK

The OK is MICROSOFT™ BASIC's way to let you know that everything is OK. No damage has been done. The computer is very patient and forgiving. It will let you make as many mistakes as you wish, then still say OK. Whenever you see OK, you know it is *your* turn to type. Note: This message may be different for your computer system or for the version of BASIC being used, but the idea is exactly the same.

3.   To avoid misunderstandings with a computer, we must learn its language. We will start with some simple, one-line statements that the computer *does* understand.

In this chapter we will use direct statements. Direct statements do not have line numbers. When you type a direct statement and press RETURN, the computer executes the statement immediately, then forgets the statement. We call this BASIC's *direct* mode of operation. Here is an example of a statement that is "executed in direct mode."

We type: `PRINT "MY HUMAN UNDERSTANDS ME"`   Then we press RETURN.

It types: `MY HUMAN UNDERSTANDS ME`
`OK`

Now you complete the following.

We type: `PRINT "WAKE UP! BURGLARS ARE IN THE HOUSE."`   Then we press RETURN.

It types: _____

_____

— — — — — — — — —

`WAKE UP! BURGLARS ARE IN THE HOUSE.`
`OK`

Along with the wake up message, we could also arrange (as we'll see later) to have the computer ring the bell on the TTY several times or to sound some other audible alarm (with appropriate electronic connections). By the way, the computer doesn't mean it is OK that burglars are in the house. It's just saying it's OK for you to type on the keyboard.

4.   The statement PRINT "MY HUMAN UNDERSTANDS ME" is called a PRINT statement. It tells the computer to print something on the printer, or on the screen if you are using a video terminal. In this case, the computer

prints the verbal message following the word PRINT. Note that the message is enclosed in quotation marks. This message, enclosed in quotation marks, is called a *string*.

PRINT "MY HUMAN UNDERSTANDS ME"

This is a string. It is enclosed in quotation marks. The quotation marks enclose the string, but are not part of the string.

A *string* may include:

Numerals (0, 1, 2, . . .)
Letters (A, B, C, . . .)
Special characters (+, −, *, /, ↑, comma, period, etc.)

Since quotation marks define the beginning and the end of a string, do you think they can be used as a character in the string? _____

— — — — — — — — — —

No, they cannot. (That would *really* confuse the computer!) However, single quotes (') can be used in a string. For example:

We type: PRINT "THEY SAID, 'ALL RIGHT.'"

It types: THEY SAID, 'ALL RIGHT.'
          OK

5.   Complete the statement so that the computer types what we say it types.

We type: PRINT _____

It types: THE ROAST IS DONE.   TURN OFF THE OVEN.
          OK

— — — — — — — — — —

"THE ROAST IS DONE. TURN OFF THE OVEN."

Did you remember the quotation marks? Someday, of course, the computer will turn off the oven! Almost anything electric can be controlled by the computer, with the proper electronic connections *and* program, of course.

Note: From now on, we will often omit the OK typed by the computer. Saves space and paper and, especially, wear and tear on the authors.

6.   Have you made any typing mistakes yet? In case you should make a typing error, BASIC has a dandy way of fixing it. Watch while we make a typing error.

We type: PTINT "DENTIST APPOINTMENT TODAY"

It types: ?SN ERROR

We misspelled PRINT, so the computer doesn't know what we want. However, if we had noticed that we hit T when we meant to hit R, we could have corrected our mistake by using the *back arrow*.

On a TTY, the back arrow (←) is on the same key as the letter O (oh). To type a back arrow, hold down the SHIFT key and press the ← key.

We type: PT←RINT "DENTIST APPOINTMENT TODAY"

It types: DENTIST APPOINTMENT TODAY

The back arrow deletes (takes out or erases) the character it points to. Two back arrows will delete the two preceding characters, three back arrows will delete three characters, and so on.

In the above example, the back arrow deleted the letter _____.

Complete the following so that the computer prints what we want it to print.

We type: PRIMR _____ "TOMORROW IS YOUR MOTHER'S BIRTHDAY!!!"

It types: TOMORROW IS YOUR MOTHER'S BIRTHDAY!!!

— — — — — — — — — —

T

←←NT (The two back arrows delete the M and R, then we type N and T to complete the word, PRINT.)

7.   But suppose we make a mistake within a string? Watch.

We type: PRINT "MY HUMAN UNNERSTANS ME"

It types: MY HUMAN UNNERSTANS ME

Well, a string is a string and the computer will type it *exactly* as *you* typed it, misspellings and all. However, if you notice a mistake, you can correct it by using the back arrow.

Deletes 2nd N⌐   ⌐Deletes S and space

We type: PRINT "MY HUMAN UNN←DERSTANS ←←DS ME"

It types: MY HUMAN UNDERSTANDS ME

Notice that the computer considers a space as a character, just like a number, letter, or symbol. Remember, to delete the last character typed, type a back arrow. To delete the last two characters, type two back arrows, and so on. To delete the last three characters, type _____ back arrows.

— — — — — — — — — —

three

Remember, a space is a character. You can delete spaces by typing back arrows.

But you *can't* delete back arrows by typing back arrows.

8.   Look at our next attempt to enter or type a one-line direct statement.

PRINT "BASIK IS←←←←C IS EASY"

(a) What four characters are deleted in this direct statement? _____

(b) When we finished typing in the statement and pressed RETURN, what did the computer print? _____

— — — — — — — — — —

(a) K, space, I, S
(b) BASIC IS EASY

9.   Back arrows are great for deleting errors that you have just made. But, suppose you are typing a long line and are almost to the end when, alas, out of the left corner of your left eye, you spot a mistake way back at the

beginning. If you complete the line and press RETURN, you will probably get an error message. You would *like* to just abort the line—that is, erase it from the beginning.

Well, you can! Simply type @ (see note below). On a TTY, @ is on the same key as P. Hold down SHIFT and press the key.

We type: PRIMT "ONCE UPON A TIME THERE WAS A @

It types: OK

After we type @, the computer voids, or deletes, the line we have been typing and types OK. Whenever we see OK, what is the computer telling us?

_____

— — — — — — — — — —

It is our turn to type.

Note: If you are not using MICROSOFT™ BASIC, but are using some other version of BASIC, this may not work. Try holding down the CTRL key and pressing the C key. If that doesn't work, check the reference manual for your version of BASIC.

10.   We can also tell the computer to do arithmetic and print the answer. In other words, we can use the computer as a calculator.

We type: PRINT 7 + 5

It types: 12

The statement PRINT 7 + 5 tells the computer to compute the value of 7 + 5 (do the arithmetic) and then print the answer.

Note that actual calculations are indicated to the computer by *not* using quotation marks in the PRINT statement. Compare the formats below.

We type: PRINT "13 + 6"   We type: PRINT 13 + 6

It types: 13 + 6   It types: 19

Your turn. Complete the following, showing what the computer typed.

We type: PRINT 23 + 45

It types: _____

We type: PRINT 1 + 2 + 3 + 4 + 5

It types: _____

We type: PRINT 6.98 + 12.49

It types: _____

— — — — — — — — — —

68
15
19.47

11.   Subtraction? Of course.

We type: PRINT 7 - 5

It types: 2

We type: PRINT 25.68 - 37.95

It types: -12.27

Uh oh! Overdrawn.

Complete the following, showing what the computer typed.

We type: PRINT 29 - 13

It types: _____

We type: PRINT 1500 - 2000

It types: _____

We type: PRINT 5.678 - 1.234

It types: _____

— — — — — — — — — —

16
−500
4.444

12.   BASIC uses + for addition and − for subtraction, just as we do with paper and pencil. However, for multiplication, BASIC uses the asterisk (*).

We type: PRINT 7 * 5

It types: 35

We type: PRINT 1.23 * 4.567

It types: 5.61741

We type: PRINT 9 * 8

It types: _____

We type: PRINT 3.14 * 20

It types: _____

— — — — — — — — — —

72
62.8

13.   For division, use the slash (/).

We type: PRINT 7/5

It types: 1.4

We type: PRINT 13/16

It types: .8125

We type: PRINT 24/3

It types: _____

We type: PRINT 3.14/4

It types: _____

— — — — — — — — — —

8
.785

14. The version of MICROSOFT™ BASIC we use in this book will print up to six (6) digits plus a decimal point as the result of an arithmetic operation. If the true result would have more than six digits, the printed result is rounded to six digits.

We type: PRINT 1.234 * 5.678

It types: 7.00665   Complete answer is 7.006652

We type: PRINT 1/3

It types: .333333   Complete answer cannot be
                                      given with a finite number of
                                      digits. It goes on forever as a
                                      repeating decimal.

We type: PRINT 2/3

It types: .666667   Rounded at the 6th digit.

Using my $10 hand calculator, I found that 12.89 * 33.456 = 431.24784.

We type: PRINT 12.89 * 33.456

It types: _____

— — — — — — — — — —

431.248 (rounded in the 6th digit from 431.24784)

Most versions of BASIC permit up to 6 digits, sufficient for most applications. Calculators usually provide 8 to 12 digits. An extended version of MICROSOFT™ BASIC provides more digits, especially useful for business and financial calculations and certain types of engineering and scientific work. As you will learn, calculators are good for number crunching; computers are good for information processing—working with ideas. We can use calculators to crunch numbers, while we use computers to expand ideas.

15. Write PRINT statements to tell the computer to evaluate each of the following numerical expressions. Also show the result printed by the computer.

Numerical expression   PRINT statement and result

(a)   10 + 6   _____

                                  _____

Numerical expression	PRINT statement and result
(b) 15 − 8	_____
	_____
(c) 23 ÷ 5	_____
	_____
(d) 3 × 13	_____
	_____
(e) 7 ÷ 3	_____
	_____
(f) 120 ÷ 7	_____
	_____

— — — — — — — — — —

(a) `PRINT 10 + 6`
      `16`
(b) `PRINT 15 - 8`
      `7`
(c) `PRINT 23/5`
      `4.6`
(d) `PRINT 3*13`
      `39`
(e) `PRINT 7/3`
      `2.33333`   Rounded to six digits
(f) `PRINT 120/7`
      `17.1429`   Rounded to six digits

16. The computer does arithmetic in *left to right* order, with all multiplications (*) and/or divisions (/) performed *before* additions (+) and/or subtractions (−).

$$\left.\begin{array}{c} * \\ / \end{array}\right\} \text{ before } \left\{\begin{array}{c} + \\ - \end{array}\right.$$

Shown on the following page are some BASIC expressions in which two or more operations are used. For some of these expressions, we have shown the value computed by the computer after it does the indicated arithmetic. You complete the rest.

Expression	Value computed by computer	How it did the arithmetic
2*3–4	2	2*3–4 = 6 – 4 = 2
2+3*4	14	2+3*4 = 2 + 12 = 14
2*3+4*5	_____	_____
2+3*4–5	_____	_____
2*3+4*5–6*7	_____	_____

– – – – – – – – – –

26   2*3+4*5 = 6 + 20 = 26
9   2+3*4–5 = 2 + 12 – 5 = 9
–16   2*3+4*5–6*7 = 6 + 20 – 42 = –16

17. Here are more examples and exercises, using division (/). Study the examples and then complete the exercises. Be sure to follow the computer's order described in frame 16.

Expression	Value computed by computer	How it did the arithmetic
3/4+5	5.75	3/4+5 = .75 + 5 = 5.75
2–3/4	1.25	2–3/4 = 2 – .75 = 1.25
2*3+4/5	6.8	2*3+4/5 = 6 + .8 = 6.8
3/4+5*6	_____	_____
2–3/4+5	_____	_____

– – – – – – – – – –

30.75   3/4+5*6 = .75 + 30 = 30.75
6.25   2–3/4+5 = 2 – .75 + 5 = 6.25

18. Following the computer's rules, give the computed value for each of the expressions below. (Remember, do arithmetic in left to right order.)

Expression	Value computed by computer
2*3/4	_____
3/4*5	_____
3/4/5	_____
2*3/4+3/4*5	_____

– – – – – – – – – –

1.5   Multiply 2 by 3, then divide result by 4.
3.75   Divide 3 by 4, then multiply result by 5.
.15   Divide 3 by 4, then divide result by 5.
5.25   First compute 2*3/4, then compute 3/4*5, then add the two results.

19. For each of the following numerical expressions, show the order in which the computer does the arithmetic by putting numbers 1, 2, or 3 in the circles above the operation symbols. We have completed the first three for you.

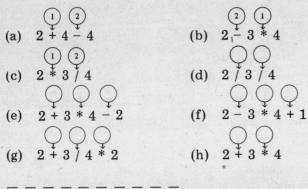

(a)   2 + 4 − 4   (b)   2 − 3 * 4

(c)   2 * 3 / 4   (d)   2 / 3 / 4

(e)   2 + 3 * 4 − 2   (f)   2 − 3 * 4 + 1

(g)   2 + 3 / 4 * 2   (h)   2 + 3 * 4

– – – – – – – – –

(d)   2 / 3 / 4

(e)   2 + 3 * 4 − 2   (f)   2 − 3 * 4 + 1

(g)   2 + 3 / 4 * 2   (h)   2 + 3 * 4

20. If you want to change the order in which operations are done by the computer, use parentheses. Operations in parentheses are done *first*.

   Starting with the leftmost inner set of parentheses, the computer does arithmetic within each set of parentheses in *left to right* order, with all multiplications (*) and/or divisions (/) performed *before* additions (+) and/or subtractions (−).

$$\left.\begin{array}{c} * \\ / \end{array}\right\} \text{before} \left\{\begin{array}{c} + \\ - \end{array}\right.$$

Look at these examples of how the order of operations can give different results.

$2*3+4 = 10$

but $2*(3+4) = 14$ Compute $3 + 4$ first because it is inside the parentheses, then multiply the result by 2.

$2+3*4+5 = 19$

but $(2+3)*(4+5) = 45$ Compute $2 + 3$, then compute $4 + 5$, and then multiply these two results.

Complete the following.

Expression	Value computed by computer
$(2+3)/(4*5)$	_____
$2+3*(4+5)$	_____
$1/(3+5)$	_____

– – – – – – – – – –

.25 $(2+3)/(4*5) = 5/20 = .25$
29     $2+3*(4+5) = 2+3*9 = 2+27 = 29$
.125 $1/(3+5) = 1/8 = .125$

21. Let's take another look at the order in which arithmetic is done. In the expressions below, the numbers in the circles show the order in which the operations are carried out. Write the final value for each expression. The operations are always done in the innermost set of parentheses first.

Expression   Value computed by computer

ⓢ ④ ③ ② ①
$2 + 3 * (4 - (5 + 6 * 7))$ _____

① ③ ② ④ ⑤
$(3 * 4 + 5 * 6 - 7) / 8$ _____

– – – – – – – – – –

−127
4.375

22.   Your next task is to write a proper PRINT statement to tell the computer to compute and print the value of each expression listed below. We have shown the actual value printed by the computer. Remember to indicate all multiplication and division operations with the proper BASIC symbol.

Expression	PRINT statement	Result
$2 \times 3 + 6 \div 7$	_____	6.85714
$16(33 - 21)$	_____	192
$3.14 \times 2 \times 2$	_____	12.56
$\dfrac{88 - 52}{18 + 47}$	_____	.553846

— — — — — — — — — —

PRINT 2*3+6/7
PRINT 16*(33–21)   (Did you remember the asterisk?)
PRINT 3.14*2*2
PRINT (88–52)/(18+47)

23.   For each numerical expression, show the order of operations by putting numbers 1, 2, 3, and so on, in the circles above the operation.

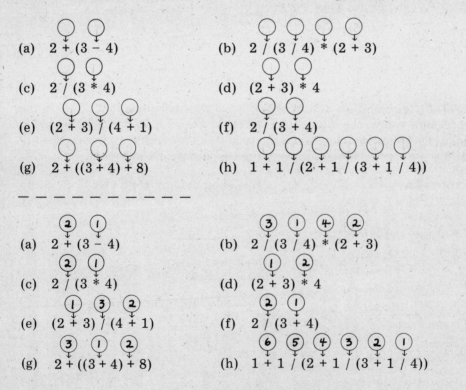

24. There is a fifth arithmetic symbol in BASIC, which indicates raising a number to a power. This operation is called *exponentiation*.

↑ means raise to a power

The volume of a cube is a good example of how exponential numbers are used.

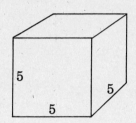

Volume of a cube: $V = S^3$, where S is the length of a side.

If $S = 5$ and $V = 5^3$, then $V = 5^3 = 5 \times 5 \times 5 = 125$.

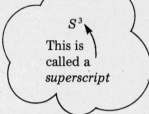

S^3

This is called a *superscript*

Since a TTY cannot print superscripts, you tell the computer to raise a number to a power by using the symbol ↑. On the TTY, depress the SHIFT key and hold it while you press the N key, where the ↑ is located.

We type: PRINT 5↑3   (5↑3 means 5^3 or $5 \times 5 \times 5$)

It types: 125

Now, complete the following.

We type: PRINT 2↑3

It types: _____

We type: PRINT 2↑4

It types: _____

We type: PRINT 2↑5

It types: _____

We type: PRINT 7↑2

It types: _____

— — — — — — — — — —

8   2↑3 = 2^3 = 2×2×2 = 8
16   2↑4 = 2^4 = 2×2×2×2 = 16
32   2↑5 = 2^5 = 2×2×2×2×2 = 32
49   7↑2 = 7^2 = 7×7 = 49

25. Write a PRINT statement to evaluate each expression. We have supplied the results.

Expression	PRINT statement	Result
3^7	_____	2187
$8 \times 8 \times 8 \times 8 \times 8$	_____	32768 (Use ↑, not *.)
1.06^{10}	_____	1.79085
$3^2 + 4^2$	_____	25

— — — — — — — — — —

PRINT 3↑7
PRINT 8↑5 (PRINT 8*8*8*8*8 will also produce the desired result.)
PRINT 1.06↑10 (We will see this type of expression later, in compound interest problems.)
PRINT 3↑2+4↑2

26. Suppose we put $123 into a savings account that pays 6% interest per year, compounded yearly. The amount of money in the account after N years can be computed using the compound interest formula shown below.

$$A = P(1 + R/100)^N$$

where:
P = Principal, or original amount put into the account.
R = Rate of interest per year, in percent.
N = Number of years.
A = Amount in account at the end of N years.

In our problem, P = $123, R = 6%, and we want to know the value of A for N = 2, N = 5, and N = 12 years.

We type: PRINT 123*(1+6/100)↑2

It types: 138.203   ◄——————— After 2 years

We type: PRINT 123*(1+6/100)↑5

It types: 164.602   ◄——————— After 5 years

Your turn. Write the PRINT statement for N = 12. We have supplied the result printed by the computer.

We type: _____

It types: 247.5   ◄─────────── After 12 years our money doubled.

— — — — — — — — — —

PRINT 123*(1+6/100)↑12

27. ˙Now here's a timesaver. Watch.

We type: ? 7+5

It types: 12

We type: ? "MY HUMAN UNDERSTANDS ME"

It types: MY HUMAN UNDERSTANDS ME

That's right. To save time, you can use a question mark (?) instead of the word PRINT in MICROSOFT™ BASIC and some other versions of BASIC.
   Note: Some versions of BASIC use the exclamation point (!) instead of the question mark as the short form for PRINT. However, still other versions of BASIC have a different use for the ! so check the reference manual for the system you use to see what, if any, short form they provide as a substitute for PRINT.
   For each expression or string below, write a PRINT statement to tell the computer to evaluate the expression and print the result, or to print the string. Use ? instead of PRINT. In each case, we have shown what we want the computer to type.

(a) Expression: 37 − 50

    We type: _____

    It types: −13

(b) String: "WANT TO PLAY?"

    We type: _____

    It types: WANT TO PLAY?

(c) String: "2*3+4"

    We type: _____

    It types: 2*3+4

— — — — — — — — — —

(a) ? 37 − 50
(b) ? "WANT TO PLAY?"
(c) ? "2*3+4"

28. Computers use a special notation to indicate very large numbers, or very small decimal fractions. This method of representing numbers is called *floating point notation.* You decipher it in the same way you do the *scientific notation* commonly used in mathematics and science textbooks.

For example, the population of the earth is about 4 billion people.

4 billion = 4,000,000,000

Now let's ask the computer to print the population of the earth.

We type: `PRINT 4000000000`   ◄─────── No commas. See note below.

It types: `4E+09`   ◄─────── What's this?

Our computer printed the population of the earth as a *floating point number.* Read it as follows.

4E+09 = four times ten to the ninth power, or
$$4E+09 = 4 \times 10^9$$

Floating point notation is simply a shorthand way of expressing very large or very small numbers. In floating point notation, a number is represented by a *mantissa* and an *exponent.*

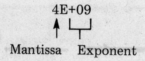

Mantissa   Exponent

The mantissa and the exponent are separated by the letter _____.

— — — — — — — — — —

E

Note: In typing numbers into the computer, we may *not* use commas as we normally do when writing numerals. Commas have a special use in BASIC PRINT statements. Please be patient. We will get to it soon.

29. Here are some examples showing numbers in good old everyday notation and again in floating point notation.

One trillion
ordinary notation: 1,000,000,000,000
floating point notation: 1E+12

Volume of the earth in bushels
ordinary notation: 31,708,000,000,000,000,000,000
floating point notation: 3.1708E+22

Speed of a snail in miles per second
    ordinary notation: .0000079
    floating point notation: 7.9E−6   (Exponent is *negative.*)

In each floating point number above, underline the mantissa and circle the exponent.

— — — — — — — — — —

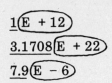

30.   Here are more examples, showing how *our* computer prints floating point numbers.

We type: PRINT 12345678

It types: 1.23457E+07

We type: PRINT 12345649

It types: 1.23456E+07

We type: PRINT 12345650

It types: 1.23457E+07

BEWARE!
Your computer
may do it
differently. Try
it and see.

Our computer prints at most six digits for the mantissa and rounds the mantissa at the sixth digit. The mantissa is printed as a nonzero digit to the left of the decimal point and up to five digits to the right of the decimal point.

We type: PRINT 3333333333

It types: _____

We type: PRINT 6666666666

It types: _____

— — — — — — — — — —

3.33333E+09
6.66667E+09

31. It works the same way with very small numbers.

We type: PRINT .00000012345678

It types: 1.23457E-07 ⌣ Negative exponent

We type: PRINT .00000012345649

It types: 1.23456E-07 ⌣ Negative exponent

We type: PRINT .00000012345650

It types: 1.23457E-07 ⌣ Negative exponent

The mantissa is printed with how many digits to the *left* of the decimal point? _____ Up to how many digits to the *right* of the decimal point? _____

— — — — — — — — — —

one; five (See frames 28 and 29 for examples of mantissas with fewer than 5 digits to the right of the decimal point.)

32. Numbers printed in floating point notation can be converted to ordinary notation, as follows. When the exponent is positive, we do the following.

   (a) Write the mantissa separately.
   (b) Move the decimal point of the mantissa to the *right* the number of places specified by the exponent. If necessary, add zeros.

Example: 6.12345E+05

(a) 6.12345   (b) 6.12345. 5 places

Therefore, 6.12345E+05 = 612,345.

Example: 4E+09

(a) 4.   (b) 4.000000000. 9 places   (add 9 zeros)

Therefore, 4E+09 = 4,000,000,000

Now you try it: 1.23456E+13

(a) _____   (b) _____

Therefore, 1.23456E+13 = _____

— — — — — — — — — —

(a)   1.23456
(b)   1.2345600000000.   13 places   (add 8 zeros)

12,345,600,000,000.

33.   When the exponent is negative, we simply change the direction that the decimal point moves.

  (a)   Write the mantissa separately.
  (b)   Move the decimal point of the mantissa to the *left* the number of places specified by the exponent. If necessary, add zeros.

Example: 7.9E−06

(a)   7.9   (b)   .000007.9   6 places   (add 5 zeros)

Therefore, 7.9E−06 = .0000079

Your turn. 1.23456E−08

(a)   _____   (b)   _____

Therefore, 1.23456E−08 = _____

− − − − − − − − − −

(a)   1.23456
(b)   .00000001.23456

.0000000123456

34.   Write each of the following floating point numbers in ordinary notation.

Floating point notation	Ordinary notation
(a) 1.23456E+06	_____
(b) 1.23456E−06	_____
(c) 1.23456E+07	_____
(d) 1.23456E−09	_____
(e) 1E+11	_____
(f) 1E−11	_____

− − − − − − − − − −

(a)   1234560 or 1,234,560
(b)   .00000123456
(c)   12345600 or 12,345,600
(d)   .00000000123456
(e)   100,000,000,000
(f)   .00000000001

35. Write each "ordinary" number in MICROSOFT™ BASIC floating point notation.

Ordinary notation	Floating point notation
(a) 1,234,560	_____
(b) .000000123456	_____
(c) 10,000,000	_____
(d) .000000001	_____
(e) 12345678	_____
(f) .0000012345678	_____
(g) 6.02×10^{21} (See note.)	_____
(h) 1.67×10^{-11} (See note.)	_____

Note: the numbers in (g) and (h) are written in scientific notation commonly used in mathematics and science.

— — — — — — — — — —

(a) 1.23456E+06
(b) 1.23456E−07
(c) 1E+07
(d) 1E−09
(e) 1.23457E+07 (Rounded off to 6 digits.)
(f) 1.23457E−06
(g) 6.02E+21
(h) 1.67E−11

36. Perhaps you have heard of the ancient story of the wise person who did a great service for a wealthy king. The king asked this person what reward would be appropriate. The person's request was simple. She asked only for grains of wheat, computed as follows. For the first square on a chess board, one grain of wheat; for the second square, 2 grains of wheat; for the third square, 4 grains of wheat and so on, doubling at each square. It goes on as shown below.

Square number	Grains of wheat
1	1
2	2
3	4
4	8
5	16
6	32
7	64

And so on. For square N, there will be 2^{N-1} grains. Let's find out how many grains on square 16.

We type: ? 2↑15   Since N = 16, N − 1 = 15.

It types: 32768

Your turn. Write a PRINT statement to find out how many grains of wheat for square number 64.

We type: _____

It types: 9.22337E+18   That's a lot of wheat!

— — — — — — — — — —

PRINT 2↑63, or ? 2↑63

SELF-TEST

Try this Self-Test, so you can evaluate how much you've learned so far.

1.   In this chapter, we used direct statements. Direct statements do not
     have line numbers. When we type a direct statement and press RETURN,
     what does the computer do? _____

     _____

     _____

2.   Assume that you are at a computer terminal, typing a statement into
     the computer, and you make a typing error. How would you correct
     the error? _____

     _____

3.   Write the symbols used in MICROSOFT™ BASIC for the following
     arithmetic operations.

     addition   _____

     subtraction   _____

     multiplication   _____

     division   _____

     exponentiation
     (raising a number to a power) _____

4.   Complete the following.

     We type: PLEASE DO THE HOMEWORK ON PAGE 157

     It types: _____

5.   Complete the following.

     We type: PRINT "PLEASE DO THE HOMEWORK ON PAGE 157"

     It types: _____

6.   Complete the following.

     We type: PRINT 9*37/5+32

     It types: _____

7. The formula to convert temperature from degrees Fahrenheit to degrees Celsius is shown below.

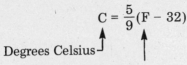

$$C = \frac{5}{9}(F - 32)$$

Degrees Celsius

Degrees Fahrenheit

Write a PRINT statement to tell the computer to compute and print the degrees Celsius (value of C) if F = 72 degrees.

_____

8. Complete the following.

We type: PRINY "THE QUICK RED FOX JUMED OVE@

It types: _____

9. What does the following statement tell the computer to do?

PRINT 23+45 _____

10. Indicate which of the following numerical expressions are valid, *as written*, in BASIC.

____ (a) 2*3*4*5

____ (b) 7(8+9)

____ (c) 1.23 ÷ 4.567

____ (d) 5↑2+12↑2

____ (e) $\dfrac{1}{37 - 29}$

____ (f) $(1 + 7/100)^3$

____ (g) 2↑2↑2

11. For each invalid numerical expression in problem 10, write a valid

BASIC numerical expression. _____

_____

12. For each of the following numerical expressions, show the order in which the computer does the arithmetic by putting numbers 1, 2, 3, and so on, in the circles above the operation symbols.

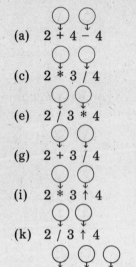

(a) 2 + 4 − 4

(b) 2 * 3 * 4

(c) 2 * 3 / 4

(d) 2 / 3 / 4

(e) 2 / 3 * 4

(f) 2 − 3 * 4

(g) 2 + 3 / 4

(h) 2 ↑ 3 * 4

(i) 2 * 3 ↑ 4

(j) 2 ↑ 3 / 4

(k) 2 / 3 ↑ 4

(l) 2 ↑ 3 ↑ 4

(m) 1 + 2 * 3 ↑ 4

(n) 2 * 3 − 4 ↑ 3 + 5 ↑ 2

13. For each numerical expression, show the order of operations by putting numbers 1, 2, 3, and so on, in the circles above the operation.

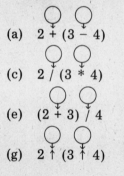

(a) 2 + (3 − 4)

(b) 2 / (3 / 4)

(c) 2 / (3 * 4)

(d) (2 − 3) * 4

(e) (2 + 3) / 4

(f) 2 ↑ (3 * 4)

(g) 2 ↑ (3 ↑ 4)

(h) 1 + 1 / (2 + 1 / (3 + 1 / 4))

14. Write each of the following floating point numbers in ordinary notation.

Floating point notation   Ordinary notation

(a) 1.23456E+05   _____

(b) 1.23456E−05   _____

(c) 1.23456E+08   _____

(d) 1.23456E−08   _____

(e) 1E+12   _____

(f) 1E−12   _____

15. Write each "ordinary" number in MICROSOFT™ BASIC floating point notation.

Ordinary notation		Floating point notation
(a)	1,234,560,000	_____
(b)	.00000000123456	_____
(c)	10,000,000,000	_____
(d)	.0000000001	_____
(e)	123456789	_____
(f)	.00000123456789	_____
(g)	6.02×10^{23} (See note.)	_____
(h)	1.67×10^{-21} (See note.)	_____

Note: The numbers in (g) and (h) are written in scientific notation commonly used in mathematics and science.

Answers to Self-Test

The frame numbers in parentheses refer to the frames in the chapter where the topic is discussed. You may wish to refer to these for quick review.

1. executes the statement, then "forgets" it   (frame 3)

2. type a back arrow ($\leftarrow$) to delete the mistake, then type the correct character   (frames 6-9)

3. addition   +
   subtraction $-$
   multiplication   *
   division   /
   exponentiation $\uparrow$
   (frames 16-20, 24)

4. SN ERROR (The computer does not understand what we want.) (frame 2)

5. PLEASE DO THE HOMEWORK ON PAGE 157   (frames 3-5)

6. 98.6   (frames 20-23)

7. PRINT 5/9*(F$-$32) or PRINT (5/9)*(F$-$32)
   Did you remember the asterisk? By the way, we will also accept
   PRINT 5*(F$-$32)/9.   (frames 20-23)

8. OK (@ deletes the entire line)   (frame 9)

9. Evaluate the numerical expression 23 + 45 and print the result. The computer will add 23 and 45, getting 68, and print 68.   (frame 10)

10. Expressions (a), (d) and (g) are valid. In (g), the computer will evaluate
    2↑2↑2, as follows: 2↑2↑2 = 4↑2 = 16. In other words, the computer will
    do it left to right, as if it were written (2↑2)↑2.   (frames 16-25)

11. (b) 7*(8 + 9)
    (c) 1.23/4.567
    (e) 1/(37 − 29)
    (f) (1 + 7/100)↑3
    (frames 16-25)

12. (a) ① ②
         2 + 4 − 4

    (b) ① ②
         2 * 3 * 4

    (c) ① ②
         2 * 3 / 4

    (d) ① ②
         2 / 3 / 4

    (e) ① ②
         2 / 3 * 4

    (f) ② ①
         2 − 3 * 4

    (g) ② ①
         2 + 3 / 4

    (h) ① ②
         2 ↑ 3 * 4

    (i) ② ①
         2 * 3 ↑ 4

    (j) ① ②
         2 ↑ 3 / 4

    (k) ② ①
         2 / 3 ↑ 4

    (l) ① ②
         2 ↑ 3 ↑ 4

    (m) ③ ② ①
         1 + 2 * 3 ↑ 4

    (n) ③ ④ ① ⑤ ②
         2 * 3 − 4 ↑ 3 + 5 ↑ 2

    (frames 16-25)

13. (a) ② ①
         2 + (3 − 4)

    (b) ② ①
         2 / (3 / 4)

    (c) ② ①
         2 / (3 * 4)

    (d) ① ②
         (2 − 3) * 4

    (e) ① ②
         (2 + 3) / 4

    (f) ② ①
         2 ↑ (3 * 4)

    (g) ② ①
         2 ↑ (3 ↑ 4)

    (h) ⑥ ⑤ ④ ③ ② ①
         1 + 1 / (2 + 1 / (3 + 1 / 4))

    (frames 16-25)

14. (a) 123,456
    (b) .0000123456
    (c) 123,456,000
    (d) .0000000123456
    (e) 1,000,000,000,000
    (f) .000000000001
    (frames 29-36)

15. (a) 1.23456E+09
    (b) 1.23456E−09
    (c) 1E+10
    (d) 1E−10
    (e) 1.23457E+08 (Mantissa is rounded to six digits.)
    (f) 1.23457E−06 (Mantissa is rounded to six digits.)
    (g) 6.02E+23
    (h) 1.67E−21
    (frames 29-36)

CHAPTER THREE

Assignment Statements, Stored Programs, and Branching

This chapter introduces some of the most useful BASIC statements. From here on, we can work with more interesting programs to illustrate home, school, and personal applications of computers.

In this chapter, you will learn the function and format for the statements and commands listed below.

Statements: LET, INPUT, GO TO, PRINT, REMARK

Commands: NEW, RUN, LIST

You will learn how you can store programs for automatic and repetitive execution. You will also learn about *variables* and be able to supply values for variables used in BASIC programs. When you have finished this chapter, you will be able to:

- write programs in which values are assigned to variables by means of LET statements or INPUT statements;

- distinguish between and use numeric variables and string variables;

- write programs in which a value calculated by a BASIC expression is assigned to a numerical variable in a LET statement;

- store a BASIC program in the computer's memory;

- erase an unwanted program from the computer's memory, LIST a program currently in the computer, and RUN (execute) a program;

- edit, correct, and delete statements in a stored program;

- write INPUT statements with messages identifying the INPUT needed;

- write programs that use the GO TO statement to repeat a portion of a program or to skip over a portion of a program;

- use REMARK statements to make programs more readable and understandable by *humans*;

- write PRINT statements which identify printed results with descriptive messages.

1.   To illustrate the concept of *variable* and the function of the LET statement in BASIC, imagine that there are 26 little boxes inside the computer. Each box can contain one number at any one time.

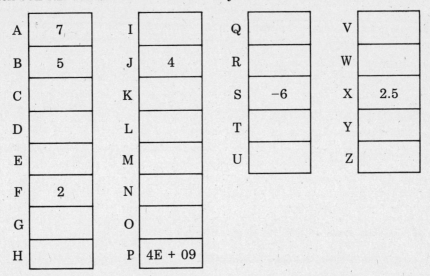

We have already stored numbers in some of the boxes. For example, 7 is in box A and 5 is in box B.

(a)   What number is in box F? _____

(b)   In J? _____

(c)   −6 is in box _____.

(d)   2.5 is in box _____.

(e)   What box contains a floating point number? _____

(f)   What is that floating point number? _____

— — — — — — — — — —

(a) 2; (b) 4; (c) S; (d) X; (e) P; (f) 4E+09

2.   Boxes C and N are shown again on the following page. Use a *pencil* to do the following.

(a)   Put 8 into box C. In other words, write the numeral "8" in the box labeled "C." Do this before you go on to (b).

(b)   Put 12 into N. Do this before you go on to (c).

(c) Put 27 into N. But wait! A box can hold only one number at a time. Before you can enter 27 into N, you must first erase the 12 that you previously entered.

C [   ]

N [   ]

Fill in the boxes before you look at the answer.

— — — — — — — — — — —

C [8   ]

N [27   ]

3.   When the computer puts a number into a box, it *automatically* erases the previous content of the box, just as you did. In order to put 27 into box N, you first erased the previous content, 12.

We call A, B, C, . . ., Z *variables.* The number in box A is the *value of A;* the number in box B is the *value of B;* the number in box C is the *value of C,* and so on.

We use the LET statement to instruct the computer to "put a number in a box." To say it more technically, we are assigning a numerical *value* to a *variable.*

We type: LET A = 7 ◄——— Put 7 into box A.

We type: PRINT A ◄——— Prints the content of box A.

It types: 7

In this program, the *variable* is _____ and the *value* assigned to it by the LET statement is _____.

— — — — — — — — — — —

A; 7

4. Complete the following.

(a) We type: LET X = 23
              PRINT X

    It types: _____

(b) We type: LET Z = −1
              PRINT Z

    It types: _____

(c) We type: LET A = 1
              LET A = 2
              PRINT A

    It types: _____

(d) We type: LET D = 7
              LET W = D
              PRINT W

    It types: _____

(e) We type: LET A = 1
              PRINT A

    It types: _____

    We type: LET A = 2
              PRINT A

    It types: _____

(f) We type: LET N = 1
              PRINT N + 1

    It types: _____

    We type: PRINT N + 2

    It types: _____

— — — — — — — — — — —

(a) 23
(b) −1
(c) 2 (The statement LET A = 2 *replaced* the value previously assigned by LET A = 1.)
(d) 7 (LET W = D copies the value in D into W. The value is still in D, also.)
(e) 1
    2
(f) 2 (Since N = 1, N + 1 = 2.)
    3 (Since N = 1, N + 2 = 3.)

5. Write a LET statement to assign the value 3.14 to P and a PRINT statement to print the value of P.

We type: _____

         _____

It types: _____

— — — — — — — — — — —

LET P = 3.14
PRINT P
 3.14

Note: In most versions of BASIC, the word LET can be omitted. For example:

We type: P = 3.14
             PRINT P

It types: 3.14

The statement P = 3.14 is called an implied LET statement. Try it on your computer. If it works, you can save time and space by omitting the word LET.

6.   Once we have assigned a value to a variable, that variable can be used in mathematical expressions.

We type: LET A = 7   A [7   ]
             LET B = 5

We now have 7 in box A and 5 in box B.
                                              B [5   ]

We type: PRINT A + B

It types: 12   Since A = 7 and B = 5, A + B = 7 + 5 = 12.

We type: PRINT A − B

It types: 2   Since A = 7 and B = 5, A − B = 7 − 5 = 2.

Your turn. Complete the following.

We type: PRINT A*B

It types: _____

We type: PRINT A/B

It types: _____

— — — — — — — — — —

35
1.4

If your computer recognizes the implied LET, you can do the above, as follows.

You type: A = 7
             B = 5
             PRINT A + B

It types: 12

7.   The variables that we have used so far are called *numeric* variables. The value assigned to a numeric variable must be a number.

BASIC has another type of variable, called a *string* variable. The value assigned to a string variable must be a string. A string variable is indicated by a letter followed by a dollar sign ($).

We type: LET N$ = "JERRY"

This assigns the value JERRY to the string variable N$.

N$ | JERRY |

Now, let's print the value of N$.

We type: PRINT N$

It types: JERRY

Complete the following.

We type: LET Z$ = "MY HUMAN UNDERSTANDS ME"
             PRINT Z$

It types: _____

— — — — — — — — — —

MY HUMAN UNDERSTANDS ME

8.   Complete the LET statement so that the computer types what we say it typed.

We type: LET C$ = _____
             PRINT C$

It types: SAN FRANCISCO, CALIFORNIA

— — — — — — — — — —

"SAN FRANCISCO, CALIFORNIA" (Did you remember the quotation marks?)

In this chapter and the next few chapters, we will make occasional use of string variables. Chapter 9 will describe string variables in detail.

9.   Let's look at a problem. We have three bicycles with wheels of 16-, 24-, and 26-inch diameters. For each bike, we want to know how far the bike

travels during one revolution of the wheel. This distance, of course, is the *circumference* of the wheel. Let's use D to represent the diameter of the wheel and C to represent the circumference.

$$C = \pi D$$

where $\pi = 3.14159 \ldots$

We will use 3.14 as a crude approximation to π. We could do this problem as follows.

We type: PRINT 3.14 * 16

It types: 50.24

We type: PRINT 3.14 * 24

It types: 75.36

We type: PRINT 3.14 * 26

It types: 81.64

Here is another way to do it. Complete the parts we have omitted.

We type: LET D = 16
              PRINT 3.14 * D

It types: 50.24

We type: LET D = 24
              PRINT 3.14 * D

It types: _____

We type: LET _____

              _____

It types: 81.64

— — — — — — — — — —

75.36
D = 26
PRINT 3.14 * D

10.   Now we are ready to take the big step from one-at-a-time *direct* statements to a *stored program*. We will store this program in the memory of the computer. (Just look at it, then read on.)

```
10 LET D = 16
20 PRINT 3.14 * D
```

The above program has two statements, each on a single line. Each statement begins with a *line number* (in this case, the 10 and 20). A line number can be an integer from 1 to 32767 on most computers using BASIC. Check your system's reference manual for the upper limit for a line number.

When we type statements with line numbers, the statements are *not* executed when you press RETURN. Instead, the statements are stored in the computer's memory for later execution.

As you learned in Chapter 2, statements without line numbers are called *direct statements*. The computer executes a direct statement immediately and then forgets it. However, this does not happen when we type a statement *with* a line number. Instead, what does happen?

_____

_____

— — — — — — — — — —

The statement is stored in the computer's memory for later execution. That is, the computer remembers the statement.

11.   The line numbers tell the computer the order in which it is to follow statements in the program. It is not necessary for line numbers to be consecutive integers (e.g., 1, 2, 3, 4, 5 . . .). It is common practice to number by tens as we do in the following program. Then, if we wish, we can easily insert or add more statements into the program between existing statements.

```
10 LET D = 16
20 PRINT 3.14 * D
```

How many additional statements could be added between line 10 and line 20? _____

— — — — — — — — — —

9 (lines 11, 12, 13, 14, 15, 16, 17, 18, 19)

Of course, you don't *have* to number by tens. If you prefer numbering by thirteens or fives or jumping around, help yourself!

12.   Before we store a program, we must first remove or erase any old program that may already be stored in the computer's memory.

_____

We type: NEW   And, of course, press RETURN.

It types: OK

The computer has erased the portion of its memory that stores BASIC programs. It is now ready to accept a new program.

How do we erase, remove, or delete an old program from the computer's memory? _____

— — — — — — — — — — —

We type NEW and press the RETURN key.

Note: If we misspell NEW, we may get an error message. For example:

We type: GNU

It types: ?SN ERROR

Our computer doesn't appreciate puns, but if we type NEW correctly and press RETURN, all is well.

Note: On some computers, you must type SCRATCH (abbreviated SCR) instead of NEW to erase an old program. If your computer is puzzled by both NEW and SCRATCH, consult the reference manual for your computer or ask someone for help.

13. Now we are ready to store our two-line program from frames 10 and 11.

First, we must erase any old program by typing _____ and pressing the RETURN key. To store the program, we type the first line or statement and press the RETURN key, then type the second line and _____

_____.

— — — — — — — — — — —

NEW; press the RETURN key

14. Let's do it.

We type: NEW

It types: OK

We type: 10 LET D = 16
         20 PRINT 3.14 * D

If we make a typing error, we start over. The program is now stored. The computer is waiting patiently for our next statement or command.

Hmmmm . . . we wonder if the program really *is* stored in the computer's memory. We can find out by typing LIST and pressing the RETURN key.

We type: `LIST`   And press RETURN.

It types:
```
10 LET D=16
20 PRINT 3.14*D
OK
```

The command LIST tells the computer to type all of the program statements that are currently stored in its memory. After listing the program, the computer types OK to let us know it is our turn again. If there is *no* program stored, the computer will simply type OK.

How do we tell the computer to type out the program that is currently stored in its memory? _____

— — — — — — — — — — —

We type LIST and press the RETURN key.

15. Listing a BASIC program lets us know whether or not a program is stored in the computer's memory. We may want to add more statements to the program. Or we may wish to see if we have typed the statements correctly. If we want the computer to execute the program, we type _____.
If we want the computer to tell us if there is a program stored in its memory, and to type out the program for us, we type _____.

— — — — — — — — — — —

RUN; LIST

16. After you type RUN to tell the computer to execute a program, or after you type LIST to command the computer to tell us "what's on its mind" (that is, what is stored in its memory), what else do you have to do before the computer will respond? _____

— — — — — — — — — — —

press the RETURN key

17. Assume you have typed our little program into the computer.

```
10 LET D = 16
20 PRINT 3.14 * D
```

The program is stored in the computer's memory. Now you want the

computer to execute (carry out) the program. Type RUN and press the
RETURN key.

We type: RUN   And press RETURN.

It types: 5Ø.24
           OK

The computer has RUN the program. That is, it has executed the statements of the program in line number order. First, the computer was told to
assign a value to a variable with this statement: 10 LET D = 16. That means

that the computer placed the value _____ in the box identified by the vari-

able _____ .

— — — — — — — — — — —

16; D

18.   After following the instruction in the statement with line number 10,
the computer went on to the next statement in line number order:
20 PRINT 3.14*D. Part of line 20 tells the computer to multiply two numbers. One number is given in the statement. The other number is stored in a
place labeled by the variable D. What are the two values that the computer

uses to multiply? _____

— — — — — — — — — — —

3.14 and 16

19.   In the last frame we saw that part of line 20 tells the computer to mul-

tiply two values. What else does line 20 tell the computer to do? _____

_____

— — — — — — — — — —

PRINT the results of the multiplication

20.   Some computers require an END statement as the last statement in the
program, as we show below. If your computer does not need END, don't use
it!

```
10 LET D = 16
20 PRINT 3.14 * D
30 END
```

Check to see if the version of BASIC your computer uses requires an END statement as the last statement in a program. MICROSOFT™ BASIC and many other microcomputer BASICs do *not* require an END statement, and we will not use it in the programs in this book except in special cases to be shown in later chapters.

If your computer's version of BASIC requires an END statement in all programs, where should that statement appear in a LISTing of the program?

_____

— — — — — — — — — —

last statement in program (the one with the highest or largest line number)

21. Let's review what happens when we use our little program that calculates the circumference of a bicycle wheel.

```
NEW
```
First, we erase any old program.

```
OK
```

```
10 LET D = 16
20 PRINT 3.14 * D
```
Then, we type in this program, which consists of two statements.

```
LIST
```
Next, we tell the computer to LIST the program.

```
10 LET D=16
20 PRINT 3.14*D
```
The computer LISTs (types) the program,

```
OK
```
then types OK and stops.

```
RUN
```
Finally, we tell the computer to RUN the program.

```
 50.24
```
It executes the program,

```
OK
```
then types OK and stops.

The program is still stored in the computer's memory. What will happen if we now type RUN? _____

_____

— — — — — — — — — —

The computer will execute the program again. Since nothing in the program has changed, the same result (50.24) will be printed.

22. What happens if we make a typing mistake in entering a program?

We type: 10 LER D = 16   We misspell LET.
        20 PRINT 3.14 * D

We type: RUN   Oops! Something is wrong here. The
                              computer might have typed ? SN ER-
It types: 0   ROR in 10. Either way, the message
                              is that the computer does not know
                              how to run the program.

We type: LIST

It types: 10 LER D=16   Sure enough, we notice that LET is
         20 PRINT 3.14*D   misspelled.

We type: 10 LET D=16   We retype line 10, correctly. This re-
                              places the old line 10.

We type: LIST   To make sure the new line 10 replaced
                              the old line 10, we LIST the corrected
It types: 10 LET D=16   program (and also check to make sure
         20 PRINT 3.14*D   we typed it right this time!).

We type: RUN

It types: 50.24

    Suppose we had seen the mistake immediately after we had typed it.

How could we have corrected it? _____

_____

— — — — — — — — — —

We could have typed a back arrow (←), then the correct letter. (See frame 6,
Chapter 2.)

23. We assume that our circumference program is still stored in memory.
Now we want to change the value assigned to D. To do this, we *replace* line
10 with a different line 10. After making this change, we will LIST the
modified program.

We type: 10 LET D = 24
        LIST

It types: 10 LET D=24   Here is the new line 10,
         20 PRINT 3.14*D   and the old line 20.

    How do we *replace* a line in a stored program? _____

_____

— — — — — — — — — —

_____

We type a new line with the same line number as the line we wish to replace.

Note: We do *not* type NEW because we want line 20 to remain in the computer while we change *only* line 10. Typing NEW would erase *both* statements from the computer's memory.

24. We will RUN the modified program of frame 23.

We type: RUN

It types: 75.36
             OK

Your turn. Complete the following.

We type: 10 LET D = 26

We type: LIST

It types: _____

             _____

             OK

We type: RUN

It types: _____

             OK

– – – – – – – – – –

10 LET D = 26 ⟵——————— New line 10
20 PRINT 3.14*D ⟵——————— Old line 20
  81.64

25. How fast does your money grow?

Problem: We put P dollars in a savings account which pays R percent interest, per year, compounded yearly. How much money will we have in the account at the end of N years?

>   P is the original amount (principal).
>   R is the interest rate, in percent, per year.
>   N is the number of years.
>   A is the amount after N years.

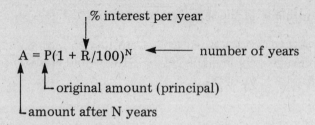

Below is a program to compute A for P = $1000, R = 6%, and N = 3 years. Complete line 40 in correct BASIC notation, using the formula above as a guide.

```
10 LET P = 1000
20 LET R = 6
30 LET N = 3

40 LET A = _____
50 PRINT A
```

— — — — — — — — — —

`P*(1+R/100)↑N`   (Did you remember the asterisk? Did you remember to use ↑ to tell the computer to raise to a power?)

26. We will store and RUN the program, then ask *you* to make some changes.

We type: `NEW`
```
10 LET P = 1000
20 LET R = 6
30 LET N = 3
40 LET A = P*(1+R/100)↑N
50 PRINT A
RUN
```

Don't forget, we are usually omitting the OK typed by the computer. We also will omit reminders to use the RETURN key after entering a statement or a command such as RUN, LIST, or NEW.

It types: `1191.02`

Now, show how to change line 30 so that N = 5.

We type: _____

       RUN

It types: 1338.23   Value of A for P = 1000, R = 6, N = 5.

— — — — — — — — — —

30 LET N = 5

27. Now change the program so that R = 7% and N = 8 years.

We type: _____

_____

RUN

It types: 1718.19

— — — — — — — — — —

20 LET R = 7
30 LET N = 8

28. Now show how the computer will respond if we type LIST.

We type: LIST

It types: _____

_____

_____

_____

_____

— — — — — — — — — —

```
1Ø LET P=1ØØØ
2Ø LET R=7
3Ø LET N=8
4Ø LET A=P*(1+R/1ØØ)↑N
5Ø PRINT A
```

29. LET statements are all fine and good, but what a hassle to change all those LET statements every time you want to change the values of variables. Ah, but leave it to BASIC to come up with a clever solution—the INPUT statement.

The INPUT statement allows the computer user to assign different values to variables each time a program is RUN *without* modifying the program itself. When the computer comes to an INPUT statement in a program, it types a question mark and waits for the user to enter a value for a variable. Below is an example:

We type: NEW   First, we erase any old program, then enter this
          1Ø INPUT A   program.
          2Ø PRINT A
          RUN   Then we tell the computer to RUN the program.

It types: ?   The computer types a question mark, then waits.

When we typed RUN, what did the computer do?_____

_____

— — — — — — — — — — —

It typed a question mark and waited for us to do something.

Note: The question mark is an example of a *prompt*. The computer types a prompt to tell you it is *your* turn to do something. The message OK is another example of a prompt.

30.   The INPUT statement causes the computer to type a question mark, then stop and wait. It is waiting for a value to assign to the variable which appears in the INPUT statement. Computers are very patient. If we don't cooperate by typing a value, the computer will simply wait, and wait, and wait.

So let's cooperate with our ever-patient computer and type in a value for A. We will enter 3 as the value to be assigned to A, then press RETURN. The computer will put our value into box A, then continue running the program.

```
NEW
10 INPUT A
20 PRINT A
```

```
RUN
?3
 3
```

After we typed 3 as the value for A and then pressed RETURN, the computer went on to line 20 and printed our value.

After we typed RUN and pressed the RETURN key, the computer

typed a _____. We then typed 3, which is our value

for the INPUT variable _____. The computer then executed the PRINT A

statement (line 20) and printed the _____ of A.

— — — — — — — — — — —

question mark; A; value

31.   The program can be RUN again with a different value of A supplied by the user. Pretend you are the computer, and show how a RUN would look if your human computer user typed 23 as the value of A.

RUN

———

———

— — — — — — — — —

? 23
 23

32.   Now let's use an INPUT statement to enter (type in) data for our familiar bicycle wheel problem. *Data* is the name for information used by a computer program.

We type: `NEW`
```
10 INPUT D
20 PRINT 3.14*D
```

It types: `RUN`
`?`

The computer wants a value for D, the diameter of our bicycle wheel. It will
then compute the distance traveled in one revolution, and print it. Let's do
it for D = 16, D = 24, and D = 26.

`RUN`   First, we RUN the program for D = 16. When the computer
`?16`   typed a question mark, we entered 16 as the value of D. The
`50.24`   computer computed and printed 3.14*D, then stopped.

`RUN`   We typed RUN again and, when the computer typed a question
`?24`   mark, we supplied 24 as the value of D. The computer zapped
`75.36`   out the answer, and stopped.

`RUN`   Your turn. Complete the third RUN.

————————

————————

— — — — — — — — —

?26
 81.64

33.   One INPUT statement can be used to assign values to *two or more* variables.

```
10 INPUT A,B          Two variables, A and B.
20 PRINT A+B
RUN
? 7,5                 Two values, 7 and 5.
 12
```

When the computer typed a question mark, we typed *two* numbers separated by a comma, then pressed the RETURN key. The computer assigned the first number as the value of A and the second number as the value of B. Note the following.

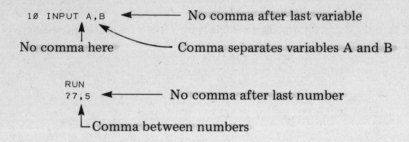

The value 7 is assigned to the variable A, and the value 5 is assigned to the variable B.

Here is the summary; you fill in the blanks. When a program containing an INPUT statement with multiple variables is RUN, the first value typed in by the user after the INPUT question mark will be assigned to the _____ variable that appears in the INPUT statement; the _____ value typed in by the user will be assigned to the second variable appearing in the INPUT statement, and so on. Both the variables in the INPUT statement in the program, and the values typed in by the user when the program is RUN, must be separated by _____.

— — — — — — — — — —

first; second; commas

34. Here is another RUN of the program in frame 33. We want to enter 73 as the value of A and 59 as the value of B.

```
RUN
? 73          Oops! We absentmindedly hit the RETURN key.
??
```

The computer typed a double question mark. This means "Didn't you forget something?"

We then completed the RUN by entering the *second* number, the value of B

```
RUN
?  73
??  59
 132
```

What happens if we don't enter a numerical value for *every* variable in an INPUT statement? _____

_____

— — — — — — — — — —

The computer types another question mark.

Note: If you enter *more* numbers than there are variables, the computer will ignore the extra values.

35.   Suppose you and a bunch of friends, all bicycle aficionados, are gathered about your computer, and they are marveling at your newly acquired computer programming skills. You decide to demonstrate how the computer works by using the program to compute the distance traveled in one turn of the wheel. However, you have to do a separate RUN of the program for each friend. But wait—first add a new statement to the program.

```
1Ø  INPUT  D
2Ø  PRINT  3.14*D
3Ø  GO  TO  1Ø          ◄——————— Something new—a GO TO statement.
```

In BASIC, a GO TO statement tells the computer to jump to or branch to the line number following the words GO TO, and then to continue following the instructions in the program in the usual line number order.
In the above program, the GO TO statement tells the computer to jump

to line _____ and start the program over again.

— — — — — — — — — —

line 10

36.   Let's see what happens when we RUN the program. (Assume that you, or someone, has typed NEW, then entered the program.)

```
RUN
?16
 5Ø.24
?24
 75.36
?26
 81.64
?
```

Following each question mark, we typed the value of D. The computer then computed the value of 3.14*D, printed the result, and typed another question mark.

Well, we are finished, but the computer doesn't know that we are finished. It is hung up on line 10, waiting for INPUT data. How do we get out of this situation? Easy! Just press the CTRL (Control) key, and while holding down CTRL, also press the C key.

? ◄——— We press CTRL and C together.
OK ◄——— It types OK.

When we press the Control and C keys simultaneously (*without* typing anything) what does the computer do? _____

_____

— — — — — — — — — —

It "escapes" from the INPUT statement and types OK.

Note: The manner of escaping from an INPUT statement varies from computer to computer. In some versions of BASIC, pressing RETURN without entering a number will assign a zero to the INPUT variable, and the program will just keep RUNning. To stop a RUN on your computer, try either holding the CTRL key down and pressing the C key, or press the ESC or ALT MODE key. Experiment with your computer to see which method works to stop the RUN of a program waiting at an INPUT question mark. If none of the above work, check the reference manual for the version of BASIC your computer uses.

37. Remember: BASIC statements are executed in line number order, unless a GO TO statement changes the order. In the program from frame 35, the statements are executed in the order shown below by the arrows.

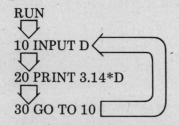

Around and around and around — until you quit by pressing the CTRL key and the C key together after the computer types a question mark (or whatever works for the version of BASIC being used).

The above program is an example of a *loop*. The GO TO statement causes the computer to "loop back" to the beginning. In this program, the computer loops back to an INPUT statement and then stops. Watch out! We can write programs with nonstop loops. Here is an example.

```
13 PRINT "TO STOP ME, PRESS 'CTRL' AND 'C' TOGETHER"
27 GO TO 13
```

Do *not* RUN this program yet! Instead, draw arrows as we did on the previous page to show how the computer executes the program.

RUN

13 PRINT "TO STOP ME, PRESS 'CTRL' AND 'C' TOGETHER"

27 GO TO 13

— — — — — — — — — —

RUN

13   PRINT "TO STOP ME, PRESS 'CTRL' AND 'C' TOGETHER"

27   GO TO 13

We have used line numbers 13 and 27 to remind you that you don't have to number by 10, although we usually do.

Note: When you press CTRL and C simultaneously, make sure that you press CTRL a fraction of a second before you press C. Another way to do it is to hold CTRL down and, while doing so, press C.

38.   Now let's enter the program of frame 37 and RUN it. Remember, to stop the computer, press CTRL and C *together.*

```
13 PRINT "TO STOP ME, PRESS 'CTRL' AND 'C' TOGETHER"
27 GO TO 13

RUN
TO STOP ME, PRESS 'CTRL' AND 'C' TOGETHER
TO STOP ME, PRESS 'CTRL' AND 'C' TOGETHER
TO STOP ME, PRESS 'CTRL' AND 'C' TOGETHER
TO STOP ME, PRESS 'CTRL' AND 'C' TOGETHER
TO STOP ME, PRESS 'CTRL' AND 'C' TOGETHER

BREAK IN 13  ◄——————
```
The computer tells us the line number of the next statement that was to be executed when we pressed CTRL and C together.

The computer executed line 13 over and over again, because the GO TO statement in line 27 repeatedly told the computer to go back to line 13. This is a "forever" loop—it just keeps going around and around until someone interrupts it. Sometimes this is referred to as an "infinite" loop, because it does not stop automatically.

How do we interrupt, or stop, the computer when it is running a program? _____

— — — — — — — — — —

press the CTRL and C keys together (simultaneously)

39.   If you should move someday, you may want to write *your* version of the following program. In this program we introduce a new statement, called REMARK. We use the REMARK statement to tell something about the program to a *human* who may be reading the program. The computer simply ignores REMARK statements.

```
100 REMARK: CHANGE OF ADDRESS PROGRAM
110 PRINT
120 PRINT "DEAR FRIENDS, MY NEW ADDRESS IS:"
130 PRINT
140 PRINT "IRENE BROWNSTONE"
150 PRINT "605 PARK AVENUE"
160 PRINT "NEW YORK NY 10016"
170 PRINT
180 GO TO 110
```

And now, dear reader, please tell us how you would use this program to obtain 10 change of address messages. _____

_____

_____

_____

— — — — — — — — — —

First, you would type NEW, then enter the program. Next you would type RUN, then count the change of address messages as they are typed by the computer. When 10 messages have been printed, you would press CTRL and C together to stop the computer.

40.   The REMARK statement has a short form that you can use. The short form is simple, the first three letters in REMark. When executing a program, the computer only "looks" at the first three letters, and if those three letters are REM, then the computer will skip on to the next statement in line number order without considering the rest of the statement. Therefore, you could use the word REMEMBER instead of REMark and the effect would be the same.

Rewrite line 100 in frame 39 using the short form of the REMark statement. _____

— — — — — — — — — —

100 REM CHANGE OF ADDRESS PROGRAM

No colon is needed after the REM, although it could be there. The computer does not look past the letters REM before going on to the next statement.

Note: Because all versions of BASIC are not standardized, some computers use the exclamation point (!) as an even shorter form for the REMark statements. But watch out! Other versions use ! instead of ? as the shorthand for PRINT.

41. When the computer executes a PRINT statement that has only the word PRINT following the line number and nothing else in the statement, it does the same thing that happens when you press the RETURN key.

(1) It does a carriage return, and
(2) It does a line feed (indexes or goes to the next line).

This has the effect on a TTY or CRT of leaving a blank line in the printout when the program is RUN. This is very handy for making the printout of a program easier to read.

Look at the change of address program in frame 39. Which statements will cause the computer to insert blank lines in the printout? _____

_____

— — — — — — — — — —

lines 110, 130, and 170

42. Here again is the bicycle wheel program from frames 35 and 36.

```
RUN
?16
  50.24
?24
  75.36
?26
  81.64
?
```

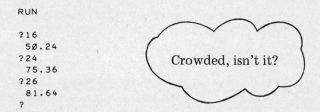

Crowded, isn't it?

We assume that the program is still stored in the computer's memory. (If you are at a computer terminal, check by using LIST and if not, store the program now.) We will add the statement on the following page, then LIST the program.

We type: `25 PRINT`   This is an "empty" PRINT statement.
                                         The space following PRINT is "empty."
We type: `LIST`

```
10  INPUT D
20  PRINT 3.14*D
25  PRINT  ◄──────────────
30  GOTO 10
```
The computer has automatically in-
serted our new statement in its proper
place, *between* line 20 and line 30.

Let's RUN it and see what happens.

```
RUN

?16
  50.24
            ◄────────  Note the line space. The "empty" line is provided by line 25.
?24
  75.36
            ◄────────  Another line space.
?26
  81.64
            ◄────────  Still another line space.
```

Compare the two RUNs. What does 25 PRINT tell the computer to do?

_____

_____

– – – – – – – – – –

It causes the computer to print a line space ("empty" line) after printing the
value of 3.14*D. Note: This happens *before* the computer execute GO TO
10 and restarts the program.

43.   When a program contains an INPUT statement, we need a way of in-
forming a user of our program what the INPUT statement is asking for. Here
is our bike program again, with a more informative INPUT statement.

```
10  INPUT "WHEEL DIAMETER";D
20  PRINT 3.14*D
25  PRINT
30  GOTO 10

RUN
WHEEL DIAMETER?
```

Note semicolon

The statement 10 INPUT "WHEEL DIAMETER"; D tells the computer to:

   (1)   print the string, WHEEL DIAMETER,
   (2)   print a question mark,
   (3)   wait for someone to type a value for D,
   (4)   continue executing the program after someone types a value of D
          (and presses RETURN).

Suppose we type 16 as the value of D and press RETURN. Show what happens next.

WHEEL DIAMETER? 16

_____

_____

— — — — — — — — — —

  50.24

WHEEL DIAMETER?

Note: When you use a string in an INPUT statement, remember to put a semicolon between the string and the variable which follows it.

44.   Now what the computer wants is clearly identified by the string enclosed in quotation marks in the INPUT statement. We use the same approach in a PRINT statement to identify the calculation performed by the computer for that statement (see line 20).

```
10 INPUT "WHEEL DIAMETER" ; D
20 PRINT "DISTANCE IN ONE TURN IS" ; 3.14*D
25 PRINT
30 GOTO 10
```

Note semicolon

The statement 20 PRINT "DISTANCE IN ONE TURN IS" ; 3.14*D tells the computer to:

   (1)   print the string DISTANCE IN ONE TURN IS,
   (2)   compute and print the value of 3.14*D.

Let's try it. Complete the RUN.

```
RUN

WHEEL DIAMETER? 16
DISTANCE IN ONE TURN IS 50.24

WHEEL DIAMETER? 24
DISTANCE IN ONE TURN IS _____

WHEEL DIAMETER? 26
```

_____

_____

— — — — — — — — — —

_____

75.36
DISTANCE IN ONE TURN IS 81.64
WHEEL DIAMETER?

Don't forget the semicolon between "DISTANCE IN ONE TURN IS" and 3.14*D. More features of the PRINT statement will be revealed as we move along.

45.   Rewrite the program in frame 44 so that a RUN looks like the one shown below.

```
RUN

IF YOU ENTER THE DIAMETER OF A BICYCLE WHEEL, THEN I WILL
TYPE THE DISTANCE TRAVELED IN ONE TURN OF THE WHEEL.

WHEEL .DIAMETER?16
DISTANCE IN ONE TURN IS 50.24

WHEEL DIAMETER?24
DISTANCE IN ONE TURN IS 75.36

WHEEL  DIAMETER?
```
... and so on. To stop, press CTRL and C together.

Write the program below.

— — — — — — — — —

```
10 REMARKABLE BICYCLE PROGRAM
20 PRINT "IF YOU ENTER THE DIAMETER OF A BICYCLE WHEEL, THEN I WILL"
30 PRINT "TYPE THE DISTANCE TRAVELED IN ONE TURN OF THE WHEEL."
40 PRINT
50 INPUT "WHEEL DIAMETER";D
60 PRINT "DISTANCE IN ONE TURN IS";3.13*D
70 GO TO 40
```

(The computer ignores everything following REM. See frame 40.)

46.   The INPUT statement, like the LET statement, belongs to the class of BASIC instructions called assignment statements. The value we type in

response to a question mark is assigned to the variable in the INPUT statement. If the INPUT variable is a string variable, we can type in a string as the value and it will be assigned to the string variable. Here is a simple example.

```
10 INPUT "WHAT IS YOUR NAME";N$
20 PRINT N$
30 PRINT
40 GO TO 10
RUN
WHAT IS YOUR NAME? "JERALD R. BROWN"
JERALD R. BROWN

WHAT IS YOUR NAME? JERALD R. BROWN
JERALD R. BROWN

WHAT IS YOUR NAME? LEROY FINKEL
```

◄────── What? No quotation marks? See note below and the next frame.

You complete this one.

_____

— — — — — — — — — —

LEROY FINKEL

Note that it is OK to omit the quotation marks enclosing a string during INPUT. However, as you will see in the next frame, sometimes the quotation marks are necessary.

47. Below is another RUN of the program in frame 46.

```
RUN
WHAT IS YOUR NAME? BROWN, JERALD R.
?EXTRA IGNORED
BROWN

WHAT IS YOUR NAME? "BROWN, JERALD R."
BROWN, JERALD R.

WHAT IS YOUR NAME?
```

When we typed BROWN, JERALD R. with a comma between BROWN and JERALD R., the computer thought we were entering *two* strings. However, the INPUT statement has only *one* string variable. So, the computer assigned BROWN to the variable N$ and politely informed us ?EXTRA IGNORED. It ignored the comma and also ignored JERALD R. It then, of course, printed the value of N$, which was BROWN.

What happened when we typed "BROWN, JERALD R."? _____

_____

— — — — — — — — — — _____

The computer typed the complete string BROWN, JERALD R.

If you wish to INPUT a string that has a comma in it, you must enclose the entire string in quotation marks.

48. String values can be assigned to two or more string variables with a single INPUT statement.

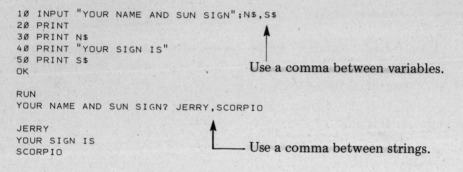

```
10 INPUT "YOUR NAME AND SUN SIGN";N$,S$
20 PRINT
30 PRINT N$
40 PRINT "YOUR SIGN IS"
50 PRINT S$
OK
```

Use a comma between variables.

```
RUN
YOUR NAME AND SUN SIGN? JERRY,SCORPIO

JERRY
YOUR SIGN IS
SCORPIO
```

Use a comma between strings.

Show how you could complete the RUN from this point.

```
RUN
YOUR NAME AND SUN SIGN? JERRY
??
```

— — — — — — — — —

```
??SCORPIO

JERRY
YOUR SIGN IS
SCORPIO
```

49. Now you write a program with three string variables in an INPUT statement. A RUN will look like the following.

```
RUN
YOUR NAME, CITY AND STATE YOU LIVE IN? JERRY,SAN FRANCISCO,CALIFORNIA

JERRY
YOU LIVE IN
SAN FRANCISCO
CALIFORNIA
```

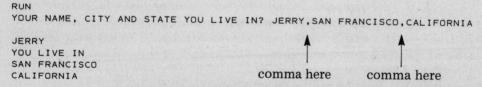

comma here   comma here

--- --- --- --- --- --- --- ---

```
10 INPUT "YOUR NAME, CITY AND STATE YOU LIVE IN";N$,C$,S$
20 PRINT
30 PRINT N$
40 PRINT "YOU LIVE IN"
50 PRINT C$
60 PRINT S$
```

Commas must be used
to separate variables.

50. Review the change of address program in frame 39. Then complete the
following RUN so that the results will be the same as in frame 39.

```
100 REMARK: CHANGE OF ADDRESS PROGRAM
110 INPUT "YOUR NAME";N$
120 INPUT "STREET ADDRESS";S$
130 INPUT "CITY,STATE AND ZIP";C$
140 PRINT
150 PRINT "DEAR FRIENDS, MY NEW ADDRESS IS:"
160 PRINT
170 PRINT N$
180 PRINT S$
190 PRINT C$
200 PRINT
210 GOTO 140
RUN

YOUR NAME? _____

STREET ADDRESS? _____

CITY,STATE AND ZIP? _____

DEAR FRIENDS, MY NEW ADDRESS IS:

IRENE BROWNSTONE
605 PARK AVENUE
NEW YORK NY 10016

DEAR FRIENDS, MY NEW ADDRESS IS:

IRENE BROWNSTONE
605 PARK AVENUE
NEW YORK NY 10016

DEAR FRIENDS, MY NEW ADDRESS IS:

IRENE BROWNSTONE
605 PARK AVENUE
NEW YORK NY 10016

BREAK IN 190
```

We pressed CTRL/C to stop the computer.

--- --- --- --- --- --- --- ---

IRENE BROWNSTONE
605 PARK AVENUE
NEW YORK NY 10016

No quotation marks were required. However, they would be required if any of the lines typed in contained a comma. For example: "NEW YORK, NEW YORK 10016"

51.   Here's a program that lets you use the computer as an adding machine, by repeating an "adding routine" with a GO TO loop. A "routine" is one or more statements to complete a computing task.

```
100 REMARK***WORLD'S MOST EXPENSIVE ADDING MACHINE!!!
110 PRINT "I AM THE WORLD'S MOST EXPENSIVE ADDING MACHINE."
120 PRINT "EACH TIME I TYPE 'X=?' YOU TYPE A NUMBER AND"
130 PRINT "PRESS THE RETURN KEY.  I WILL THEN TYPE THE TOTAL"
140 PRINT "OF ALL THE NUMBERS YOU HAVE ENTERED."
150 LET T = 0
160 PRINT
170 INPUT "X=" ; X
180 LET T = T + X
190 PRINT "TOTAL SO FAR IS" ; T
200 GO TO 160
```

Lines 160 through 200 are a GO TO loop. These lines are done for each number entered by the user.

Notice the LET statements using the variable T in lines 150 and 180. Line 150 is *outside* the GO TO loop. It is executed *once* before the loop begins, setting T equal to zero. This is called *initializing*, giving an initial or starting value to a variable.

Line 180 is *inside* the GO TO loop. Therefore line 180 will be executed *each time* through the loop. In line 180, a *new* value of T is computed by adding the old value stored in box T to the INPUT value of X entered by the computer user.

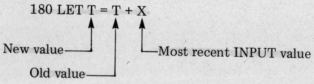

$$180 \text{ LET } T = T + X$$

New value———┘   └———Most recent INPUT value

Old value———┘

(a)   Suppose the *old* value of T is zero and the INPUT value of X is 12. What is the *new* value of T? _____

(b)   Suppose the *old* value of T is 12 and the INPUT value of X is 43. What is the *new* value of T? _____

— — — — — — — — — —

(a) 12;   (b) 55

52.   Note how the PRINT statements (lines 110-140) are used to provide the user with an explanation and instructions for using the program. Are the PRINT statements inside or outside the GO TO loop? _____

— — — — — — — — — —

outside

53.   It's RUN time. Let's see how the program works.

```
RUN
I AM THE WORLD'S MOST EXPENSIVE ADDING MACHINE.
EACH TIME I TYPE 'X=?' YOU TYPE A NUMBER AND
PRESS THE RETURN KEY.  I WILL THEN TYPE THE TOTAL
OF ALL THE NUMBERS YOU HAVE ENTERED.

X=? 12
TOTAL SO FAR IS 12

X=? 43
TOTAL SO FAR IS 55

X=? 33
TOTAL SO FAR IS 88

X=? 92
TOTAL SO FAR IS 180

X=? 76.25
TOTAL SO FAR IS 256.25

X=?
```
◄——————————— Do you remember how to get out of this? If not, check frame 36.

Let's focus on the statement in line 180. For the RUN above, the *first* time through the program the values of the variables to the right of the = symbol in 180 LET T = T + X will be:

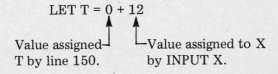

LET T = 0 + 12

Value assigned⌐   ⌐Value assigned to X
T by line 150.   by INPUT X.

So the *new* value for T is 12. The value is printed. Notice that the computer substitutes the current values in the boxes for the variables to the right of = each time it executes line 180.

For the *second* time through the "loop" section of the program show the values:

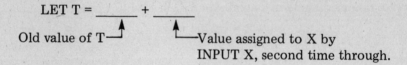

LET T = _____ + _____

Old value of T ⎤   ⎤—Value assigned to X by
                                    INPUT X, second time through.

The *new* value of T is _____.

— — — — — — — — — —

LET T = 12 + 43
55

54. Now that you know how to stop a "runaway" computer, try this program, which causes the computer to print counting numbers, 1, 2, 3, 4, 5, and so on, until you press CTRL and C, together.

```
10 LET N=1
20 PRINT N
30 LET N=N+1
40 GO TO 20

RUN

 1
 2
 3
 4
 5
 6
 7

BREAK IN 20
```

How does it work? Follow the arrows.

10 LET N=1
    ⇩
20 PRINT N ⇐
    ⇩
30 LET N=N+1
    ⇩
40 GO TO 20

This program is another example of a *loop*. Line 10 is outside the loop. Lines 20, 30, and 40 comprise the loop; they are repeated over and over and over. Line 10 is done *once*, initializing N equal to one.

Line 30 is *inside* the loop. It will be done each time through the loop. In line 30, a new value of N is computed by adding 1 to the old value of N.

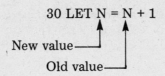

$$30 \text{ LET } N = N + 1$$

New value⸻⏌

Old value⸻⏌

(a) Suppose the old value of N is 1. What will the new value of N be? _____

(b) Suppose the old value of N is 2. What will the new value of N be? _____

— — — — — — — — — — —

(a) 2; (b) 3 (Line 20 will print the new value next time around the loop.)

55. With a counting loop and a few other statements, we can write a program to show how our money grows, year by year. Here it is.

```
100 REM***WATCH YOUR MONEY GROW
110 PRINT "IF YOU TYPE THE AMOUNT OF PRINCIPAL AND THE"
120 PRINT "INTEREST RATE PER YEAR, I WILL SHOW YOU HOW"
130 PRINT "YOUR MONEY GROWS, YEAR BY YEAR. TO STOP ME,"
140 PRINT "PRESS THE 'CTRL' AND 'C' KEYS TOGETHER."
150 PRINT
160 INPUT "PRINCIPAL";P
170 INPUT "INTEREST RATE";R
180 LET N=1            ◄——————————— Start year (N) at 1.
190 PRINT
200 LET A=P*(1+R/100)↑N ⎫
210 PRINT "YEAR =";N     ⎬ ————— Compute and print results for year N.
220 PRINT "AMOUNT =";A   ⎭
230 LET N=N+1         ◄——————————— Increase year (N) by 1 and go around
240 GOTO 190                        again.
RUN
IF YOU TYPE THE AMOUNT OF PRINCIPAL AND THE
INTEREST RATE PER YEAR, I WILL SHOW YOU HOW
YOUR MONEY GROWS, YEAR BY YEAR. TO STOP ME,
PRESS THE 'CTRL' AND 'C' KEYS TOGETHER.

PRINCIPAL? 1000
INTEREST RATE? 6

YEAR = 1
AMOUNT = 1060

YEAR = 2
AMOUNT = 1123.6

YEAR = 3
AMOUNT = 1191.02
```

And so on, until someone presses CTRL and C. Which statements are part of the loop? Give the line numbers. _____

— — — — — — — — — — —

190, 200, 210, 220, 230, and 240

We suggest that you also draw a box around the loop with a felt tip pen. Note that lines 100 through 180 are outside the loop. They are done once during a RUN, while lines 190 through 240 are repeated over and over until you press CTRL and C.

SELF-TEST

Try this Self-Test, so you can evaluate how much you have learned in this chapter.

1. Before entering a program, we usually first type NEW and press RETURN. Why? _____

    _____

2. How do we tell the computer to type a complete listing of a program stored in its memory? _____

3. Assume that we have just stored a program in the computer's memory. How do we tell the computer to execute the program? _____

    _____

4. Assume that the following program is stored in the computer's memory.

    ```
    10 PRINT "MY COMPUTER UNDERSTANDS ME"
    20 PRINT "MY COMPUTER CONFUSES ME"
    ```

    Describe how to replace the second statement (line 20) without erasing the entire program. _____

    _____

5. What is the difference between direct statements and statements to be stored in the computer's memory for later execution? _____

    _____

6. We store the following program and RUN it.

    ```
    100 PRINT "I PROMISE NOT TO CHEW BUBBLE GUM IN CLASS"
    200 GO TO 100
    ```

    How do we stop the computer? _____

    _____

7. Each of the following statements contains an error. Mark the error and show the statement in correct BASIC format (syntax, that is).

    (a)   10 INPUT WHEEL DIAMETER; D

    _____

(b)   20 PRINT DISTANCE IN ONE TURN IS; 3.14*D

_____

(c)   20 "DISTANCE IN ONE TURN IS"; 3.14*D

_____

(d)   20 LET P*(1 + R/100)↑N = A

_____

(e)   20 TYPE "X="; X _____

8.   Describe what is wrong with each statement.

(a)   99999 LET A = 7 _____

_____

(b)   30 GO TO 3.14 _____

_____

(c)   30 GO TO − 100 _____

_____

(d)   10 INPUT, Z _____

_____

(e)   10 INPUT Z, _____

_____

9.   Describe what is wrong with each program.

(a)
```
10 INPUT A
20 INPUT B
30 PRINT A+B
40 GO TO 12
```
_____

_____

_____

(b)
```
10 LET A = 7
20 LET B = 5
30 PRINT X + Y
```
_____

_____

_____

10.   Complete the RUN on the line provided.

```
10 INPUT "A=";A
20 INPUT "B=";B
30 PRINT "A+B =";A+B

RUN
A=? 7
B=? 5
```

_____

11. Show the RUN for the following program.

```
10 LET A$="   XXXXX"
20 LET B$=" X       X"
30 LET C$="(X O O X)"
40 LET D$=" X   V   X"
50 LET E$=" X < > X"
60 LET F$="  X   X"
70 LET G$="    XXX"
80 PRINT A$
90 PRINT B$
100 PRINT C$
110 PRINT D$
120 PRINT E$
130 PRINT F$
140 PRINT G$

RUN
```

12. Write a program to convert temperatures, given in degrees Celsius, to degrees Fahrenheit, using the following formula.

$$F = \frac{9}{5}C + 32$$

A RUN of your program should look like this.

```
RUN
YOU ENTER DEGREES CELSIUS. I WILL TYPE DEGREES FAHRENHEIT.

DEGREES CELSIUS? 0
DEGREES FAHRENHEIT = 32

DEGREES CELSIUS? 100
DEGREES FAHRENHEIT = 212

DEGREES CELSIUS? 37
DEGREES FAHRENHEIT = 98.6

DEGREES CELSIUS?
```
And so on.

13. Congratulations! You are the big winner on a TV show. Your prize is selected as follows.

A number from 1 to 1000 is chosen at random. Call it N. You then select one, and only one, of the following prizes. You have 60 seconds to make your selection.

PRIZE NO. 1: You receive N dollars
PRIZE NO. 2: You receive D dollars, where $D = 1.01^N$

Perhaps you recognize the formula for D. It is the amount you would receive if you invested \$1 at 1% interest per day, compounded daily for N days.

The question, of course, is: For a given value of N, which prize do you take, PRIZE NO. 1 or PRIZE NO. 2? Write a program to help you decide. A RUN might look like this.

```
RUN

N=? 100
PRIZE NØ. 1 = 100            Take PRIZE NO. 1
PRIZE NØ. 2 = 2.70478

N=? 500
PRIZE NØ. 1 = 500            Take PRIZE NO. 1
PRIZE NØ. 2 = 144.764

N=? 1000
PRIZE NØ. 1 = 1000           Take PRIZE NO. 2
PRIZE NØ. 2 = 20956.7

N=?                          And so on.
```

14. Write this program to assist you in performing that tiresome task called "balancing the checkbook." Here is a RUN of our program.

```
RUN
I WILL HELP YOU BALANCE YOUR CHECKBOOK.
ENTER CHECKS AS NEGATIVE NUMBERS AND
DEPOSITS AS POSITIVE NUMBERS.

OLD BALANCE? 123.45

CHECK OR DEPOSIT? -3.95      Remember to enter checks as
NEW BALANCE: 119.5          negative numbers.

CHECK OR DEPOSIT? -25
NEW BALANCE: 94.5.

CHECK OR DEPOSIT? -73.69
NEW BALANCE: 20.81

CHECK OR DEPOSIT? -8.24
NEW BALANCE: 12.57

CHECK OR DEPOSIT? 50         At last! A deposit, and just in time!
NEW BALANCE: 62.57

CHECK OR DEPOSIT?            And so on. Do you remember how to get
                            out of this? If not, see frame 36.
```

15. Suppose we enter this program and then type RUN. Show the first seven numbers printed by the computer.

```
10 LET N = 1
20 PRINT N
30 LET N = N + 1
50 GO TO 20

RUN
```

_____

_____

_____

_____

_____

_____

_____

How do we stop the computer from continuing to print numbers? ____

16. The U.S. is going metric, so here is a metric problem. Write a program to convert feet and inches to centimeters, as indicated by the following RUN.

```
RUN

FEET =? 5
INCHES =? 11
CENTIMETERS =100.34

FEET =? 3
INCHES =? 0
CENTIMETERS =91.44

FEET =?
```

We enter, as requested, the number of feet, and the number of inches.
The computer computes and prints the number of centimeters.

And so on.

Answers to Self-Test

The frame numbers in parentheses refer to the frames in the chapter where the topic is discussed. You may wish to refer to these for quick review.

1. This erases, or removes, any old program that might be in the computer's memory. If we *don't* do this, statements of an old program might be intermingled with statements of the new program, thus causing mysterious and unpredictable behavior when we try to RUN the new program.   (frames 12, 13)

2. Type LIST and press the RETURN key.   (frames 14, 15)

3. Type RUN and press the RETURN key.   (frames 15, 17)

4. Type a new line numbered 20 and press the RETURN key. The old statement 20 is automatically erased and we may now replace it. If we type the line number (and only the line number) of a statement and press RETURN, the computer deletes from its memory the statement (if any) with that line number.   (frames 22, 23)

5. Direct statements do *not* have line numbers and are executed immediately after we press RETURN. A statement to be stored must have a line number; the computer "remembers" it for later execution (at "RUN time" as we sometimes say).   (frame 10)

6. Press the CTRL key and the C key at the same time.   (frames 36-38)

7. (a)   10 INPUT WHEEL DIAMETER ; D   Quotation marks missing.
      10 INPUT "WHEEL DIAMETER" ; D   (frame 44)

   (b)   20 PRINT DISTANCE IN ONE TURN IS ; 3.14*D
                                                Quotation marks missing.
      20 PRINT "DISTANCE IN ONE TURN IS" ; 3.14*D   (frame 45)

   (c)   20 "DISTANCE IN ONE TURN IS" ;3.14*D
      PRINT or ? is missing.
      20 ? "DISTANCE IN ONE TURN IS" ;3.14*D   (frame 45)

(d)   20 LET P*(1 + R/100)↑N = A
Left side of = must be *only* a variable.
20 LET A = P*(1 + R/100)↑N   (frames 1-4)

(e)   20 TYPE "X=" ; X
Computer doesn't know what TYPE means.
20 PRINT "X=" ; X   Either is OK.   (Chapter 2)
20 ?"X=" ; X

8.   (a)   line number too big   (frame 10)

     (b)   3.14 is not a valid line number because it is not an *integer* in the range 1 to 32767   (frame 10)

     (c)   −100 is not a valid line number   (frame 10)

     (d)   should not be a comma following the word INPUT   (frame 33)

     (e)   should not be a comma at the end of the INPUT statement (INPUT statements with two or more variables have commas *between* variables.)   (frame 33)

9.   (a)   The program does not have a line number 12. Therefore, the computer cannot execute the statement 40 GO TO 12. Instead, it will type US IN 40 (which means Undefined Statement reference in line 40) or a similar error message.   (frames 35, 37, 38)

     (b)   The PRINT statement does not use the same variables assigned values in the first two statements. (In MICROSOFT™ BASIC, the computer would print a 0 (zero) for the PRINT statement.) We probably should have done one of the following.

        10 LET A = 7   10 LET X = 7
        20 LET B = 5   20 LET Y = 5
        30 PRINT A + B   30 PRINT X + Y   (frames 1-8)

10.   Here is the complete RUN.

```
RUN
A=? 7
B=? 5
A+B = 12
```

This statement: 30 PRINT "A+B =" ; A+B
Caused this: A+B = 12
(frame 45)

11.
```
 XXXXX
 X     X
(X O O X)
 X  V  X
 X < > X
  X   X
   XXX
```
(Chapter 2 and frame 45)

12.
```
100 REM***PROGRAM TO CONVERT CELSIUS TO FAHRENHEIT
110 PRINT "YOU ENTER DEGREES CELSIUS. I WILL TYPE DEGREES FAHRENHEIT."
120 PRINT
130 INPUT "DEGREES CELSIUS";C
140 PRINT "DEGREES FAHRENHEIT =";(9/5)*C+32
150 GOTO 120
```

(frames 45, 46)

13.
```
100 REM***TV SHOW PRIZE PROBLEM
110 PRINT
120 INPUT "N=";N
130 PRINT "PRIZE NØ. 1 =";N
140 PRINT "PRIZE NØ. 2 =";1.Ø1↑N
150 GOTO 110
```

(frames 45, 46)

14.
```
100 REM***CHECKBOOK BALANCING PROGRAM
110 PRINT "I WILL HELP YOU BALANCE YOUR CHECKBOOK."
120 PRINT "ENTER CHECKS AS NEGATIVE NUMBERS AND"
130 PRINT "DEPOSITS AS POSITIVE NUMBERS."
140 PRINT
150 INPUT "OLD BALANCE";B
160 PRINT
170 INPUT "CHECK OR DEPOSIT";X
180 LET B=B+X ◄───────── Compute new balance as shown below.
190 PRINT "NEW BALANCE:";B
200 GOTO 160
```

$$180 \text{ LET } B = B + X$$

└─check or deposit

└─old balance

└─new balance

(frames 52-54)

15.
```
RUN
  1
  2
  3
  4
  5
  6
  7 And so on.
```
This program illustrates a *counting loop*. Once you type RUN, the computer will begin counting. It will count and count and count and keep on counting until the power fails or the computer breaks down or you press CTRL and C together to stop the computer.   (frames 51-54)

16.
```
100 REM***CONVERT FEET AND INCHES TO CENTIMETERS
110 PRINT
120 INPUT "FEET =";F
130 INPUT "INCHES =";I
140 LET T = 12*F+I
150 LET C = 2.54*T
160 PRINT "CENTIMETERS =";C
170 GO TO 110
```
T is total number of inches in F'I".
C is number of centimeters in T".

(frame 45)

CHAPTER FOUR

Decisions Using IF-THEN Statements

By now you have probably gotten the idea that a computer only does what you very specifically tell it to do. So how can a computer ever decide anything on its own? Well, it can't decide "on its own," but it can make certain comparisons that you instruct it to make, and then either execute or skip other statements in the program according to whether the comparison you specified is true or false. The statement that you use to set up such comparisons is the IF-THEN statement. (As you will see, IF-THEN is actually a whole family of statements.) When you finish this chapter, you will be able to:

- use the IF-THEN statement;

- use the following comparisons in an IF-THEN statement:

Symbol	Meaning
<	less than
>	greater than
=	equal to
<> (or #)	not equal to
=> (or > =)	greater than or equal to
= < (or < =)	less than or equal to

- use the RND function to generate random numbers;

- use the INT function to "drop" the fractional part of a number;

- use the INT and RND functions together to generate random digits;

- use the ON-GOTO statement to selectively branch to various statements in a program;

- use a colon (:) to separate multiple statements in the same line as a means to organize your programs and to save computer memory space;

- use multiple statements per line to increase the usefulness of IF-THEN statements.

1.   In this chapter, we present a very important capability of BASIC—the ability to compare and decide. We will begin with the IF-THEN statement, which tells the computer to carry out a specified operation IF a given condition is TRUE. However, if the condition is FALSE (not true), the operation will not be done. An IF-THEN statement is shown below.

150 IF X > 0 THEN PRINT "YOUR NUMBER IS POSITIVE"

This IF-THEN statement tells the computer: If the value of X is greater than zero, then print the message, YOUR NUMBER IS POSITIVE, and go on to the next statement in line number order. The symbol > means "is greater than."

If the value of X is *less than* zero or *equal to* zero, the computer does *not* print the message. Instead, it simply continues executing the program in the line number order.

Here is another way to look at it. Follow the arrows.

The condition.

150 IF X > 0 THEN [   ] ⟹ PRINT "YOUR NUMBER IS POSITIVE"

Follow this
path if the
condition is
FALSE.

Follow this path if the
condition is TRUE.

What is the *condition* in the above IF-THEN statement? _____

_____

— — — — — — — — —

X > 0 or X is greater than zero

2.   Using our sample statement from frame 1:

(a)   Suppose X = 3. Is the condition TRUE or FALSE? _____

(b)   Suppose X = -7. Is the condition TRUE or FALSE? _____

(c)   Suppose X = 0. Is the condition TRUE or FALSE? _____

— — — — — — — — — —

(a) TRUE. The computer *will* print the message: YOUR NUMBER IS POSITIVE.
(b) FALSE. The computer will *not* print the message.
(c) FALSE. The computer will *not* print the message.

3. The symbol > in an IF-THEN comparison means "is greater than." The symbol = means "is equal to." You can guess that the symbol < used in an

IF-THEN comparison means _____.

— — — — — — — — — —

"is less than"

4. Here is a simple program illustrating the use of the IF-THEN statement. This program has three IF-THEN statements that tell the computer to "compare and decide." Remember, the message in an IF-THEN PRINT statement will be printed only if the comparison is true.

```
100 REM***DETERMINE IF X IS POSITIVE, NEGATIVE OR ZERO
110 PRINT "WHEN I ASK, YOU ENTER A NUMBER AND I WILL TELL YOU"
120 PRINT "WHETHER YOUR NUMBER IS POSITIVE, NEGATIVE OR ZERO."
130 PRINT
140 INPUT "WHAT IS YOUR NUMBER";X
150 IF X>0 THEN PRINT "YOUR NUMBER IS POSITIVE"
160 IF X<0 THEN PRINT "YOUR NUMBER IS NEGATIVE"
170 IF X=0 THEN PRINT "YOUR NUMBER IS ZERO"
180 GOTO 130
```

```
RUN
WHEN I ASK, YOU ENTER A NUMBER AND I WILL TELL YOU
WHETHER YOUR NUMBER IS POSITIVE, NEGATIVE OR ZERO.

WHAT IS YOUR NUMBER? -7
YOUR NUMBER IS NEGATIVE
```
◄——————— This message printed by line 160.

```
WHAT IS YOUR NUMBER? 3
YOUR NUMBER IS POSITIVE
```
◄——————— This message courtesy of line 150.

```
WHAT IS YOUR NUMBER? 0
YOUR NUMBER IS ZERO
```
◄———————Thank you, line 170.

```
WHAT IS YOUR NUMBER?
```
◄——————— And so on. (Do you remember how to stop a program waiting at the IN-PUT question mark?)

(a) What is the condition in line 150? _____

(b) What is the condition in line 160? _____

(c) What is the condition in line 170? _____

— — — — — — — — — —

(a)   X > 0 or X is greater than zero
(b)   X < 0 or X is less than zero
(c)   X = 0 or X is equal to zero

5.   In running the program from frame 4, the computer executes lines 100, 110, and 120 once, since they are "outside the loop." Lines 130 through 180 are included in the loop and are executed for each value of X supplied by the user after an INPUT question mark. Suppose the user runs the program and types 13 after the INPUT question mark, then presses RETURN. This assigns the value 13 to the variable X. Now look back at the program. Since X = 13 (13 is the value of X), the condition in line 150 is TRUE and the conditions in lines 160 and 170 are FALSE. So, the computer will print the message in line 150, but will *not* print the messages in lines 160 and 170.

(a)   Suppose X = −7. The condition in line 160 is (TRUE or FALSE)

_____ and the conditions in lines 150 and 170 are (TRUE or

FALSE) _____.

(b)   Suppose X = 0. Which condition is TRUE? (Give line number.) _____

Which conditions are FALSE? (Give line numbers.) _____

— — — — — — — — — —

(a)   TRUE; FALSE. The computer will print the message in line 160, but will *not* print the messages in lines 150 and 170.
(b)   line 170; lines 150 and 160. The computer will print the message in line 170, but will *not* print the messages in lines 150 and 160.

6.   The program on the following page compares two numbers, A and B, and prints an appropriate message. Complete lines 160 and 170 so that the program will RUN as shown.

```
100 REM***COMPARE TWO NUMBERS, A AND B
110 PRINT "WHEN I ASK, ENTER VALUES FOR A AND B."
120 PRINT
130 INPUT "A ="; A
140 INPUT "B ="; B
150 IF A>B THEN PRINT "A IS GREATER THAN B"

160 IF A<B _____

170 _____
180 GOTO 120

RUN
WHEN I ASK, ENTER VALUES FOR A AND B.

A =? 1
B =? 2
A IS LESS THAN B

A =? 7
B =? 2
A IS GREATER THAN B

A =? 55
B =? 55
A IS EQUAL TO B

A =?
```

— — — — — — — — — —

160 IF A < B THEN PRINT "A IS LESS THAN B"
170 IF A = B THEN PRINT "A IS EQUAL TO B"

7. Let's look at another IF-THEN statement.

This statement: `190 IF X=-1 THEN GO TO 230`

Tells the computer: If the value of X is equal to -1, then go to line 230. If the value of X is *not* equal to -1, the computer continues in usual line number order.

In general, the IF-THEN statement has the following form.

IF *condition* THEN *statement*

The statement could be almost any BASIC statement. The condition is usually a comparison between a variable and a number, between two variables, or between two BASIC expressions. On the following page is a handy table of comparison symbols.

BASIC symbol	Comparison	Math symbol
=	is equal to	=
<	is less than	<
>	is greater than	>
<= (or =<)	is less than or equal to	≤
>= (or =>)	is greater than or equal to	≥
<> (or #)*	is not equal to	≠

*for most versions of BASIC

Write each of the following conditions in proper BASIC.

(a) M is greater than 10. _____

(b) Z is less than or equal to A squared. _____

(c) X is not equal to Y. _____

(d) 3 times P is equal to Z times Q. _____

— — — — — — — — — —

(a) M > 10
(b) Z <= A↑2 or Z <= A * A
(c) X <> Y or X # Y
(d) 3 * P = Z * Q

8.   So far you have seen two members of the IF-THEN family of statements.

> IF-THEN PRINT (message in quotes)
> IF-THEN GOTO (line number)

The second IF-THEN statement shown above tells the computer to branch or GOTO the line number given, if the comparison is true. You may omit the instruction GOTO following THEN, and just specify the line number. Show how you could write the following statement in shorter form.

```
190 IF X = -1 THEN GOTO 230 _____
```

— — — — — — — — — —

```
190 IF X = -1 THEN 230
```


9.   Remember, the basic form of the IF-THEN statement is as follows.

> IF (condition) THEN (almost any BASIC statement)

Since almost any BASIC statement can follow THEN, we could have the computer assign a value or ask for an INPUT (provided that the condition or comparison is true) in an IF-THEN statement.

```
IF Y = 3*Q THEN LET X = 1
IF 2*Y = 6↑N THEN INPUT "WHAT IS YOUR GUESS"; G
```

It's your turn to practice writing the IF-THEN statements that will assign values if the comparison is true. From the following descriptions, write an IF-THEN statement.

(a) If A does not equal B then assign the new value 10 to variable B.

_____

(b) If X is equal to or greater than Y then ask the computer user for another guess and assign the guess to variable G. _____

_____

— — — — — — — — — —

(a) IF A <> B THEN B = 10 (Remember, you can omit the LET in an assignment statement.)
(b) IF X >= Y THEN INPUT "ANOTHER GUESS"; G or
     IF X => Y THEN INPUT "ANOTHER GUESS"; G
     (Either >= or => will be understood by the computer.)

10. For each description, write an IF-THEN statement.

(a) If the value of A is less than or equal to 10, go to line 100.

_____

(b) If A is less than 2*B, then increase the old value of T by 1.

_____

(c) If X is greater than 2 times Y, then print the message X IS MORE THAN Y DOUBLED. _____

(d) If Z does not equal −1, then INPUT a new value for X.

_____

— — — — — — — — — —

(a) IF A <= 10 THEN 100 (The GOTO is optional and usually omitted.)
(b) IF A < 2*B THEN T = T+1 or
     IF A < 2*B THEN LET T = T+1
     (The LET may be included or omitted.)
(c) IF X > 2*Y THEN PRINT "X IS MORE THAN Y DOUBLED."
(d) IF Z <> −1 THEN INPUT X

11. One common use of the IF-THEN statement is to recognize a signal called a "flag" that terminates one process and begins another. Here is

another version of the "World's Most Expensive Adding Machine" which you first encountered in Chapter 3, frame 51. You may wish to review that frame before plunging onward. Notice that we have used MICROSOFT™ BASIC's shortcuts for many of the statements, just to give you practice in recognizing them.

```
100 REM***WORLD'S MOST EXPENSIVE ADDING MACHINE
110 ? "I AM THE WORLD'S MOST EXPENSIVE ADDING MACHINE."
120 ? "EACH TIME I TYPE 'X = ?' YOU TYPE A NUMBER. WHEN"
130 ? "YOU ARE FINISHED ENTERING NUMBERS, TYPE -1 AS YOUR"
140 ? "NUMBER AND I WILL TYPE THE TOTAL OF YOUR PREVIOUS INPUTS."
150 T=0
```

```
160 ?
170 INPUT "X ="; X
180 IF X=-1 THEN 210
190 T=T+X
200 GOTO 160
```
Lines 160 through 200 are a GOTO loop. However, if someone types −1 for the value of X, line 180 will cause the computer to jump out of the loop and go to line 210.

```
210 ?
220 ? "TOTAL ="; T
230 ?
240 GOTO 110
```
This section of the program tells the computer to print a line space, the total of the numbers, and then another line space, then go back to line 110 and start over.

```
RUN
I AM THE WORLD'S MOST EXPENSIVE ADDING MACHINE.
EACH TIME I TYPE 'X = ?' YOU TYPE A NUMBER. WHEN
YOU ARE FINISHED ENTERING NUMBERS, TYPE -1 AS YOUR
NUMBER AND I WILL TYPE THE TOTAL OF YOUR PREVIOUS INPUTS.

X =? 6.95

X =? .47

X =? 1.28

X =? 8.49

X =? 3.06

X =? -1
```
◄─────────Aha! Here is our flag saying "that's all folks."

```
TOTAL=20.25

I AM THE WORLD'S MOST EXPENSIVE ADDING MACHINE.
```
And so on.

The flag used in our program is −1; statement 180 checks each and every input value of X and, if it is −1, causes the computer to jump out of the loop to line 210. Lines 210 through 240 print the total (T) and then cause the computer to jump back to line 110 and start over.

Any unusual number that will not be used as a normal INPUT value could be used as a flag.

Modify the program so that, instead of using −1 as the flag, we use 999999 as the flag. You will have to change lines 130 and 180.

130 _____

180 _____

─ ─ ─ ─ ─ ─ ─ ─ ─ ─

```
130 ? "YOU ARE FINISHED ENTERING NUMBERS,TYPE 999999 AS YOUR"
180 IF X=999999 THEN 210
```

12.   In our program in frame 11 we first used −1 as the flag. This may not be a good idea if some of the values we wish to use are negative. For example, here are temperatures recorded during one cold week in Minneapolis, Minnesota.

S	M	T	W	T	F	S
10	3	−9	−15	−23	−25	−30

In this case, using 999999 as the flag would prevent confusion between a temperature of −1 and an end-of-data flag of −1.

With a few changes, we can modify the program in frame 11 and obtain a program to compute the mean, or average, of a set of numbers. The formula for determining the mean of a set of N numbers is as follows.

$$\text{Mean} = \frac{\text{Sum or total of the Numbers}}{\text{Number of Numbers}} = \frac{T}{N}$$

In the Friendly "Mean" Program, we use the variable T for the total (sum) of the numbers, and N for the number of numbers. Complete the program.

```
100 REM***A FRIENDLY 'MEAN' PROGRAM
110 PRINT "I WILL COMPUTE THE MEAN, OR AVERAGE, OF NUMBERS ENTERED."
120 PRINT "WHEN I TYPE 'X =?' YOU TYPE A NUMBER.  WHEN YOU ARE"
130 PRINT "FINISHED ENTERING NUMBERS, TYPE 999999."

140 LET T=0

150 LET N= _____    ◄─────────────  We will use N to count the
                                              numbers.
160 PRINT
170 INPUT "X ="; X
180 IF X=999999 THEN 220
190 LET T=T+X

200 LET N= _____    ◄─────────────  Increase the count by one.
210 GOTO 160
220 PRINT

230 PRINT "N ="; _____   ◄───────  First, print the number of
240 PRINT "TOTAL ="; T                        numbers.

250 PRINT "MEAN ="; _____   ◄─────  Compute and print the
260 PRINT                                     mean.
270 GOTO 110
```

The RUN is on the next page.

```
RUN
I WILL COMPUTE THE MEAN, OR AVERAGE, OF NUMBERS ENTERED.
WHEN I TYPE 'X =?' YOU TYPE A NUMBER.  WHEN YOU ARE
FINISHED ENTERING NUMBERS, TYPE 999999.

X =? 10

X =? 3

X =? -9

X =? -15

X =? -23

X =? -25

X =? -30

X =? 999999  ◄──────The flag!

N = 7
TOTAL =-89
MEAN =-12.7143
```

N is the number of numbers. One week's worth. That was the cold week that was, or yes, that was a *mean* week.

— — — — — — — — — —

```
150 LET N=0
200 LET N=N+1
230 PRINT "N ="; N
250 PRINT "MEAN ="; T/N
```

13. For temperatures in Minneapolis, 999999 is a good flag. We assume, of course, that the temperature *never* reaches 999999 degrees, even in the summer. For other types of data, 999999 may not be a good flag. One of the most outrageous and least likely BASIC numbers we can think of is the floating point number, 1E38. For most data, 1E38 would be a good flag. So, modify lines 130 and 180 in the program of frame 12 so that the flag is 1E38.

130 _____

180 _____

— — — — — — — — — —

```
130 PRINT "FINISHED ENTERING NUMBERS, TYPE 1E38."
180 IF X=1E38 THEN 220
```

14. You have helped us write several computer programs using IF-THEN comparisons. Now it is time for you to do a solo flight and write a program on your own. Think carefully about the use of IF-THEN comparisons, and what the computer will do if the conditions are TRUE or if they are FALSE. On the following page is a RUN of the program we want you to write.

```
RUN
INPUT A NUMBER AND I WILL TELL YOU IF IT IS
100 OR LESS, OR OVER 100.

YOUR NUMBER?  99
YOUR NUMBER IS 100 OR LESS.

YOUR NUMBER? 101
YOUR NUMBER IS OVER 100.

YOUR NUMBER? 100
YOUR NUMBER IS 100 OR LESS.

YOUR NUMBER?
```

Now you write the program.

— — — — — — — — — —

```
100 REM***NUMBER SIZE PROGRAM
110 PRINT "INPUT A NUMBER AND I WILL TELL YOU IF IT IS"
120 PRINT "100 OR LESS, OR OVER 100."
130 PRINT
140 INPUT "YOUR NUMBER"; N
150 IF N <= 100 THEN PRINT "YOUR NUMBER IS 100 OR LESS."
160 IF N > 100 THEN PRINT "YOUR NUMBER IS OVER 100."
170 GOTO 130
```

15. Soon we will enter the fun-filled realm of computer games. But first, you should learn about random numbers and the unpredictable BASIC function known as RND.

Random numbers are numbers chosen at random from a given set of numbers. Many games come with dice or a spinner or some other device for generating random numbers. Roll the dice; they come up 8. Move 8 spaces.

Functions are automatic features of BASIC that you use to perform special operations. These functions are like built-in programs; most of them could be replaced by a program or segment of a program. However, computers are called upon often enough to do the operations accomplished by these functions that it is worthwhile to "build them in" to the computer language.

BASIC provides a special function, called the RND function, that generates numbers that seem to be chosen at random, like picking numbers out of a hat. The program on the following page shows the use of the RND function. We show you the program (enclosed in a box) and two different runs of that program. We interrupted the first RUN by pressing CONTROL/C, then typed RUN again.

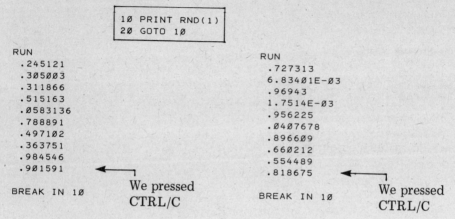

```
10 PRINT RND(1)
20 GOTO 10
```

RUN
```
 .245121
 .305003
 .311866
 .515163
 .0583136
 .788891
 .497102
 .363751
 .984546
 .901591
```
BREAK IN 10   ← ⌐ We pressed
                      CTRL/C

RUN
```
 .727313
6.83401E-03
 .96943
1.7514E-03
 .956225
 .0407678
 .896609
 .660212
 .554489
 .818675
```
BREAK IN 10   ← ⌐ We pressed
                      CTRL/C

Two runs of the program are shown. Are the lists of random numbers in the two runs the same? _____

— — — — — — — — — — —

No. In fact, *don't* expect to enter our program into your computer, type RUN, and get either list. That's the idea of random numbers. They are, well, random!

16.   The statement 10 PRINT RND(1) causes the computer to produce a *different* list of random numbers each time the program is RUN. The RND function generates numbers that appear to be chosen at random. On our computer, the RND function is written RND(1).

We use the number 1 in parentheses. However, *any* positive number is OK, even numbers with decimal fractions! On our computer, a positive number in parentheses following RND will cause the computer to produce a different list of random numbers each time. This will not be true if zero (0) or a negative number is used. Consult your reference manual, or ask someone, how RND works on your computer for zero or negative numbers, or experiment when you have the opportunity.

Examine the random numbers in frame 15.

(a)   Is any number less than zero (negative)? _____

(b)   Is any number equal to zero? _____

(c)   Is any number greater than one? _____

(d)   Is any number equal to one? _____

(e)   From the evidence, it appears that random numbers produced by the

RND function are _____ zero and _____ one.

— — — — — — — — — —

(a)   no
(b)   no
(c)   no
(d)   no
(e)   greater than; less than. However, we haven't shown much evidence—
      only a few random numbers. When you have a computer to use, we
      suggest you run off a bunch of random numbers on your computer in
      order to get more evidence. (But remember! Evidence is not proof.)

17.   It's true that random numbers produced by the RND function *are*
greater than zero and less than one. Another way to say it: random numbers
produced by the RND function are *between* 0 and 1. Or, in still another
way: $0 < \text{RND}(1) < 1$.

However, random numbers between 0 and 1 are not always convenient.
Sometimes we would like random *digits* (the numbers 0, 1, 2, 3, 4, 5, 6, 7,
8, and 9) or random integers (whole numbers) from 1 to 100. Below is a
RUN in which the computer acts as a teaching machine to teach *one-digit*
addition to children.


```
RUN

  1 + 4 =? 5            ◄──────────────  Computer typed: 1 + 4 = ?
RIGHT ON...GOOD WORK!!!                  Student typed the answer, 5,
                                         and pressed RETURN.
  9 + 6 =? 14
HMMM...I GET A DIFFERENT ANSWER.  ◄───── Student missed this one.

  9 + 6 =? 15          ◄──────────────  Computer repeats problem.
RIGHT ON...GOOD WORK!!!                  This time student gets it cor-
                                         rect.
  7 + 2 =? 9
RIGHT ON...GOOD WORK!!!

  8 + Ø =?                               New problem. . . . And so on.
```

Undoubtedly, you are anxious to see the program. Patience! Let's
build it, piece by piece. First, how do we generate *random digits*?

The random numbers produced by the RND function are *uniformly
distributed* between 0 and 1. That is, they are "spread evenly" between 0
and 1. Each random number is about as likely (or unlikely) to occur as any
other random number.

RND(1) is *between* 0 and 1, but is never 0 or 1. Therefore, 10*RND(1)

is between 0 and _____.

— — — — — — — — — —

10. But 10*RND(1) is never *equal* to zero or ten.

18. Below is a program to print random numbers between 0 and 10. We show you two RUNs to remind you that you get a different list each time.

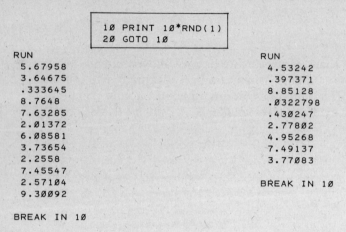

```
10 PRINT 10*RND(1)
20 GOTO 10
```

RUN
5.67958
3.64675
.333645
8.7648
7.63285
2.01372
6.08581
3.73654
2.2558
7.45547
2.57104
9.30092

BREAK IN 10

RUN
4.53242
.397371
8.85128
.0322798
.430247
2.77802
4.95268
7.49137
3.77083

BREAK IN 10

Each random number in the runs is greater than zero and less than ten. Each random number can be thought of as having an *integer* part to the left of the decimal point and a fractional part to the right of the decimal point. For example:

The integer part of 8.35007 is 8 and the fractional part is .35007.

Although it is not actually printed, the integer part of .717177 is zero (0). The fractional part is .717177.

(a) What is the integer part of 2.81303? _____ The fractional

part? _____

(b) What is the integer part of .0523684? _____ The frac-

tional part? _____

— — — — — — — — — —

(a) 2; .81303
(b) 0; .0523684

19. Now you write three short program to print random numbers in the ranges specified.

(a) between 0 and 100

(b)   between 0 and 50

(c)   between 0 and 6

— — — — — — — — — —

(a)
```
10 PRINT 100*RND(1)
20 GOTO 10

RUN
 73.3308
 12.7318
 37.9114
 87.8885
 2.109
 20.1256
 69.579
 4.26022

BREAK IN 10
```

(b)
```
10 PRINT 50*RND(1)
20 GOTO 10

RUN
 28.9513
 35.5718
 44.6059
 11.434
 6.48894
 15.2396

BREAK IN 10
```

(c)
```
10 PRINT 6*RND(1)
20 GOTO 10

RUN
 2.60018
 1.31444
 3.24057
 .115358
 .0228755
 2.90792
 5.721
 2.03216

BREAK IN 10
```

20.   For each random number *between* 0 and 10, the integer (whole number) part is a *single digit.* Wouldn't it be nice if we could direct the computer to delete the fractional part and keep the integer part?

Well, as you may suspect, we can. BASIC has another clever and useful function called INT. Here are some examples.

$$INT (3) = 3 \qquad INT (7) = 7$$
$$INT (3.14159) = 3 \qquad INT (7.99999) = 7$$
$$INT (1.23456) = 1 \qquad INT (.999999) = 0$$

(Say it like this: "The integer part of 3.14159 is 3.")

In general, if X is any positive number, INT(X) is the *integer part* of X. Now, you apply INT to some of the random numbers from frame 18.

(a)   INT (7.45547) = _____   (b)   INT (.333645) = _____

(c)   INT (2.57104) = _____   (d)   INT (.032279) = _____

— — — — — — — — — — —

(a)   7
(b)   0   (Think of .333645 as being equal to 0.333645.)
(c)   2
(d)   0   (Think of .032279 as being equal to 0.032279.)

21.   Caution. INT works as shown in frame 20 only for *positive* numbers or zero. In general, INT(X) computes *the greatest integer less than or equal to X.* For example:

$$\begin{array}{lll} \text{INT } (3.14) = 3 & \text{but} & \text{INT } (-3.14) = -4 \\ \text{INT } (7) = 7 & \text{and} & \text{INT } (-7) = -7 \\ \text{INT } (.999) = 0 & \text{but} & \text{INT } (-.999) = -1 \end{array}$$

For positive numbers, or zero, INT(X) computes the integer part of X. In a program, the *value* assigned to X will be substituted for X in the INT parentheses when the program is RUN. The computer then performs the INT function on the numerical value. Of course, any variable could be used instead of the letter X, as long as it has been assigned a value earlier in the program.

You be the computer and show what you will print when your human tells you to RUN the following programs.

(a)
```
10 X=15.77
20 ? INT(X)
RUN
```
_____

(b)
```
10 A=99.999
20 ? INT(A)
RUN
```
_____

(c)
```
10 F=98.6
20 ? INT(F)
RUN
```
_____

— — — — — — — — — — —

(a) 15; (b) 99; (c) 98

22.   Instead of a number, we can write a variable, a function, or any BASIC expression in the parentheses that follow the word INT.

INT(   )

└── Any BASIC number, variable, function or expression here

You should be able to distinguish between *values*, *variables*, *expressions*, *functions*, and *strings*. To show that you can, identify each of the following with one of the words given above in italics.

(a)   X   _____

(b)   X*2   _____

(c)   RND(1)   _____

(d)   "A+B IS AN EXPRESSION"   _____

(e)   22   _____

(f)   1+1   _____

(g)   INT(52.88)   _____

(h)   "="   _____

(i)   4*(3+X)   _____

(j)   Which of the above could be used in the parentheses of a function such
      as INT or RND? _____

_ _ _ _ _ _ _ _ _ _

(a)   variable
(b)   expression
(c)   function
(d)   string
(e)   value
(f)   expression
(g)   function
(h)   string
(i)   expression
(j)   a, b, c, e, f, g, and i

23.   Remember, the general form for the INT function is as follows.

   INT(   )

   └─────── Any BASIC number, variable, function or expression here

      So, it is OK to write INT(10*RND(1)). This is an expression containing
a function as part of the expression.

         RND(1) is a random number between 0 and 1.
         10*RND(1) is a random number between 0 and 10.
         INT(10*RND(1)) is a *random digit*.

      The program on the following page causes the computer to generate
and print random digits. Digits are the numbers 0, 1, 2, 3, 4, 5, 6, 7, 8, and
9, or 0 to 9, inclusive. Note that "inclusive" means it includes both 0 and 9,
as well as the digits between 0 and 9.

```
10 PRINT INT(10*RND(1))
20 GOTO 10.
```

```
RUN               RUN
 5                 4
 3                 6
 2                 3
 0                 9
 6                 4
 3                 0
 4                 1
 1                 2
 7
                  BREAK IN 10
BREAK IN 10
```

This program prints random digits, which are integers from _____ to _____, inclusive.

— — — — — — — — — —

0; 9

24. Now write a short program to print random integers (whole numbers) from 0 to 19, inclusive. Our RUN looks like this.

```
RUN
 3
10
17
 5
 9
19
 7
 2
```

— — — — — — — — — —

```
10 PRINT INT(20*RND(1))
20 GOTO 10
```

Be sure to match the parentheses. There must be a right, or closing, parenthesis for every left, or opening, parenthesis; if not, the computer will give you an error message when you RUN the program.

25. What if we want random integers from 1 to 20, inclusive, instead of from 0 to 19? Well, that's easy. Simply add a 1 to the random integer. You could do it in two ways.

```
10 PRINT INT(20*RND(1)+1)
20 GOTO 10
```

or

```
10 PRINT INT(20*RND(1))+1
20 GOTO 10

RUN
 14
 20
 20
 16
 19
  7
 20
  2
 15
```

The "+1" can be added to the random number either before or after taking the integer part of 20*RND(1). The resulting random integer will be the same in either case.

Now you write three simple programs to print a list of random integers.

(a)   from 1 to 10 inclusive   (b)   from 1 to 100, inclusive

(c)   from 1 to 12, inclusive

— — — — — — — — — —

(a)   10 PRINT INT(10*RND(1))+1   or   10 PRINT INT(10*RND(1)+1)
      20 GOTO 10   20 GOTO 10
(b)   10 PRINT INT(100*RND(1))+1 or   10 PRINT INT(100*RND(1)+1)
      20 GOTO 10   20 GOTO 10
(c)   10 PRINT INT(12*RND(1))+1   or   10 PRINT INT(12*RND(1)+1)
      20 GOTO 10   20 GOTO 10

26.   What if we want random integers from 5 to 10 inclusive? Here is a hint: to get random integers from 1 to 10 instead of 0 to 9, we added a +1. Look at it like this.

$$\frac{\begin{array}{cc} 0 \text{ to } 9 \\ +1 \quad +1 \end{array}}{1 \text{ to } 10}$$

(a)   The function INT(6*RND(1)) will generate what random digits? _____

_____

(b) What should we add to this expression INT(6*RND(1)) in order to generate integers from 5 to 10 inclusive? _____

(c) What should we add in order to generate integers from 11 to 16 inclusive? _____

— — — — — — — — — —

(a) 0 to 5 inclusive, that is, 0, 1, 2, 3, 4, and 5, a total of 6 digits.
(b) +5   0 to   5

$$\begin{array}{cc} +5 & +5 \\ \hline 5 & 10 \end{array}$$

(c) +11   0 to   5

$$\begin{array}{cc} +11 & +11 \\ \hline 11 & 16 \end{array}$$

27. Look back at the RUN in frame 17 before we continue. Now we are ready to build the addition practice program. Here is the first section of the program that produced the RUN.

```
100 REM***ADDITION PRACTICE PROGRAM
200 REM***GENERATE RANDOM NUMBERS, A AND B
210 LET A=INT(10*RND(1))
220 LET B=INT(10*RND(1))
```

The values of A and B will be _____.

— — — — — — — — — —

random digits (0, 1, 2, 3, 4, 5, 6, 7, 8, or 9)

28. Ready for the next piece? Here we go.

```
300 REM***PRINT PROBLEM AND ASK FOR ANSWER
310 PRINT
320 PRINT A; "+"; B; "=";
330 INPUT C
```

Line 320 is something new. The statement PRINT A; "+"; B; "="; tells the computer to print the *value* of A, then print +, then print the *value* of B, then print =. These items are separated by semicolons. The fourth semicolon, at the very end, tells the computer *not* to return the carriage on the TTY and *not* to go to the next line down on the CRT. In other words, it tells the computer to stay where it stopped printing.

Do you remember? The INPUT statement causes the computer to print a *question mark*. This question mark will be printed on the same line as the information from the PRINT statement, because of that semicolon at the end of line 320.

For example, if A = 7 and B = 5, then lines 320 and 330 will cause the computer to print the following.

$$7 + 5 = ?$$

from line 320 ⌐⌐   ⌐ from line 330 (INPUT question mark)

If A = 3 and B = 4, what will be printed by lines 320 and 330? _____

_____

— — — — — — — — — —

3 + 4 = ? (This, of course, is the *random problem* which helps the eager young learner practice addition.)

29. After the learner types an answer and presses the RETURN key, the computer assigns the answer value to variable C and continues.

Note how we are using REM (REMARK) statements to tell something about each piece of the program. This doesn't help the computer, but it does help *people* read and understand how the program works.

```
400 REM***IS THE ANSWER CORRECT?
410 IF C=A+B THEN 610
```

If the student's answer (C) is correct, the computer will go to line _____.

— — — — — — — — — —

610 (If the answer is not correct, the computer continues in regular line number order.)

30. If the student's answer is not correct, then the IF-THEN condition is false. The computer next does the following as it continues on in the program in line number order.

```
500 REM***ANSWER IS NOT CORRECT
510 PRINT "HMMM...I GET A DIFFERENT ANSWER."
520 GOTO 310
```

Assume an incorrect answer. The computer prints HMMM . . . I GET A DIFFERENT ANSWER, then goes to line 310. From there (check previous frames if necessary), what happens next? _____

— — — — — — — — — —

The computer repeats the problem.

Note: In a previous book, we had the computer type YOU GOOFED. TRY

AGAIN. Now that we know more about learners, we wish to make the computer seem friendly and compassionate, rather than nasty and authoritarian. Remember that what the computer "says" depends on the person who writes the program, and not the machine itself.

31. Review frame 29, which shows lines 400 and 410 of the program. If the learner's answer is correct, line 410 causes the computer to go to line 610.

```
600 REM***ANSWER IS CORRECT
610 PRINT "RIGHT ON...GOOD WORK!!! "
620 GOTO 210
```

Assume a correct answer. The computer prints RIGHT ON . . . GOOD WORK!!! and then goes to line 210. What happens next? _____

_____

— — — — — — — — — —

The computer generates a new problem (new values for A and B) and prints the new problem.

32. Below is a listing of the complete ADDITION PRACTICE PROGRAM.

```
100 REM***ADDITION PRACTICE PROGRAM
200 REM***GENERATE RANDOM NUMBERS, A AND B
210 LET A=INT(10*RND(1))
220 LET B=INT(10*RND(1))
300 REM***PRINT PROBLEM AND ASK FOR ANSWER
310 PRINT
320 PRINT A; "+"; B; "=";
330 INPUT C
400 REM***IS THE ANSWER CORRECT?
410 IF C=A+B THEN 610
500 REM***ANSWER IS NOT CORRECT
510 PRINT "HMMM...I GET A DIFFERENT ANSWER."
520 GOTO 310
600 REM***ANSWER IS CORRECT
610 PRINT "RIGHT ON...GOOD WORK!!!"
620 GOTO 210
```

Change line 210 so that the value of A is a random integer from 0 to 19, inclusive, instead of 0 to 9.

210 LET A = _____

— — — — — — — — — —

210 LET A=INT(20*RND(1))

_____

33. Careful on this one! Change line 220 so that the value of B is a random integer from 10 to 20, inclusive.

220 LET B = _____

— — — — — — — — — — —

220 LET B=INT(11*RND(1))+10

That gives us 10 to 20 inclusive, eleven numbers in all.

$$\begin{array}{r} 0 \text{ to } 10 \\ +10 \quad +10 \\ \hline 10 \text{ to } 20 \end{array}$$

We changed lines 210 and 220 of the program in frame 32 to look like the answer to frame 32, and ran the modified program. Remember, a RUN on your computer will probably show different numbers in the problems. These are random numbers, after all.

```
RUN

 16 + 14 =? 30
RIGHT ON...GOOD WORK!!!

 16 + 15 =? 31
RIGHT ON...GOOD WORK!!!

 4 + 10 =? 15
HMMM...I GET A DIFFERENT ANSWER.

 4 + 10 =? 14
RIGHT ON...GOOD WORK!!!

 6 + 16 =?      And so on.
```

34. When the learner's answer is correct, the computer always prints: RIGHT ON . . . GOOD WORK!!! To relieve the monotony, let's modify the program so that the computer selects at random from three possible replies to a correct answer. The changes are in the portion of the program beginning at line 600.

```
600 REM***ANSWER IS CORRECT
610 LET R=INT(3*RND(1))+1   ◄——————— Note the +1.
620 IF R=1 THEN 630
621 IF R=2 THEN 650
622 IF R=3 THEN 670
630 PRINT "RIGHT ON...GOOD WORK!!!"
640 GOTO 210
650 PRINT "YOU GOT IT! TRY ANOTHER."
660 GOTO 210
670 PRINT "THAT'S GREAT! KEEP IT UP!"
680 GOTO 210
```

The possible values of R are _____, _____, and _____.

— — — — — — — — — — —

1, 2, and 3 (Not 0, 1, and 2, because we added +1 at the end of line 610.)

35.   So, we see, R can be 1 or 2 or 3.

(a)   If R = 1, the computer will print _____.

(b)   If R = 3, the computer will print _____.

(c)   If R = 2, the computer will print _____.

— — — — — — — — — — —

(a)   RIGHT ON . . . GOOD WORK!!!
(b)   THAT'S GREAT! KEEP IT UP!
(c)   YOU GOT IT! TRY ANOTHER.

36.   We made the changes in response (frame 34) from the original program (frame 32) and ran the modified program. Here is what happened.

```
RUN

 9 + 19 =? 28
THAT'S GREAT! KEEP IT UP!

 6 + 15 =? 21
YOU GOT IT! TRY ANOTHER.

 17 + 12 =? 29
THAT'S GREAT! KEEP IT UP!

 12 + 11 =? 23
RIGHT ON...GOOD WORK!!!

 Ø + 19 =? 19
RIGHT ON...GOOD WORK!!!

 8 + 17 =? 22
HMMM...I GET A DIFFERENT ANSWER.

 8 + 17 =?
```

If the learner's answer is incorrect, the computer always prints: HMMM . . . I GET A DIFFERENT ANSWER. Modify the program in frame 32 so that, for an incorrect response, the computer selects randomly one of the two following responses.

HMMM . . . I GET A DIFFERENT ANSWER
TRY A DIFFERENT ANSWER. GOOD LUCK!

500 REM***ANSWER IS NOT CORRECT

510 LET R = _____

520 IF _____

_____

530 IF _____

540 PRINT _____

550 GOTO 310

560 _____

570 GOTO 310

— — — — — — — — — —

```
500 REM***ANSWER IS NOT CORRECT
510 LET R=INT(2*RND(1))+1
520 IF R=1 THEN 540
530 IF R=2 THEN 560
540 PRINT "HMMM...I GET A DIFFERENT ANSWER. "
550 GOTO 310
560 PRINT "TRY A DIFFERENT ANSWER.   GOOD LUCK! "
570 GOTO 310
```

Again, we are trying to make the computer seem friendly and helpful, instead of harsh and unforgiving.

37.   The three statements: 620 IF R=1 THEN 630
                              621 IF R=2 THEN 650
                              622 IF R=3 THEN 670

can be replaced by a single statement.

620 ON R GOTO 630,650,670

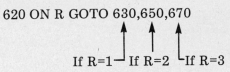

If R=1 — If R=2 ⌐If R=3

With this change, the program segment in frame 34 can be rewritten as follows.

```
600 REM***ANSWER IS CORRECT
610 LET R=INT(3*RND(1))+1
620 ON R GOTO 630,650,670
630 PRINT "RIGHT ON...GOOD WORK!"
640 GOTO 210
650 PRINT "YOU GOT IT! TRY ANOTHER."
660 GOTO 210
670 PRINT "THAT'S GREAT! KEEP IT UP!"
680 GOTO 210
```

(a)   Look at line 610. What are the *possible* values of R? _____

(b)   Suppose, during a RUN, the random number generated by RND(1) in

line 610 is .34319. What value will R have? _____

(c)   In this case, which line will the ON R GOTO statement send the computer to?_____

— — — — — — — — — —

(a)   1, 2, 3
(b)   2. INT(3*.34319)+1 = INT(1.02957)+1 = 1 + 1 = 2
(c)   line 650

38.   In general, the ON . . . GOTO statement has the following form.

ON e GOTO $\ell_1, \ell_2, \ell_3, \ldots, \ell_n$

Where e can be any BASIC expression and $\ell_1, \ell_2, \ell_3, \ldots, \ell_n$ are line numbers. Valid values for e are integers 1, 2, 3, . . ., n. If $e = 1$, the computer goes to line ℓ_1. If $e = 2$, the computer goes to ℓ_2. And so on. To find out what happens if the value of e is *not* an integer from 1 to n, consult the reference guide for *your* BASIC. Usually, the fraction part is dropped, and the remaining integer part of the number will be used.

Use an ON . . . GOTO to replace the two IF statements (lines 520 and 530) in our solution to frame 36.

```
500 REM***ANSWER IS NOT CORRECT
510 LET R=INT(2*RND(1))+1

520 ON _____
540 PRINT "HMMM...I GET A DIFFERENT ANSWER."
550 GOTO 310
560 PRINT "TRY A DIFFERENT ANSWER.  GOOD LUCK!"
570 GOTO 310
```

— — — — — — — — — —

520 ON R GOTO 540,560

39.   And now, a wonderful space saving method! Here is the first part of our addition practice program, featuring *multiple statements per line*.

```
100 REM***ADDITION PRACTICE PROGRAM
200 REM***GENERATE RANDOM NUMBERS, A AND B
210 LET A=INT(20*RND(1))
220 LET B=INT(11*RND(1))+10
300 REM***PRINT PROBLEM AND ASK FOR ANSWER
310 PRINT : PRINT A; "+"; B; "="; : INPUT C
400 REM***IS THE ANSWER CORRECT?
410 IF C=A+B THEN 600
500 REM***ANSWER IS NOT CORRECT
510 LET R=INT(2*RND(1))+1
520 ON R GOTO 540,560
540 PRINT "HMMM...I GET A DIFFERENT ANSWER." : GOTO 310
560 PRINT "TRY A DIFFERENT ANSWER.  GOOD LUCK!" : GOTO 310
```

Line 310 has 3 statements.

Lines 540 and 560 each have 2 statements per line.

In the program, line 310 contains three statements, and lines 540 and 560 each contain two statements. In a line that contains more than one statement, what symbol, or character, is used between statements?_____

— — — — — — — — — —

a colon (:)

┌—colon   colon—┐
310 PRINT : PRINT A; "+"; B; "="; : INPUT C

40.   For readability, we usually put a space on each side of the colon. However, this is not necessary. For example, we could have typed line 310 as shown below.

```
310 PRINT:PRINT A; "+"; B; "=";:INPUT C
```

In fact, leaving out all of the unnecessary spaces, and using our BASIC's shortcuts, line 310 could look like this.

```
310?:?A;"+";B;"=";:INPUTC
```

However, we will include spaces to make the statements easier to read. The computer understands either way.

We didn't show you the entire program in the last frame, because we want you to rewrite the part of the program beginning with line 600 as shown in frame 37, using multiple statements in those lines where it makes sense to group statements to work together.

```
600 REM***ANSWER IS CORRECT
610 LET R=INT(3*RND(1))+1
620 ON R GOTO 630,640,650

630 _____

640 _____

650 _____
```

— — — — — — — — — —

```
630 PRINT "RIGHT ON...GOOD WORK!!!" : GOTO 210
640 PRINT "YOU GOT IT! TRY ANOTHER." : GOTO 210
650 PRINT "THAT'S GREAT! KEEP IT UP!" : GOTO 210
```

41.   Here is the computer game we promised you earlier in the chapter. Note the use of multiple statements per line in lines 150, 160, 170, and 180.

```
100 REM***GUESS MY NUMBER - A COMPUTER GAME
110 LET X=INT(100*RND(1))+1
120 PRINT
130 PRINT "I'M THINKING OF A NUMBER FROM 1 TO 100."
140 PRINT "GUESS MY NUMBER!"
150 PRINT : INPUT "YOUR GUESS"; G
160 IF G < X THEN PRINT "TRY A BIGGER NUMBER." : GOTO 150
170 IF G > X THEN PRINT "TRY A SMALLER NUMBER." : GOTO 150
180 IF G = X THEN PRINT "THAT'S IT! YOU GUESSED MY NUMBER!" : GOTO 110

RUN

I'M THINKING OF A NUMBER FROM 1 TO 100.
GUESS MY NUMBER!

YOUR GUESS? 50
TRY A BIGGER NUMBER.

YOUR GUESS?  75
TRY A SMALLER NUMBER.

YOUR GUESS? 68
TRY A BIGGER NUMBER.

YOUR GUESS? 72
TRY A BIGGER NUMBER.

YOUR GUESS? 73
THAT'S IT! YOU GUESSED MY NUMBER!

I'M THINKING OF A NUMBER FROM 1 TO 100.
GUESS MY NUMBER!

YOUR GUESS?
```
And so on.

Line 110 tells the computer to generate a random number and store it in variable X. This number will be a(n) _____ from _____ to _____.

— — — — — — — — — —

integer (or whole number); 1; 100

42.   Multiple statements per line give us another nice shortcut. You'll recall that if the comparison in an IF-THEN statement is false, the computer skips the rest of the statement and goes on to the next line in the program in line number order. The nice thing is that the computer will also skip any statements that follow a false IF-THEN comparison if they are on the same multiple statement line. The rest of the statements on a line will be executed if the IF-THEN comparison is true. Therefore, in one line, you can have the computer do more than one thing if an IF-THEN comparison is true. Consider line 170 as it is shown on the following page. The computer will both

PRINT and GOTO if the condition is true, but it won't do either if the condition is false.

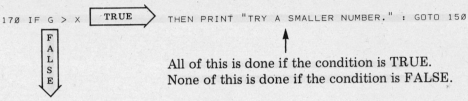

```
170 IF G > X    TRUE    THEN PRINT "TRY A SMALLER NUMBER." : GOTO 150
```

All of this is done if the condition is TRUE.
None of this is done if the condition is FALSE.

The *condition* is: $G > X$

(a) Suppose G = 90 and X = 73. Is the condition TRUE or FALSE?_____

(b) Suppose G = 70 and X = 73. Is the condition TRUE or FALSE?_____

(c) Suppose G = 73 and X = 73. Is the condition TRUE or FALSE?_____

— — — — — — — — — —

(a) TRUE; (b) FALSE; (c) FALSE

43. Line 150 causes the computer to print YOUR GUESS? When the player types a guess, the computer stores it in variable G. Lines 160, 170, and 180 compare the guess G with the random number X. Let's look at line 160.

```
160 IF G < X THEN PRINT "TRY A BIGGER NUMBER." : GOTO 150
```

If the guess G is less than the number X, the computer will print the message TRY A BIGGER NUMBER and will then GOTO line 150 to ask for another guess. However, if G is greater than X or equal to X, *neither* the PRINT *nor* the GOTO will be done. Here is another way to "picture" that idea.

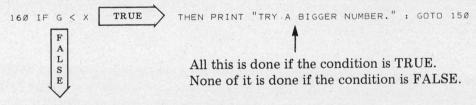

```
160 IF G < X    TRUE    THEN PRINT "TRY A BIGGER NUMBER." : GOTO 150
```

All this is done if the condition is TRUE.
None of it is done if the condition is FALSE.

So, if G < X is FALSE, the computer goes on to line 170. Describe what happens when the computer executes line 170.

```
170 IF G > X THEN PRINT "TRY A SMALLER NUMBER." : GOTO 150
```

(a) If G *is* greater than X (G > X is TRUE), then _____

_____.

(b) However, if G is *not* greater than X (G > X is FALSE), then _____

_____.

— — — — — — — — — —

(a) the computer will print the message TRY A SMALLER NUMBER and then GOTO line 150 for another guess
(b) neither the PRINT nor the GOTO will be done

44. If G < X is FALSE *and* G > X is FALSE, the computer will finally arrive at line 180. Here is a picture of the entire process of arriving at line 180.

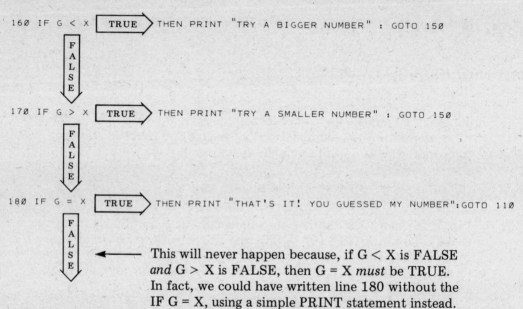

Suppose the player has guessed the number. Therefore, G < X is FALSE, G > X is FALSE, and, of course, G = X is TRUE. What happens?

_____

_____

_____

— — — — — — — — — —

The computer prints the message THAT'S IT! YOU GUESSED MY NUMBER, then goes to line 110, where it is directed to "think of" a new number and start the game again.

45. For very young children, we may wish to reduce the range of integers generated by the statement that uses the RND functions (line 110). For example, instead of generating a number from 1 to 100, we may wish a number from 1 to 25. Conversely, advanced players may prefer a larger range, say 1 to 1000.

(a) Modify lines 110 and 130 so that the range is 1 to 25.

110 _____

130 _____

(b) Modify lines 110 and 130 so that the range is 1 to 1000.

110 _____

130 _____

— — — — — — — — — —

(a) 110 LET X=INT(25*RND(1))+1
    130 PRINT "I'M THINKING OF A NUMBER FROM 1 TO 25."
(b) 110 LET X=INT(1000*RND(1))+1
    130 PRINT "I'M THINKING OF A NUMBER FROM 1 TO 1000."

46. Here is a convenient way to make it easy to change the range.

```
100 REM***GUESS MY NUMBER – A COMPUTER GAME
105 LET R=100
110 LET X=INT(R*RND(1))+1
120 PRINT
130 PRINT "I'M THINKING OF A NUMBER FROM 1 TO"; R
```

Now the range is 1 to R, where R is assigned a value in line 105, then used in lines 110 and 130. So, to change the range, you simply change line 105. Suppose you want the range to be 1 to 500. What do you write for line 105?

105 _____

— — — — — — — — — —

105 LET R=500 or simply 105 R=500

47. Using IF-THEN statements and multiple statements per line, modify and rewrite your NUMBER SIZE PROGRAM from frame 14 so that it will RUN like the one on the following page.

```
RUN
INPUT A NUMBER AND I WILL TELL YOU IF IT IS
LESS THAN 100, BETWEEN 100 AND 1000, OR OVER 1000.

YOUR NUMBER? 99
YOUR NO. IS LESS THAN 100.

YOUR NUMBER? 100
YOUR NO. IS BETWEEN 100 AND 1000.

YOUR NUMBER? 999
YOUR NO. IS BETWEEN 100 AND 1000.

YOUR NUMBER? 1000
YOUR NO. IS BETWEEN 100 AND 1000.

YOUR NUMBER? 1001
YOUR NO. IS OVER 1000.

YOUR NUMBER?
```

— — — — — — — — —

```
100 REM***NEW NUMBER SIZE PROGRAM
110 PRINT "INPUT A NUMBER AND I WILL TELL YOU IF IT IS"
120 PRINT "LESS THAN 100, BETWEEN 100 AND 1000, OR OVER 1000."
130 PRINT : INPUT "YOUR NUMBER"; N
140 IF N<100 THEN PRINT "YOUR NO. IS LESS THAN 100." : GOTO 130
150 IF N<=1000 THEN PRINT "YOUR NO. IS BETWEEN 100 AND 1000." : GOTO 130
160 IF N>1000 THEN PRINT "YOUR NO. IS OVER 1000." : GOTO 130
```

48. Now we want you to put your accumulated knowledge of BASIC to work and write a program to provide practice for a person learning or reviewing the "times table," that is, multiplication from 1 times 1 to 12 times 12. Of course, we are calling this program COMPASSIONATE MULTIPLICATION PRACTICE. Study the RUN and our notes, then build your program. If you have a computer handy to use, check your own program before looking at our way of doing it.

Generate a problem, using random numbers from 1 to 12. Print the problem and ask for an answer. Compare the player's answer with the correct answer.

If the answer is smaller than the correct answer, print TRY A BIGGER NUMBER and repeat the problem.

If the answer is bigger than the correct answer, print TRY A SMALLER NUMBER and repeat the problem.

If the answer is correct, tell the player that she or he has typed the correct answer.

Our program uses three different replies to a correct answer. These are chosen at random from the following three possibilities.

THAT'S IT!
CORRECT ANSWER
GOOD WORK! KEEP IT UP

```
RUN

 2 × 4 =? 8
GOOD WORK! KEEP IT UP!

 2 × 2 =? 4
GOOD WORK! KEEP IT UP!

 2 × 8 =? 15
TRY A BIGGER NUMBER.

 2 × 8 =? 16
CORRECT ANSWER!

 10 × 1 =? 10
CORRECT ANSWER!

 10 × 9 =? 100
TRY A SMALLER NUMBER.

 10 × 9 =? 90
GOOD WORK! KEEP IT UP!

 11 × 7 =?
```

_____

```
100 REM***COMPASSIONATE MULTIPLICATION PRACTICE
110 LET A=INT(12*RND(1))+1 : LET B=INT(12*RND(1))+1
120 PRINT : PRINT A; "×"; B; "="; : INPUT C
130 IF C<A*B THEN PRINT "TRY A BIGGER NUMBER." : GOTO 120
140 IF C>A*B THEN PRINT "TRY A SMALLER NUMBER." : GOTO 120
150 LET R=INT(3*RND(1))+1 : ON R GOTO 160,170,180
160 PRINT "THAT'S IT!" : GOTO 110
170 PRINT "CORRECT ANSWER!" : GOTO 110
180 PRINT "GOOD WORK! KEEP IT UP!" : GOTO 110
```

49. We mentioned in Chapter 2 that some of the older versions of BASIC required an END statement as the last statement in a program. Most versions of BASIC for home computers do not need this final END. However, the END statement, and its relative, the STOP statement, can be handy for terminating a program in some place other than the last line numbered statement.

It is often handy to be able to end or stop a program as a result of an IF-THEN decision. END or STOP can be the condition to fulfill after THEN if the condition is TRUE. Examples:

    20 IF X = 10 THEN STOP
    20 IF X = 10 THEN END

For our version of BASIC, using STOP will cause the computer to type a message, as shown below, giving the line number where the STOP statement was encountered and the RUN ended.

    BREAK IN 20
    OK

However, a RUN that ends when an END statement is encountered just gives the standard OK.

In a multiple-statement line with IF-THEN, END or STOP could be used as below:

120 IF Y * Q = 100 THEN PRINT "THAT'S ALL, FOLKS" : END
120 IF Y * Q = 100 THEN PRINT "THAT'S ALL, FOLKS" : STOP

At the end of a math drill or game playing program, you could use the following approach.

310 INPUT "ANOTHER GAME (YES OR NO)"; A$
320 IF A$ = "NO" THEN END
330 GOTO 100

In a counting loop program, insert a line to tell the computer to quit counting when F is greater than 6.

10 LET F = 1

20 _____

30 PRINT "F ="; F
40 LET F = F + 1
50 GOTO 20

— — — — — — — — — —

20 IF F > 6 THEN END or
20 IF F > 6 THEN STOP

SELF-TEST

Try this Self-Test, so you can evaluate how much you have learned in Chapter 4.

1. Give the BASIC symbols for each of the following comparisons.

    _____ is equal to

    _____ is less than

    _____ is greater than

    _____ is less than or equal to

    _____ is greater than or equal to

    _____ is not equal to

2. Describe each IF-THEN statement in words. That is, describe what the statement tells the computer to do.

    (a) `IF G = X THEN 200` _____

    _____

    _____

    (b) `IF X>=0 THEN C = C+1` _____

    _____

    _____

    (c) `IF N <> INT(N) THEN PRINT "N IS NOT AN INTEGER." : GOTO 210`

    _____

    _____

    _____

    (d) `IF A↑2+B↑2=C↑2 THEN PRINT "YES, IT IS A RIGHT TRIANGLE."`

    _____

    _____

    _____

3. For each description, write an IF-THEN statement.

    (a) If the value of N is less than or equal to 7, go to line 15.

    _____

    _____

(b) If A is less than 2*P, then increase the value of N by 1 and go to line 180. _____

(c) If M/N is equal to INT(M/N), then print the message M IS EVEN-LY DIVISIBLE BY N. _____

_____

4. Complete the following program to tell how many years are needed to "double your money." Use multiple statements in line 190.

```
100 REM***HOW MANY YEARS TO DOUBLE YOUR MONEY
110 PRINT "IF YOU TYPE THE AMOUNT OF PRINCIPAL AND THE"
120 PRINT "INTEREST RATE PER YEAR, I WILL SHOW YOU HOW"
130 PRINT "MANY YEARS TO DOUBLE YOUR MONEY."
140 PRINT
150 INPUT "PRINCIPAL"; P
160 INPUT "INTEREST RATE"; R
170 LET N=1
180 LET A=P*(1+R/100)↑N
190 _____
200 PRINT
210 PRINT "YEARS TO DOUBLE YOUR MONEY:"; N
220 PRINT "THE ACTUAL AMOUNT WILL BE $"; A
```

This is a loop { 180 ... 190 }

```
RUN
IF YOU TYPE THE AMOUNT OF PRINCIPAL AND THE
INTEREST RATE PER YEAR, I WILL SHOW YOU HOW
MANY YEARS TO DOUBLE YOUR MONEY.

PRINCIPAL? 1000      ⎫
INTEREST RATE? 6     ⎬── 1000 at 6% per year.

YEARS TO DOUBLE YOUR MONEY: 12
THE ACTUAL AMOUNT WILL BE $ 2012.2
```

5. What will be the result of running the following program? Show the RUN.

```
10 LET K=1
20 PRINT K
30 LET K=K+1
40 IF K<=5 THEN 20
RUN
```

6. What will the RUN look like for this program?

```
10 LET K=1
20 IF K<5 THEN K=K+1 : GOTO 20
30 PRINT K
```

7. Describe the random numbers generated by each of the following expressions.

(a)   RND(1) _____

_____

(b)   2*RND(1) _____

_____

(c)   INT(2*RND(1)) _____

_____

(d)   INT(2*RND(1))+1 _____

_____

(e)   INT(3*RND(1))-1 _____

_____

(f)   3.14159*RND(1) _____

_____

8.   Here is an incomplete program to simulate (imitate) flipping a coin. Please complete the program. (Hint: C should be 0 or 1, at random.)

```
100 REM***COIN FLIPPER

110 LET C = _____
120 IF C=0 THEN PRINT "TAILS" : GOTO 110
130 IF C=1 THEN PRINT "HEADS" : GOTO 110

RUN
HEADS
HEADS
TAILS
TAILS
HEADS
HEADS
HEADS
HEADS
TAILS
HEADS
TAILS
TAILS
HEADS
HEADS
```

Answers to Self-Test

The frame numbers in parentheses refer to the frames in the chapter where the topic is discussed. You may wish to refer to these for quick review.

1.   =   is equal to
      <   is less than
      >   is greater than
      <=   is less than or equal to (=< is also acceptable)
      >=   is greater than or equal to (=> is also acceptable)
      <>   is not equal to (# is acceptable for most versions of BASIC)
      (frame 7)

2.   (a)   If the value of G is equal to the value of X, go to line 200. Otherwise (G = X is FALSE), continue in the usual line number order. (frames 1-8)
      (b)   If the value of X is greater than or equal to zero, increase the value of C by 1. Otherwise (X >= 0 is FALSE), do not execute the LET portion. In either case, continue in regular line number order. (frame 10)
      (c)   If N <> INT(N) is TRUE, this means that the value of N is not an integer. In this case, print the string N IS NOT AN INTEGER and then go to line 210. However, if N *is* an integer, N <> INT(N) will be FALSE. In this case, neither the PRINT nor the GOTO will be executed and the computer will simply continue in regular line number order.   (frames 1-8, 20-23, 42)
      (d)   If the value of A squared plus B squared is equal to the value of C squared, print the string YES, IT IS A RIGHT TRIANGLE.

Otherwise (A↑2 + B↑2 = C↑2 is FALSE), *don't* print the string. In either case, continue in regular line number order.   (frames 1-8)

3.   (a)   `IF N<=7 THEN GOTO 15`
     (b)   `IF A<2*P THEN LET N=N+1 : GOTO 180`
     (c)   `IF M/N = INT(M/N) THEN PRINT "M IS EVENLY DIVISIBLE BY N"`

(frames 1-10)

4.   190 IF A < 2*P THEN LET N = N + 1 : GOTO 180
     In other words, if the newly computed amount A is still less than twice the original principal P, increase the year N by 1, and go back to line 180 to compute a new amount A.   (frames 9-10)

5.   RUN   The PRINT statement is *inside* the loop. Therefore, it is done
     1   every time.
     2
     3
     4
     5   (frame 8)

6.   RUN   This time, the PRINT statement is *outside* the loop. It is done
     5   only once, after the loop has been completed.   (frame 8)

7.   (a)   Numbers between 0 and 1. Each random number is greater than zero, but less than one. This answer is also acceptable: $0 < RND(1) < 1$.   (frames 16, 17)
     (b)   Numbers between 0 and 2. Each random number will be greater than 0, but less than 2. Also: $0 < 2*RND(1) < 2$.   (frames 17-19)
     (c)   0 or 1 No other values are possible.   (frames 20, 23-26)
     (d)   1 or 2   (frames 20, 23-26)
     (e)   −1, 0, or 1   (frames 20, 23-26)
     (f)   Numbers between 0 and 3.14159. Each random number is greater than 0, but less than 3.14159. Also: $0 < 3.14159*RND(1) < 3.14159$. Since 3.14159 is an approximation to π, we might also say, although somewhat imprecisely, that these numbers are between 0 and π.   (frames 20, 23-26)

8.   110 LET C = INT(2*RND(1))   (frames 26, 27)

CHAPTER FIVE

READ and DATA
Work Together

This chapter is designed to give you practice using the BASIC statements and programming skills you have learned so far and to add to your bag of programming tricks. You will be able to extend your understanding of the capabilities of the PRINT statement, in order to better control the output of your programs and write more efficient instructions or programming code. In addition, you will learn two frequently used statements that always work together to assign values to variables: the READ and DATA statements. When you finish this chapter, you will be able to:

- use READ statements to assign values or strings to one or more variables at a time, from items in DATA statements;

- control the spacing of output through the use of commas and semicolons separating items in PRINT statements;

- identify the standard print positions in printout and write PRINT statements using comma spacing;

- show the way numbers are printed or displayed as compared to strings.

1. You've seen how LET statements and INPUT statements can be used to assign values to variables. (We hope you've been able to use them at a terminal, too.) A third method uses two statements in combination, READ and DATA, to assign values to variables.

```
10 READ X
20 ? "THIS TIME THROUGH THE LOOP, X ="; X
30 GOTO 10
40 DATA 10, 15, 7, 3.25, 11

RUN
THIS TIME THROUGH THE LOOP, X = 10
THIS TIME THROUGH THE LOOP, X = 15
THIS TIME THROUGH THE LOOP, X = 7
THIS TIME THROUGH THE LOOP, X = 3.25
THIS TIME THROUGH THE LOOP, X = 11
?OD ERROR IN 10
```

This statement 10 READ X tells the computer to READ one value from the DATA statement, and assign the value to the variable X. Every time the READ statement is executed (each time through the loop), the computer reads the next value from the DATA statement, and assigns the new value to the variable X. The computer keeps track of each value as it is read out, in effect, moving a pointer across the items in the DATA statement, one notch at a time.

How many values are in the DATA statement? _____

— — — — — — — — — —

5

2. As the computer executed the program, each time through the loop it read and printed one value from the DATA statement. Then on the sixth trip through the loop, it tried to find still another number. Since it couldn't find another number to read from the DATA statement, the computer printed OD ERROR IN 10, which means "Out of Data error in line 10." It isn't really an error. It just informs you that the computer has used up all the available data, tried to find more, but couldn't. The "out of data" message may be different on your computer.

When the program in frame 1 was RUN, how many times was a new value assigned to the READ variable? _____

— — — — — — — — — —

5 values were assigned

3. Look at the format for DATA statements.

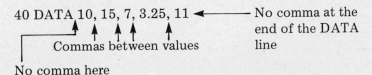

40 DATA 10, 15, 7, 3.25, 11 ◄——— No comma at the end of the DATA line

Commas between values

No comma here

DATA statements may contain whole numbers, numbers with decimal fractions (such as 3.25 above), numbers in floating point or "E" notation, or negative numbers.

DATA statements may *not* contain variables, arithmetic operations, other functions, or fractions. (Most computers can't handle these. What about yours? Try it and find out.)

This is OK: 90 DATA 3, 8, 2.5
This is NOT OK: 95 DATA 2+3, 1/4, 2/5, 7*8

Write a DATA statement for these values.

342	60.25
1256	−412
205	2.05E8

_ _ _ _ _ _ _ _ _ _

60 DATA 342, 1256, 205, 60.25, −412, 2.05E8

Your line number may be different. And remember, no commas can be used in large numbers, such as 1256 above. However, floating point or "E" notation may be used.

4.   Data statements may be placed anywhere in the program.

```
10 READ N          10 DATA  123
20 PRINT N         20 READ N
30 DATA 123        30 PRINT N
RUN                RUN
 123                123
```

Can the DATA statement be placed as shown in the following program?

_____

```
10 READ N
20 DATA 123
30 PRINT N
```

_ _ _ _ _ _ _ _ _ _

yes

5.   These DATA statements are not written in correct BASIC. Tell what is wrong with each one.

(a)   20 DATA, 15, 32, 85, 66 _____

(b) 30 DATA 22.3; 81.1; 66.66; 43.22 _____

(c) 40 DATA 266, 985, 421, 968, 420, _____

— — — — — — — — — —

(a) should not have comma after DATA
(b) should use commas instead of semicolons to separate values in a DATA statement
(c) should not have comma after last item in DATA statement

6.   This program converts inches to centimeters. One inch = 2.54 centimeters. When the program is RUN, the computer prints the value in inches on one line, and the equivalent in centimeters on the next. Fill in the missing statement (line 20).

```
10 REM***CONVERT INCHES TO CENTIMETERS

20 _____
30 PRINT
40 PRINT "INCHES =";I
50 PRINT "CENTIMETERS =";2.54*I
60 GOTO 20
90 DATA 1, 8, 12

RUN

INCHES = 1
CENTIMETERS = 2.54

INCHES = 8
CENTIMETERS = 20.32

INCHES = 12
CENTIMETERS = 30.48
?OD ERROR IN 20
```

— — — — — — — — — —

20 READ I

7.   Now you write a program to convert ounces to grams. One ounce = 28.35 grams (rounded to two decimal places). Use a DATA statement to hold the values in ounces that you want converted to grams. Here is what your program should print when it is RUN.

```
RUN

OUNCES = 1
GRAMS = 28.35

OUNCES = 13
GRAMS = 368.55

OUNCES = 16
GRAMS = 453.6
?OD ERROR IN 20
```

— — — — — — — — —

```
10 REM***CONVERT OUNCES TO GRAMS
20 READ Z
30 PRINT
40 PRINT "OUNCES ="; Z
50 PRINT "GRAMS ="; 28.35*Z
60 GOTO 20
90 DATA 1, 13, 16
```

We used Z to represent ounces because O (oh) can be confused with 0 (zero) on some terminals.

8.   Write a "World's Most Expensive Adding Machine" program (from Chapter 3, frame 51) using READ and DATA statements instead of an INPUT statement so that a RUN of the program will look like the one below. Examine the RUN to determine the values in the DATA statement.

```
RUN
X = 12
TOTAL SO FAR IS 12

X = 43
TOTAL SO FAR IS 55

X = 33
TOTAL SO FAR IS 88

X = 92
TOTAL SO FAR IS 180

X = 76.25
TOTAL SO FAR IS 256.25

?OD ERROR IN 120
```
◄ This line number may be different for your program.

— — — — — — — — —

```
100 REM***WORLD'S MOST EXPENSIVE ADDING MACHINE
110 LET T=0
120 READ X
130 LET T=T+X
140 PRINT "X ="; X
150 PRINT "TOTAL SO FAR IS"; T
160 PRINT
170 GOTO 120
180 DATA 12,43,33,92,76.25
```

Your line numbers may be different.

9.   Do you remember our program to compute the mean, or average, of a group of numbers? If not, review Chapter 4, frame 12. Below is a rewrite of that program, using READ and DATA statements. We use lots of REMs (REMARKS) to explain what is happening.

```
100 REM***A FRIENDLY 'MEAN' PROGRAM
110 REM***INITIALIZE T (FOR TOTAL) AND N (FOR NUMBER OF NUMBERS)
120 T=0 : N=0
130 REM***READ A NUMBER, X. IF IT IS THE FLAG 1E38
140 REM***GOTO PRINTOUT. OTHERWISE, UPDATE T AND X
150 READ X : IF X=1E38 THEN 180
160 T=T+X : N=N+1 : GOTO 150
170 REM***PRINT ANSWERS
180 PRINT "N ="; N
190 PRINT "TOTAL ="; T
200 PRINT "MEAN ="; T/N
900 REM**.*DATA FOLLOWS
910 DATA 10,3,-9,-15,-23,-25,-30,1E38  ◄─────── The flag
```

```
RUN
N = 7
TOTAL =-89
MEAN =-12.7143
```

To RUN this program for a different set of data, simply replace line 910 by one or more DATA statements containing the new data and the flag 1E38. (You'll recall from Chapter 3 that to replace a statement, just type the new statement using the old line number.) For example, suppose we wish to use this data: 63, 72, 50, 55, 75, 67, 59, 61, 64. Write the DATA statement.

910 DATA _____

– – – – – – – – – – –

910 DATA 63, 72, 50, 55, 75, 67, 59, 61, 64, 1E38

> Did you remember the flag?

10.   The following program causes the computer to read numbers from a DATA statement and print only the numbers that are *positive* (greater than zero). Numbers that are less than zero or equal to zero are not printed.

```
10 READ X
20 IF X>0 THEN PRINT "X ="; X
30 GOTO 10
40 DATA 3,7,0,-2,5,-1,7,8,0,-3
RUN
X = 3
X = 7
X = 5
X = 7
X = 8
?OD ERROR IN 10
```

Note: 7 is printed *twice* because it occurs twice in the DATA statement.

Look at the numbers in the DATA statement.

(a)   For which numbers is the condition X > 0 TRUE? _____

(b)   When X > 0 is TRUE, what does line 20 cause the computer to do?

_____

(c)   For which numbers is the condition X > 0 FALSE? _____

(d)   When X > 0 is FALSE, what happens in line 20? _____

– – – – – – – – – – –

(a)   3, 7, 5, 7, 8
(b)   print the message X = followed by the value of X
(c)   0, −2, −1, 0, −3
(d)   Nothing. The PRINT portion of line 20 is not executed and the computer goes on to line 30.

11.   What will the RUN look like for this program?

```
10 READ X
20 IF X<0 THEN PRINT"X =";X
30 GOTO 10
40 DATA 3,7,0,-2,5,-1,7,8,0,-3
RUN
```

– – – – – – – – – – –

```
RUN
X = -2
X = -1
X = -3
?OD ERROR IN 10
```
◄——————— Did you remember this?

12.   Complete the following program so that the RUN will occur as shown.

```
10 READ X

20 _____
30 GOTO 10
40 DATA 3, 7, 0, -2, 5, -1, 7, 8, 0, -3

RUN
X = 0
X = 0
?OD ERROR IN 10
```
Two zeros are printed because there are two zeros in the DATA statement.

— — — — — — — — — —

20 IF X=0 THEN PRINT "X ="; X

13.   For more practice, do each of the following. If possible, try each one on your computer.

(a)   Complete line 20 so that only *nonzero* numbers are printed.

20 IF _____ THEN PRINT "X ="; X

(b)   Complete line 20 so that the computer prints numbers that are greater than or equal to zero.

20 IF _____ THEN PRINT "X ="; X

(c)   Complete line 20 so that the computer prints numbers that are less than or equal to 3.

20 IF _____ THEN PRINT "X ="; X

— — — — — — — — — —

(a)   X <> 0 (The computer will print 3, 7, -2, 5, -1, 7, 8, and -3.)
(b)   X >= 0 or X => 0 (The computer will print 3, 7, 0, 5, 7, 8, and 0.)
(c)   X <= 3 or X =< 3 (The computer will print 3, 0, -2, -1, 0, and -3.)

If you need review, see Chapter 4, frame 7.

14.   In BASIC you may have more than one variable following a READ instruction. On the following page is an example. Use commas to separate the variables.

10 READ X,Y,Z

No comma here ———— No comma here

This will cause the computer to take three values from the DATA statement and assign them in order to the three READ variables.

Complete the RUN of this program (fill in blanks).

```
1Ø  READ X,Y,Z
2Ø  PRINT X,Y,Z
3Ø  GOTO 1Ø
4Ø  DATA 1Ø, 2Ø, 3Ø, 4Ø, 5Ø, 6Ø
RUN
  1Ø          2Ø          3Ø

_____    _____    _____

?OD ERROR IN 1Ø
```

– – – – – – – – – –

40   50   60

The second time through the loop, these values were assigned to X, Y, and Z, and printed by line 20. (We'll discuss the spacing of items in PRINT statements later on.)

15. Fill in the blank spaces in the program and in the RUN.

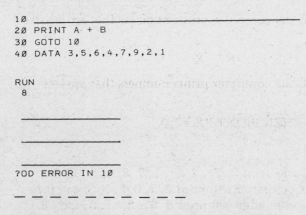

```
1Ø  _____
2Ø  PRINT A + B
3Ø  GOTO 1Ø
4Ø  DATA 3,5,6,4,7,9,2,1

RUN
  8

_____

_____

_____

?OD ERROR IN 1Ø
```

– – – – – – – – – –

10 READ A,B

RUN
   8
  10
  16
   3

16.   You may have more than one READ statement in a program. However, all READ statements assign values to their variable(s) from the same DATA statement. An item from DATA is assigned to a READ variable in the order that the computer comes to READ statements when the program is RUN.

```
10 READ P
20 READ Q
30 PRINT P
40 PRINT Q
50 GOTO 10
60 DATA 3,5,6,4,7,9
RUN
 3 ]—First data item assigned to P, second assigned to Q.
 5 ]
 6 ]__ Second trip through the loop: third data item is assigned to P, fourth
 4 ]     to Q.
 7
 9
?OD ERROR IN 10
```

For the third trip through the loop, what value is assigned to P?_____

What value is assigned to Q? _____

— — — — — — — — — — —

7; 9

17.   Write a program that:

uses three READ statements to assign values to three different READ variables X, Y, and Z;

then prints the *sum* of X + Y + Z;

then loops back to repeat the process until the data are all used up.

Show what the computer will print when your program is RUN. Here are the data for the DATA statement: 3, 5, 6, 4, 7, 9, 2, 5, 2.

— — — — — — — — — —

```
10 READ X
20 READ Y
30 READ Z
40 PRINT X + Y + Z
50 GOTO 10
60 DATA 3,5,6,4,7,9,2,5,2
RUN
 14
 20
 9
?OD ERROR IN 10
```

18.   Here is a questionnaire we gave to 50 people.

DOES YOUR COMPUTER UNDERSTAND YOU?

1.   YES
2.   NO

Each of the 50 responses was either 1 (YES) or 2 (NO). The responses are shown below in five DATA statements. The last response is followed by –1, the flag signalling end of data.

```
900 REM***DATA* 1=YES, 2=NO, -1=END OF DATA
910 DATA 1,2,2,2,1,2,1,2,1,2
920 DATA 2,1,1,1,2,1,2,2,2,1
930 DATA 2,2,2,1,2,1,2,2,1,2
940 DATA 1,1,1,1,2,1,2,2,1,1
950 DATA 2,2,2,2,1,1,1,2,1,2,-1
```

How many YES answers? _____

How many NO answers? _____

     Write the number of YES answers in the box labeled "Y" and the number of NO answers in the box labeled "N."

Y ☐

N ☐

_ _ _ _ _ _ _ _ _ _

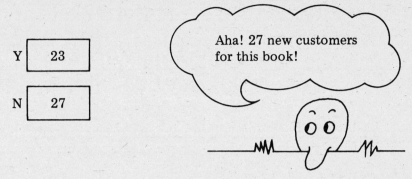

19. Here is a program to read the answers from the DATA statements and count the number of YES answers and NO answers. The variable Y is used to count YES answers. The variable N is used to count NO answers.

```
100 REM***QUESTIONNAIRE ANALYSIS PROGRAM
110 REM***INITIALIZE:  SET COUNTING VARIABLES TO ZERO
120 Y=0 : N=0
200 REM***READ AND COUNT VOTES
210 READ A : IF A=-1 THEN 410
220 IF A=1 THEN LET Y=Y+1 : GOTO 210
230 IF A=2 THEN LET N=N+1 : GOTO 210
400 REM***PRINT THE RESULTS
410 PRINT
420 PRINT "YES:"; Y
430 PRINT " NO:"; N
900 REM***DATA* 1=YES, 2=NO, -1=END OF DATA
910 DATA 1,2,2,2,1,2,1,2,1,2
920 DATA 2,1,1,1,2,1,2,2,2,1
930 DATA 2,2,2,1,2,1,2,2,1,2
940 DATA 1,1,1,1,2,1,2,2,1,1
950 DATA 2,2,2,2,1,1,1,2,1,2,-1

RUN

YES: 23
 NO: 27
```

Note the multiple statements in lines 120, 210, 220, and 230.

(a) Which section of the program is a loop that is repeated for each value in the DATA statements? Lines _____ to _____.

(b) Which statement reads a value corresponding to one vote and puts it into box A? _____

(c) Which line determines whether a vote is YES and, if it is, increases the YES count by one? _____

(d) Which line determines whether a vote is NO and, if it is, increases the NO count by one? _____

— — — — — — — — — —

(a) lines 210 to 230; (b) line 210; (c) line 220; (d) line 230

20. Now look at this new questionnaire.

DOES YOUR COMPUTER UNDERSTAND YOU?

1. YES
2. NO
3. SOMETIMES

Modify the program in frame 19 so that the computer counts the YES, NO, and SOMETIMES answers. Use the variable Y to count YES answers. Use the variable N to count NO answers. Use the variable S to count SOMETIMES answers. Use the following data.

2, 1, 3, 2, 3, 3, 1, 3, 3, 2, 1, 2, 1, 2, 1, 1, 3, 3, −1

Using this data, the results when the program is RUN should be printed as follows.

```
YES: 6
 NO: 5
SOMETIMES: 7
```

Here are our changes.

```
120 Y=Ø : N=Ø : S=Ø
240 IF A=3 THEN LET S=S+1 : GOTO 210
440 PRINT "SOMETIMES:" ; S
900 REM***DATA: 1=YES, 2=NO, 3=SOMETIMES, -1=END OF DATA
910 DATA 2,1,3,2,3,3,1,3,3,2,1,2,1,2,1,1,3,3,-1
920
930
940
950
```

We deleted lines 920, 930, 940, and 950 from the program of frame 19. If the program is in the computer, we can do this by typing the line number and pressing RETURN. If you have a computer handy, LIST the program to show the modifications and to prove that the deleted lines have disappeared from the computer's memory. On the following page is our listing.

```
LIST

100 REM***QUESTIONNAIRE ANALYSIS PROGRAM
110 REM***INITIALIZE: SET COUNTING VARIABLES TO ZERO
120 Y=0 : N=0 : S=0
200 REM***READ AND COUNT VOTES
210 READ A : IF A=-1 THEN 410
220 IF A=1 THEN LET Y=Y+1 : GOTO 210
230 IF A=2 THEN LET N=N+1 : GOTO 210
240 IF A=3 THEN LET S=S+1 : GOTO 210
400 REM***PRINT THE RESULTS
410 PRINT
420 PRINT "YES:"; Y
430 PRINT " NO:"; N
440 PRINT "SOMETIMES:"; S
900 REM***DATA: 1=YES, 2=NO, 3=SOMETIMES, -1=END OF DATA
910 DATA 2,1,3,2,3,3,1,3,3,2,1,2,1,2,1,1,3,3,-1
OK
```

21. Back in Chapter 2, we used PRINT statements in the following form.

> PRINT *e*

> where *e* is a numerical expression

For example:

> PRINT 7 + 5

> numerical expression

A PRINT statement of this form tells the computer to compute and evaluate (do the arithmetic of) the numerical expression and then print the result.

The following PRINT statement tells the computer to evaluate *four* numerical expressions and print the four results.

We type: PRINT 7 + 5, 7 – 5, 7 * 5, 7 / 5

It types: 12 ⤶   2   35   1.4

In the above, draw arrows connecting each numerical expression with its computed and printed value. We have drawn the first arrow, connecting the expression, 7 + 5, with its printed result, 12.

— — — — — — — — — —

PRINT 7 + 5, 7 – 5, 7 * 5, 7 / 5
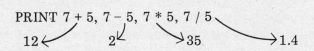
12 ⤶   2 ↙   ↘35   →1.4

22.   If a PRINT statement has more than one expression, then the expressions are separated by commas.

$$\text{PRINT } 7+5, \; 7-5, \; 7*5, \; 7/5$$

comma   comma   comma

The following PRINT statement directs the computer to compute and print the values of $2 + 3$, $2 - 3$, $2 * 3$, and $2/3$. However, we forgot to put in commas. Please insert commas in the correct BASIC form.

PRINT   2+3   2-3   2*3   2/3

— — — — — — — — — —

PRINT 2+3, 2-3, 2*3, 2/3

Note: *No* comma following PRINT and no comma following 2/3. A comma following PRINT will cause an SN ERROR message. A comma following 2/3 (at the very end of the PRINT statement) has a special purpose which we will discuss later.

23.   Complete the following. (Remember, for direct statements, you do not need a line number and you only have to press RETURN to have the computer execute the statement.)

We type: PRINT 3*3, 5*5, 7*7

It types: _____   _____   _____

We type: PRINT 2*3+4*5, (2+3)*(4+5)

It types: _____   _____

— — — — — — — — — —

9   25   49

26   45

24.   Your turn. Let's go back to our three bicycles, with wheels of 20-, 24-, and 26-inch diameters. You want to find out, for each bike, how far it travels during *one turn* of the wheel. In other words, you want to evaluate the following three expressions.

20-inch wheel:	3.14*20	First expression
24-inch wheel:	3.14*24	Second expression
26-inch wheel:	3.14*26	Third expression

Write a PRINT statement to tell the computer to evaluate the three expressions and PRINT the results.

You type: _____

It types: 62.8   75.36   81.64

— — — — — — — — — —

```
PRINT 3.14*20, 3.14*24, 3.14*26
```

25.   A teletypewriter line has five standard print positions. A comma in a PRINT statement causes the TTY to move to the next available standard print position. Look at the example below and fill in the blanks.

We type: `PRINT 1,2,3,4,5`

It types: 1   2   3   4   5

   ↑   ↑   ↑   ↑   ↑
   Position 1   Position 2   Position 3   Position ___   Position ___

— — — — — — — — — —

4; 5

Note: Our computer programs and runs have been reduced to fit the book's page size.

26.   Did you notice that the arrows in the above example seem to be pointing to the space to the left of the number? This is where the print positon actually begins. When the computer prints a positive number or zero, it prints a space first, then prints the digits of the number. Watch what happens when *negative* numbers are printed.

We type: `PRINT -1,-2,-3,-4,-5`

It types: -1   -2   -3   -4   -5

 ↑   ↑   ↑   ↑   ↑
 Position 1   Position 2   Position 3   Position 4   Position 5

How does the printing of negative numbers differ from that of positive numbers? _____

— — — — — — — — — —

Negative numbers are printed with a minus sign (−) followed by the digits of the number, while positive numbers are printed with a space followed by the digits of the number. (That space, called a leading space, is where the plus sign (+) to indicate a positive number would go, but BASIC doesn't print the sign for positive numbers.)

27.   What happens if there are *more than* five items in a PRINT statement? Look at the direct statement below and also at how the computer executed it.

We type: PRINT 1,2,3,4,5,6,7,8

It types:

1	2	3	4	5
6	7	8		

Describe what happened. _____

_____

– – – – – – – – – –

The computer printed the 8 numbers on 2 lines, with 5 numbers on the first line and 3 numbers on the second line.

28.   Following the rules for items or expressions separated by commas, show what the computer will print in response to the following PRINT statement.

We type: PRINT 1,2,3,4,5,6,7,8,9,1Ø,11,12

It types:

– – – – – – – – – –

1	2	3	4	5
6	7	8	9	1Ø
11	12			

29.   Instead of commas, we can also use *semicolons* as separators in a PRINT statement. Watch what happens.

We type: PRINT 1;2;3;4;5

It types: 1   2   3   4   5

We type: PRINT 1;2;3;4;5;6;7;8

It types: 1   2   3   4   5   6   7   8

We type: `PRINT 1;12;123;1234;12345;123456;1234567`

It types: `1   12   123   1234   12345   123456   1.23457E+06`

    With semicolon spacing and positive numbers (or zero), the computer prints a space, followed by the digits of the number, followed by a space. We call the first space the leading space, and the space after the number the trailing space.
    Complete the following. With semicolon spacing and positive numbers

the computer prints a _____ followed by the

_____ of the number, followed by a _____.

— — — — — — — — — —

(leading) space; digits; (trailing) space

30.   Let's see what happens when we use semicolon spacing with *negative* numbers.

We type: `PRINT -1;-2;-3;-4;-5;-6;-7`

It types: `-1  -2  -3  -4  -5  -6  -7`

    With semicolon spacing, negative numbers are printed as a minus sign, the digits of the number, and a trailing space.
    Another example? Of course. Here it is.

We type: `PRINT -1;-12;-123;-1234;-12345;-123456;-1234567`

It types: `-1  -12  -123  -1234  -12345  -123456  -1.23457E+06`

    Semicolon spacing *catenates* numbers. That is, it directs the computer to print numbers close together, in a linked series. Comma spacing causes numbers to be printed in predetermined print positions. So, to print results

close together, use _____.

— — — — — — — — — —

semicolons

31.   A TTY has 72 character positions across one line. (Other terminals may have anywhere from 32 positions to 132 positions.) The TTY character positions are numbered from 0 to 71, starting from the left margin. Complete the diagram on the following page.

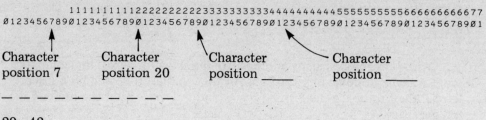

Character   Character   Character   Character
position 7   position 20   position _____   position _____

— — — — — — — — — —

29; 42

32.   The five standard print positions, used in *comma* spacing, begin at
character positions 0, 14, 28, 42, and 56. We've marked print positions 1
and 2; you mark print positions 3, 4, and 5 on the following diagram.

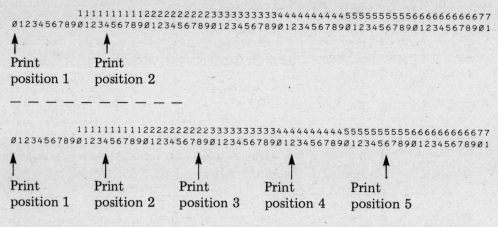

Print   Print
position 1   position 2

— — — — — — — — — —

```
          1111111111222222222233333333334444444444555555555566666666667
012345678901234567890123456789012345678901234567890123456789012345678901
```

Print   Print   Print   Print   Print
position 1   position 2   position 3   position 4   position 5

Note: A standard print position is 14 character positions wide. For example,
print position 1 occupies character positions 0 through 13, or 14 character
positions in all. Print position 2 occupies character positions 14 through 27,
and so on.

33.   Now watch what happens when we put a comma at the *end* of a
PRINT statement.

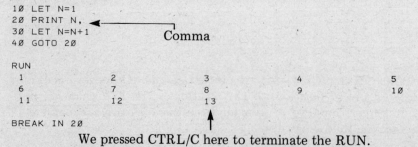

```
10 LET N=1
20 PRINT N,
30 LET N=N+1
40 GOTO 20
```
Comma

```
RUN
 1            2            3            4            5
 6            7            8            9           10
11           12           13
```

BREAK IN 20

We pressed CTRL/C here to terminate the RUN.

Remember what the comma does. It tells the computer to move to the next standard print position. So, after printing number 1, the computer moves to print position 2; after printing 2, the computer moves to standard print position 3, and so on. As we have seen, after printing something in standard print position 5, it returns the carriage to the left margin, spaces the paper up one line (performs a "line feed"), and continues printing at standard print position 1.

Show the first 8 items printed by the following program.

```
1Ø LET N=1
2Ø PRINT N,
3Ø LET N=N+2
4Ø GOTO 2Ø

RUN
```

— — — — — — — — —

```
1              3           5              7           9
11             13          15
```

34. Now, what do you suppose happens if we put a semicolon at the end of a PRINT statement? As always with computers, if we don't know, we EXPERIMENT. Let's try it.

```
1Ø LET N=1
2Ø PRINT N;
3Ø LET N=N+1
4Ø GOTO 2Ø
RUN
 1   2   3   4   5   6   7   8   9   1Ø   11   12   13   14   15   16   17   18   19   2Ø
 21  22  23  24  25  26  27  28  29
BREAK IN 2Ø
```

We pressed CTRL/C again to stop the RUN.

Remember, with semicolon spacing, the computer prints positive numbers as space, digit(s), space. When it gets to the end of a line, it returns the carriage, indexes up one line (still another way of saying it does a "line feed"), and keeps chunking away. Show what happens if we RUN the following program.

```
10 PRINT 1;◄————————┐ Semicolons
20 PRINT 2;◄————————┘
30 PRINT 3 ◄———————— No semicolon
40 PRINT 4;◄———————— Semicolon
50 PRINT 5 ◄———————— No semicolon
RUN
```

— — — — — — — — —

```
1  2  3  ◄──────  Printed by lines 10, 20, 30
4  5     ◄──────  Courtesy of lines 40 and 50
```

Since there was no semicolon at the end of the statement PRINT 3 (line 30) to hold the printer on the same line, the computer did a carriage return and line feed.

35.   Write a program using *two* PRINT statements, to compute and print the values of 2*2, 3*3, 4*4, 5*5, and 6*6. When you RUN your program, the results should be printed as follows.

```
RUN
 4              9              16   25   36
```

— — — — — — — — — —

Method 1:

```
1Ø PRINT 2*2,3*3,4*4;
2Ø PRINT 5*5;6*6

RUN
 4              9              16   25   36
OK
```

Method 2:

```
1Ø PRINT 2*2,3*3,
2Ø PRINT 4*4;5*5;6*6

RUN
 4              9              16   25   36
OK
```

Method 3:

```
1Ø PRINT 2*2,
2Ø PRINT 3*3,4*4;5*5;6*6

RUN
 4              9              16   25   36
OK
```

You might have thought of still more ways to do it!

36. We have spent some time with comma spacing and semicolon spacing with *numbers.* Next, let's try *strings.*

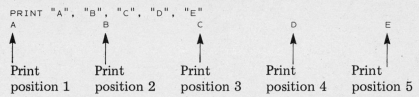

```
PRINT "A", "B", "C", "D", "E"
A             B             C             D             E
```

Print position 1   Print position 2   Print position 3   Print position 4   Print position 5

Your turn. Complete the output for this direct statement the way the computer would do it.

```
PRINT "A", "B", "C", "D", "E", "F", "G", "H"
A             B             C             D             E
```

_ _ _ _ _ _ _ _ _ _

```
A             B             C             D             E
F             G             H
```

With strings, as with numbers, the comma causes the computer to move to the next standard print position. However, no leading spaces are printed as there are with numbers.

37. Comma spacing is useful for printing *headings.* For example, here is a rewrite of our inches to centimeters program in frame 6.

```
1Ø REM***INCHES VERSUS CENTIMETERS TABLE
2Ø PRINT "INCHES","CENTIMETERS"
3Ø READ I
4Ø PRINT I,2.54*I
5Ø GOTO 3Ø
9Ø DATA 1,8,12

RUN
INCHES          CENTIMETERS
  1               2.54
  8              2Ø.32
 12              3Ø.48
?OD ERROR IN 3Ø
```

Note the use of comma spacing in lines 20 and 40. The numerical values printed by line 40 line up nicely under the headings printed by line 20.

Your turn. Rewrite the ounces to grams program (frame 7), so that a RUN looks like the one on the following page.

```
RUN
OUNCES        GRAMS
 1              28.35
 13            368.55
 16            453.6
?OD ERROR IN 30
```

— — — — — — — — — —

```
10 REM***OUNCES TO GRAMS TABLE
20 PRINT "OUNCES","GRAMS"
30 READ Z
40 PRINT Z,28.35*Z
50 GOTO 30
90 DATA 1,13,16
```

38. Now, let's look at semicolon spacing with strings.

```
PRINT "A"; "B"; "C"; "D"; "E"
ABCDE          ◄——————————— Look ma! No spaces.
```

Semicolon spacing causes the computer to catenate strings, that is, to print them one after the other with no spaces.

Show what happens when the computer executes the following PRINT statement.

```
PRINT "THIS"; "IS"; "COMPUTER"; "PROGRAMMING?"
```

_____

— — — — — — — — — —

```
THISISCOMPUTERPROGRAMMING?
```

39. The output in frame 38 was rather crowded and hard to read. If you want spaces between strings, you must put them where you want them. For example:

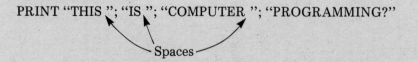

PRINT "THIS "; "IS "; "COMPUTER "; "PROGRAMMING?"

Spaces

Show what the computer will print this time.

_ _ _ _ _ _ _ _ _ _

THIS IS COMPUTER PROGRAMMING?

40.   Let's try a program that uses strings stored by string variables to print information.

```
10 LET A$="COMPUTERS "
20 LET B$="ARE"
30 LET C$=" INTERESTING."
40 PRINT A$;B$;C$
50 PRINT A$,B$,C$
```

Note the spaces inside the quotation marks in lines 10 and 30.

Show what the computer will print when the program is RUN.

RUN

_____

_____

_ _ _ _ _ _ _ _ _ _

```
RUN
COMPUTERS ARE INTERESTING.
COMPUTERS      ARE           INTERESTING.
```

41.   You may have guessed by now that a READ statement may also be used to assign strings to string variables. Show how you think the RUN for the following program to print the names of computer club members will look.

```
10 READ M$
20 PRINT M$
30 GOTO 10
40 DATA JERRY,BOBBY,MARY,DANNY
50 DATA MIMI,KARL,DOUG,SCOTT
```

_ _ _ _ _ _ _ _ _ _

```
RUN
JERRY
BOBBY
MARY
DANNY
MIMI
KARL
DOUG
SCOTT
?OD ERROR IN 10
```

42.   We have made a special point of explaining how strings and values are printed when semicolons and colons are used to separate items in PRINT statements. Now we would like to emphasize how strings assigned to string variables from DATA statements must be handled in order to leave the desired spacing between printed strings.

```
10 READ L$,M$,N$
20 PRINT L$;M$;N$
30 DATA    COMPUTERS,    ARE,    INTERESTING.
RUN
COMPUTERSAREINTERESTING.
```

     Notice that even though we left leading spaces around the string items in the DATA statement, the computer ignored those spaces when it assigned the string characters to the string variables. We replaced line 30 with the following line and ran the program again.

```
30 DATA COMPUTERS," ARE ",INTERESTING

RUN
COMPUTERS ARE INTERESTING
```

     Based upon your examinations of the two DATA statements and RUNs, explain how you can include leading and/or trailing spaces in strings assigned to variables from DATA statements. _____

_____

_____

— — — — — — — — — —

Enclose strings in quotation marks, and include leading or trailing spaces, in order to assign strings to string variables that will include leading or trailing spaces.

Note: MICROSOFT™ BASIC will include *trailing* spaces in a DATA string. For example, line 30 could also be written as it is on the following page.

30 DATA COMPUTERS ,ARE ,INTERESTING

trailing spaces

However, to include leading spaces, you must enclose the string in quotation marks.

43.   And now, it's your turn again to write a program. You have probably used dice before, either in "board" games or other games. We want you to apply your accumulated knowledge of BASIC to write a program that simulates (imitates) the roll of a die. (A "die" is one "dice.") Below is a RUN of our program. Examine it and use it as a guide to writing a program that will produce a RUN similar to this one. Use standard print positions. Take your time, and try *your* solution on a computer before looking at ours, if possible.

```
RUN

HOW MANY ROLLS? 7

ONE         THREE         THREE         SIX           FIVE
FOUR        FIVE

HOW MANY ROLLS? 2

ONE         SIX

HOW MANY ROLLS?      And so on.
```

— — — — — — — — — —

```
100 REM***DIE ROLLER
110 PRINT : INPUT "HOW MANY ROLLS"; R
120 K=1 : PRINT
200 REM***'ROLL THE DIE' R TIMES
210 S=INT(6*RND(1))+1
220 ON S GOTO 230,240,250,260,270,280
230 PRINT "ONE", : GOTO 290
240 PRINT "TWO", : GOTO 290
250 PRINT "THREE", : GOTO 290
260 PRINT "FOUR", : GOTO 290
270 PRINT "FIVE", : GOTO 290
280 PRINT "SIX",
290 IF K<R THEN LET K=K+1 : GOTO 210
300 PRINT : GOTO 110
```

SELF-TEST

Try this Self-Test, so you can evaluate how much you have learned so far.

1. Pretend that *you* are the computer and complete each RUN.

    (a)
    ```
    10 READ A
    20 PRINT A
    30 DATA 27
    RUN
    ```

    (b)
    ```
    10 READ A
    20 READ B
    30 PRINT A-B
    40 DATA 27,15
    RUN
    ```

    (c)
    ```
    10 READ A,B
    20 PRINT A-B
    30 DATA 27,15
    RUN
    ```

    (d)
    ```
    10 READ A,B
    20 PRINT A-B
    30 DATA 27
    40 DATA 15
    RUN
    ```

2. Show the RUNs for the following programs.

    (a)
    ```
    10 READ X
    20 PRINT X,   ←——————— Comma at end of PRINT statement
    30 GOTO 10
    40 DATA 3,7,0,-2,5,-1,7,8,0,-3
    RUN
    ```

    (b)
    ```
    10 READ X
    20 PRINT X;   ←——————— Semicolon at end of PRINT statement
    30 GOTO 10
    40 DATA 3,7,0,-2,5,-1,7,8,0,-3
    RUN
    ```

3. Complete each RUN as if *you* were the computer.

    (a)
    ```
    10 READ X
    20 IF X >= 0 THEN PRINT "X ="; X,   ←——————— Comma
    30 GOTO 10
    40 DATA 3,7,0,-2,5,-1,7,8,0,-3
    RUN
    ```

    (b)
    ```
    10 READ X
    20 IF X >= 0 THEN PRINT "X ="; X;   ←——————— Semicolon
    30 GOTO 10
    40 DATA 3,7,0,-2,5,-1,7,8,0,-3
    RUN
    ```

4. Show the results if we RUN the following short program. Watch out! We are using *comma* spacing, and assuming 72-character TTY lines and 14-character print position spaces.

```
420 PRINT "ANSWER","NUMBER OF","PERCENT OF"
430 PRINT "(YES OR NO)","ANSWERS","TOTAL"
```

5. Modify the questionnaire analysis program beginning in frame 18 so that the results are printed as follows.

```
ANSWER          NUMBER OF       PERCENT OF
(YES OR NO)     ANSWERS         TOTAL

YES                23              46
NO                 27              54
TOTAL              50             100
```

Hint: Rewrite beginning with line 420. The required information is printed in three columns, occupying the first three standard print positions.

6. Write a program, using READ and DATA statements, to compute the distance traveled in one turn of the rear wheel for bicycles with various wheel diameters. Use the following DATA statement with the line number of your choice.

DATA 16,20,24,26,27 ◄————— Wheel diameters

On the following page is a RUN of *our* program.

```
RUN

WHEEL DIAMETER: 16
DISTANCE IN ONE TURN: 50.24

WHEEL DIAMETER: 20
DISTANCE IN ONE TURN: 62.8

WHEEL DIAMETER: 24
DISTANCE IN ONE TURN: 75.36

WHEEL DIAMETER: 26
DISTANCE IN ONE TURN: 81.64

WHEEL DIAMETER: 27
DISTANCE IN ONE TURN: 84.78

?OD ERROR IN LINE _____
```

Remember, distance in one turn is circumference of the wheel. C = 3.14*D where D = diameter of the wheel.

←——— Line number of *your* READ statement

7. Write a program to simulate coin flipping. The program should direct the computer to do the following steps. Type H for HEADS and T for TAILS *across* the page as shown in the RUN below. Also ask *how many* flips the user wants and do exactly that many, then stop. In other words, count the flips, and, when the count has reached the number requested, stop. Here are two RUNs of our program.

```
RUN

HOW MANY FLIPS? 20

H H H H T T T H T H H T T H T T T T H T
```

Note the spaces between flips

```
RUN

HOW MANY FLIPS? 100

H H H H T T T H T T T H H H T H T T T H T T T H H T H H H H H H H T H T H T T H
T H T H H T T T H T H H T T H H H T H H H T H H T H T H T H T H H T T
H T H H H H H H H T T T T H T H T H T H H T T T T H H T T T T
```

The first RUN of our program on our computer produced 9 heads (H) and 11 tails (T). The second RUN produced 53 heads (H) and 47 tails (T). Your computer may give quite different results.

8. Why not let the computer count the number of heads and the number of tails? Modify your program for question 7 so that the computer counts the number of heads and tails. Use the variable H to keep track of the number of heads and the variable T to keep track of the number of tails. Two RUNs of the modified program are shown below.

```
RUN

HOW MANY FLIPS? 20

T H H T T H H H T H H H T H H T T T H T

  11 HEADS AND 9 TAILS


RUN

HOW MANY FLIPS? 100

H T H H H T T T T H T T H T T T H H H H T T H T H T H T H T H H T T T T H H T
T H H H H T H T T T T T T T T H T T H T H T H H T T T T H H H H H T T T T
H H H T T H T T T T T T H T H H T H H H T T T T H H H H

  45 HEADS AND 55 TAILS
```

9. Write a program to *count* the numbers in all the DATA statements in *a* program. Do *not* count the *flag*! For example, if the following DATA statements are in the program, the computer should dutifully tell us that there are 25 numbers.

```
15Ø DATA 2,3,5,7,11,13,17,19,23,29,31,37,41
16Ø DATA 43,47,53,59,61,67,71,73,79,83,89,97,1E38
```
                                                          ↑
                                                     The flag

Our program RUNs like this.

```
RUN
THERE ARE 25 ITEMS IN THE DATA STATEMENTS.
```

10. Now write a program that will print a pattern of asterisks according to a plan entered as DATA statement values. This might be a way of laying a pattern of floor tiles, or loom weaving patterns, or just "computer art." Use a flag to avoid an out-of-data error message. Shown on the following page are our DATA statement values and the pattern produced by our program. Our program prints five different lines of asterisks and spaces.

```
3,4,4,5,1,5,1,5,1,5,2,2,2,5,1,5,1,5,1,5,4,4,3
```
◄── DATA values

```
RUN

* * * * * * * * * * * * * * * * * * * * * *
*  *  *  *  *  *  *  *  *  *  *
*  *  *  *  *  *  *  *  *  *  *
*** . ***     ***      ***
*******  ***  *******
***   ***     ***     ***
*******  ***  *******
***   ***     ***     ***
*******  ***   *******
***   ***   ***     ***
*** *****     ***** ***
*** *****     ***** ***
*** *****     ***** ***
***   ***     ***     ***
*******  ***  *******
***   ***     ***     ***
*******  ***  *******
***   ***     ***     ***
*******  ***  *******
***   ***     ***     ***
*  *  *  *  *  *  *  *  *  *  *
*  *  *  *  *  *  *  *  *  *  *
* * * * * * * * * * * * * * * * * * * * * *
```

Hint: The pattern consists of five different types of lines. The first and last lines are "type 3" lines. The first and last numbers in the DATA statement are 3. Got the idea?

Answers to Self-Test

The frame numbers in parentheses refer to the frames in the chapter where the topic is discussed. You may wish to refer to these for quick review.

1. (a) RUN
        27

    (b) RUN
        12

    (c) RUN
        12

    (d) RUN
        12

    (frames 1-6)

2. (a) RUN

3	7	Ø	-2	5
-1	7	8	Ø	-3

        ?OD ERROR IN 1Ø

    (b) RUN
          3 7 Ø -2 5 -1 7 8 Ø -3
        ?OD ERROR IN 1Ø

    (frames 1-10, 33-34)

3. (a) RUN

X = 3	X = 7	X = Ø	X = 5	X = 7
X = 8	X = Ø			

(b) RUN

```
X = 3 X = 7 X = Ø X = 5 X = 7 X = 8 X = Ø
```

(frames 11, 33-35)

4. RUN

```
ANSWER          NUMBER OF       PERCENT OF
(YES OR NO)     ANSWERS         TOTAL
```

(frame 36)

5.
```
420 PRINT "ANSWER","NUMBER OF","PERCENT OF"
430 PRINT "(YES OR NO)","ANSWERS","TOTAL"
440 PRINT
450 LET T=Y+N
460 PRINT "YES", Y,100*Y/T
470 PRINT "NO",N,100*N/T
480 PRINT "TOTAL",T,100
```

In the above program segment, we have used T to computer the *Total* number of votes (T = Y + N). Then, in lines 460 and 470, the expressions 100*Y/T and 100*N/T are the percent Yes votes and No votes. (frames 35-37)

6.
```
100 REM***DISTANCE IN ONE TURN OF A WHEEL
110 READ D
120 PRINT
130 PRINT "WHEEL DIAMETER:";D
140 PRINT "DISTANCE IN ONE TURN:";3.14*D
150 GOTO 110
160 DATA 16,20,24,26,27
```

(frame 36)

7.
```
100 REM***COIN FLIPPER
110 PRINT : INPUT "HOW MANY FLIPS";N
120 IF N<1 THEN END
130 REM***FLIP COIN N TIMES
140 K=Ø : PRINT
150 C=INT(2*RND(1))
160 IF C=Ø THEN PRINT "T ";
170 IF C=1 THEN PRINT "H ";
180 K=K+1
190 IF K<N THEN 150
200 END
```

There is more than one way to write this program. In ours, we use the variable K to count the number of times the coin has been flipped. In line 140, we set K to zero. Then, each time through the loop, we increase K by 1 (line 180) and compare K with N (line 190). If K is still less than N, we increase K by 1 and go around again. If N is less than one, no flips are done—this is checked by line 120. Your program may be entirely different. If it works, you have solved the problem! (frames 37, 42)

8.   We modified our program of question 7. The complete program is
     shown below. The variable T is used to count the number of tails and
     the variable H to count the number of heads. Look for T and H in lines
     140, 160, 170, and 210.

```
100 REM***COIN FLIPPER
110 PRINT : INPUT "HOW MANY FLIPS";N
120 IF N<1 THEN END
130 REM***FLIP COIN N TIMES
140 K=0 : T=0 : H=0 : PRINT
150 C=INT(2*RND(1))
160 IF C=0 THEN PRINT "T "; : T=T+1
170 IF C=1 THEN PRINT "H "; : H=H+1
180 K=K+1
190 IF K<N THEN 150
200 PRINT : PRINT
210 PRINT H;"HEADS AND";T;"TAILS"
220 END
```

(frames 33, 37, 42)

9.
```
100 REM***COUNT ITEMS IN DATA STATEMENTS, EXCEPT FLAG
110 K=0
120 READ N
130 IF N<>1E38 THEN LET K=K+1 : GOTO 120
140 IF N=1E38 THEN PRINT "THERE ARE";K;"ITEMS IN THE DATA STATEMENTS."
150 DATA 2,3,5,7,11,13,17,19,23,29,31,37,41
160 DATA 43,47,53,59,61,67,71,73,79,83,89,97,1E38
999 END
```

Do you recognize the numbers in the DATA statements? They are all
the prime numbers (those numbers with themselves and 1 as their only
factors) less than 100.   (frames 10, 11, 18, 32)

10.
```
100 REM***PATTERN PRINTING PROGRAM
110 READ X : IF X=-1 THEN END
120 ON X GOTO 210,220,230,240,250
200 REM***PATTERN LINES
210 PRINT "*******  ***  *******" : GOTO 110
220 PRINT "*** *****   ***** ***" : GOTO 110
230 PRINT "********************" : GOTO 110
240 PRINT "* * * * * * * * * *" : GOTO 110
250 PRINT "***   ***   ***   ***" : GOTO 110
300 REM*** DATA TO MAKE A RUG DESIGN
310 DATA 3,4,4,5,1,5,1,5,1,5,2,2,2,5,1,5,1,5,1,5,4,4,3,-1
RUN
********************
* * * * * * * * * *
* * * * * * * * * *
***   ***   ***   ***
*******  ***  *******
***   ***   ***   ***
*******  ***  *******
***   ***   ***   ***
*******  ***  *******
***   ***   ***   ***
*** *****   ***** ***
*** *****   ***** ***
*** *****   ***** ***
***   ***   ***   ***
*******  ***  *******
***   ***   ***   ***
*******  ***  *******
***   ***   ***   ***
*******  ***  *******
***   ***   ***   ***
* * * * * * * * * *
* * * * * * * * * *
********************
```

Here is another way to do it.

```
10 REMARK PATTERN PRINTING PROGRAM
20 READ X
30 IF X=-1 THEN END
40 IF X=1 THEN 100
50 IF X=2 THEN 120
60 IF X=3 THEN 140
70 IF X=4 THEN 160
80 IF X=5 THEN 180
90 GOTO 20
100 PRINT "*******  ***  *******"
110 GOTO 20
120 PRINT "*** *****   ***** ***"
130 GOTO 20
140 PRINT "********************"
150 GOTO 20
160 PRINT "* * * * * * * * * *"
170 GOTO 20
180 PRINT "***   ***   ***   ***"
190 GOTO 20
900 DATA 3,4,4,5,1,5,1,5,1,5,2,2
910 DATA 2,5,1,5,1,5,1,5,4,4,3,-1
```

(frames 18, 19, 37, 42)

CHAPTER SIX

FOR-NEXT Loops

In this chapter we introduce another important computer programming concept: the FOR-NEXT loop. The IF-THEN statement and the FOR-NEXT loop greatly extend the usefulness of the computer as a tool. Close attention to the explanation and problems in this chapter will help you understand the functions of these statements in BASIC and will open a new dimension in your computer programming capability. When you complete this chapter you will be able to:

- use the FOR and NEXT statements;
- use the STEP clause in FOR statements.

1.   The Loop Demonstration Program on the following page is a counting program that prints the value for F as we increase F from 1 through 8. Line 10 merely initializes F at 1. To initialize, remember, means to assign the first value to a variable. Line 20 prints the current value for F. Line 30 increases F by 1 each time through the program.

Line 40 is an IF statement that tests the value of F. As long as F is less than or equal to 6, line 40 sends the computer back to line 20 to print the value of F. Once F exceeds 6, the program will stop since there are no more statements in the program. Just for practice, rewrite the program on the following page using multiple statements in one line. But think carefully: Can you do the *entire* program in just one line?

```
5 REM***LOOP DEMONSTRATION
10 LET F=1
20 PRINT "F ="; F
30 LET F=F+1
40 IF F <= 6 THEN 20

RUN
F = 1
F = 2
F = 3
F = 4
F = 5
F = 6
```
— — — — — — — — — — —

```
10 LET F=1
20 PRINT "F ="; F : LET F=F+1 : IF F <= 6 THEN 20
RUN
F = 1
F = 2
F = 3
F = 4
F = 5
F = 6
```

This means go back and start executing line 20 again (only if the comparison is true, of course). Notice that line 10 would also fit on this line, but the value for F would get "initialized" back to 1 every time the statement was executed. So we could *not* put the entire program in just one line.

2.   The space-saving, time-saving FOR-NEXT loop accomplishes a given number of *iterations* or repetitions more easily. Look at the FOR-NEXT loop below. Instead of IF-THEN, this time we use the FOR and NEXT statements to tell the computer how many times to go through the loop.

```
5 REM***FOR-NEXT LOOP DEMONSTRATION
10 FOR F=1 TO 6
20 PRINT "F ="; F
30 NEXT F
RUN
F = 1
F = 2
F = 3
F = 4
F = 5
F = 6
```

    In every FOR-NEXT loop, the FOR statement is the beginning point of the loop and the NEXT statement is always the last statement in the loop. The statement or statements between FOR and NEXT are executed, in order, over and over again, with the FOR statement indicating to the computer how many times the loop is to be executed.

(a)   You can see from the RUN of the FOR-NEXT loop that each time through the loop the value of F is automatically increased by _____.

(b)   How many times did the computer go through the loop? _____

(c)   Why did the computer stop after going through the loop the above number of times? _____

_____

(d)   What other statement must you have? _____

— — — — — — — — — —

(a)   1
(b)   6
(c)   because the FOR statement told it to go from 1 to 6.
(d)   a NEXT statement

3.   As you can see in the program below, the computer will continue with the rest of the program when it has completed the loop as specified by the FOR statement.

```
5 REM***ANOTHER FOR-NEXT LOOP
10 FOR D=5 TO 10  ◄──────────── Note that the loop doesn't have to
20 PRINT "D ="; D                start with 1.
30 NEXT D
40 PRINT
50 PRINT "AHA! OUT OF THE LOOP BECAUSE"
60 PRINT "D ="; D; "WHICH EXCEEDS 10."

RUN
D = 5
D = 6
D = 7
D = 8
D = 9
D = 10

AHA! OUT OF THE LOOP BECAUSE
D = 11 WHICH EXCEEDS 10.
```

In the program, the FOR-NEXT loop occupies which lines? _____

— — — — — — — — — —

lines 10, 20, and 30

4.   How does the FOR-NEXT loop work? Follow the arrows.

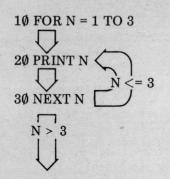

In line 10, N is set equal to 1.

In line 30, N is increased by one, and the computer compares the increased value of N to the upper limit for N indicated in the FOR statement.

Let's look at the FOR statement.

When N goes past this value, the computer stops executing the loop and continues on with the rest of the program past the FOR-NEXT loop (if there is more to the program). We call this the *limit* of N, or the limit of the FOR variable.

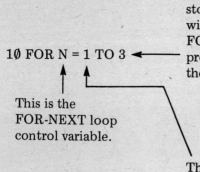

10 FOR N = 1 TO 3 ←—————

This is the FOR-NEXT loop control variable.

This is the first value N will have.

Here is a RUN of the program above.

```
10 FOR N=1 TO 3
20 PRINT N
30 NEXT N
RUN
 1
 2
 3
```

Each time the computer comes to a NEXT N statement, it increases the value of N by one, and checks the new value against the limit for N. In this case, the limit is 3, because the FOR statement reads: FOR N = 1 TO 3. When the value of N is greater than 3, the computer continues on to the next statement after the NEXT statement, if there is one. If not, the computer has finished executing the program and stops. Got that? Let's see.

    Statement 10 means that for the first time through the loop, N = 1. The second time through, N = N + 1 = 1 + 1 = 2. The third time through,

N = _____ = _____ = _____.

— — — — — — — — — — —

$N = N + 1 = 2 + 1 = 3$

5. Write a program with three statements that will print the word LOOP six times. Use a FOR-NEXT loop, and use C as the FOR-NEXT loop control variable. Show what your program will print when it is RUN.

— — — — — — — — — —

```
10 FOR C = 1 TO 6
20 PRINT "LOOP"
30 NEXT C
RUN
LOOP
LOOP
LOOP
LOOP
LOOP
LOOP
```

6. FOR-NEXT statements can be used in a multiple statement line. Here is a FOR-NEXT program, all on one line. Follow the arrows.

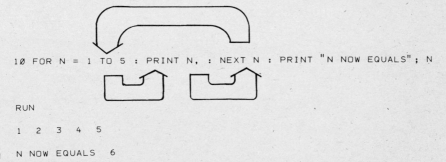

```
10 FOR N = 1 TO 5 : PRINT N, : NEXT N : PRINT "N NOW EQUALS"; N

RUN

1   2   3   4   5

N NOW EQUALS   6
```

When the computer had finished the FOR-NEXT loop and had made its exit from the loop, what was the value for N? _____

— — — — — — — — — —

6

Notice that the value for N after loop exit is one more than the upper limit for N as given in the FOR statement. That is how the computer recognized that it had performed the proper number of loops and was ready to go on to the next statement in the program beyond the FOR-NEXT loop.

7.   You can use FOR-NEXT in DIRECT mode, too. Remember, in direct mode you can enter a one-line statement without a line number, and the computer executes the statement as soon as you press RETURN. Let's say you enter the following multiple-statement line.

```
PRINT "TESTING"; : FOR X = 1 TO 4 : PRINT X; : NEXT X
```

What would your computer print when you pressed RETURN? _____
_____

— — — — — — — — —

```
TESTING 1   2   3   4
```

8.   Finish writing this program so that the computer will produce the RUN shown. Use a FOR-NEXT loop with Y as the control variable.

```
10 PRINT "THIS YEAR CATHY IS 10 YEARS OLD"
20 _____
30 _____
40 _____
RUN
THIS YEAR CATHY IS 10 YEARS OLD
AND THE NEXT YEAR SHE WILL BE 11
AND THE NEXT YEAR SHE WILL BE 12
AND THE NEXT YEAR SHE WILL BE 13
AND THE NEXT YEAR SHE WILL BE 14
```

— — — — — — — — —

```
20 FOR Y = 11 TO 14
30 PRINT "AND THE NEXT YEAR SHE WILL BE"; Y
40 NEXT Y
```

9.　Another thing to notice about FOR-NEXT loops is that variables may be used instead of numbers, providing, of course, that the variables have been assigned values earlier in the program. In the example below, values are assigned by LET statements. Values could also have been assigned by INPUT or READ statements.

```
1Ø A=3 : B=8
2Ø FOR C=A TO B
3Ø PRINT C;  ◄─────── Semicolon keeps printout on one line.
4Ø NEXT C
RUN
 3  4  5  6  7  8
```

Rewrite the FOR statement (line 20), substituting numerical values for variables A and B. Use the values that were assigned by the program above.

20 _____

— — — — — — — — — —

20 FOR C = 3 TO 8

10.　Play computer and show the RUN for this FOR-NEXT demonstration program.

```
1Ø X=Ø : Y=4
2Ø FOR Z=X TO Y
4Ø PRINT Z;
5Ø NEXT Z
RUN
```

_____

— — — — — — — — — —

```
RUN
 Ø  1  2  3  4
```

11.　Now you write a program where variables are used to set the initial and upper limits of the FOR-NEXT loop control variable. Have your program READ the values to be used for the initial and upper limits from a DATA statement.

　　　Use Z for the control variable, and use X and Y for the variables that set the initial and upper limits. Select your DATA statement values so that your program will produce the following RUN.

```
RUN
 1ØØ  1Ø1  1Ø2  1Ø3  1Ø4  1Ø5
```

— — — — — — — — — —

```
10 READ X
20 READ Y
30 FOR Z=X TO Y
40 PRINT Z;
50 NEXT Z
60 DATA 100,105
```

Statements 10 and 20 could be combined in one statement: 10 READ X, Y.

12.   In this next program, an INPUT value (line 40) is used to establish the upper limit of the FOR statement (line 100), which tells the computer how many times to repeat "X = ?" When the program is RUN, the PRINT statements in lines 10-80 tell the user how to use the program.

```
5 REM***FRIENDLY MEAN FROM INPUT VALUES
10 PRINT "FOR MY NEXT ENCORE I WILL COMPUTE"
20 PRINT "THE MEAN (AVERAGE) OF A LIST OF NUMBERS."
30 PRINT
40 INPUT "HOW MANY NUMBERS IN THE LIST"; N
50 PRINT
60 PRINT "EACH TIME I TYPE 'X =?' YOU TYPE IN"
70 PRINT "ONE NUMBER AND THEN PRESS THE RETURN KEY."
80 PRINT
90 T=0
100 FOR K=1 TO N
110 INPUT "X ="; X
120 T=T+X
130 NEXT K
140 M=T/N
150 PRINT
160 PRINT "TOTAL ="; T
170 PRINT "MEAN ="; M
```

(a)   In the program above, the FOR-NEXT loop occupies lines _____

_____.

(b)   What is the FOR-NEXT loop control variable? _____

(c)   The upper limit for the control variable is determined by the value assigned to which other variable? _____

— — — — — — — — — —

(a)   100, 110, 120, 130
(b)   K
(c)   N

13.   In the program of frame 12, which line in the FOR-NEXT loop will keep a running tally of the values entered for line 110?_____

— — — — — — — — — —

120 T = T + X

14.   This is a RUN of the program in frame 12.

```
RUN
FOR MY NEXT ENCORE, I WILL COMPUTE
THE MEAN (AVERAGE) OF A LIST OF NUMBERS.

HOW MANY NUMBERS IN THE LIST? 5

EACH TIME I TYPE 'X =?' YOU TYPE IN
ONE NUMBER AND THEN PRESS THE RETURN KEY.

X =? 16
X =? 46
X =? 38  }——————— Values entered by user.
X =? 112
X =? 23

TOTAL = 235
MEAN = 47
```

Show the numerical values in the FOR statement for the above RUN.

100 FOR K = _____ TO _____

— — — — — — — — — —

1 TO 5 (The value entered for INPUT N was 5.)

15.   Here is the beginning of another RUN of the same program.

```
RUN
FOR MY NEXT ENCORE, I WILL COMPUTE
THE MEAN (AVERAGE) OF A LIST OF NUMBERS.

HOW MANY NUMBERS IN THE LIST? 4 ◄——————— Value entered by user.
```

How many times will "X = ?" be printed? _____ How many times will the statements between the FOR-NEXT statements be executed?_____

— — — — — — — — — —

4; 4

Just to prove it to you, this is the rest of the same RUN.

```
EACH TIME I TYPE 'X =?' YOU TYPE IN
ONE NUMBER AND THEN PRESS THE RETURN KEY.

X =? 2
X =? 4
X =? 6
X =? 8

TOTAL = 20
MEAN = 5
```

16. Do you remember this program from frame 39 in Chapter 3?

```
100 REM***CHANGE OF ADDRESS PROGRAM
110 PRINT
120 PRINT "DEAR FRIENDS, MY NEW ADDRESS IS:"
130 PRINT
140 PRINT "IRENE BROWNSTONE"
150 PRINT "605 PARK AVENUE"
160 PRINT "NEW YORK, NY 10016"
170 PRINT
180 GOTO 110
```

Show how you would modify this program to use a FOR-NEXT loop
that will ask the user how many messages to print, and then print just that
many address change messages. Insert, replace, or delete lines as needed. A
RUN should look like this.

```
RUN
HOW MANY TIMES? 2

DEAR FRIENDS, MY NEW ADDRESS IS:

IRENE BROWNSTONE
605 PARK AVENUE
NEW YORK, NY 10016

DEAR FRIENDS, MY NEW ADDRESS IS:

IRENE BROWNSTONE
605 PARK AVENUE
NEW YORK, NY 10016


— — — — — — — — —


105 INPUT "HOW MANY TIMES"; T
115 FOR X=1 TO T
180 NEXT X
```

Line numbers need not be the same as those we used. However, the INPUT statement *must* be inserted between lines 100 and 110, and the FOR statement *must* appear between lines 110 and 120. Also, you might have used another letter for the FOR-NEXT loop control variable where we used X, or for the INPUT variable T.

17. Complete the following program to compute the product (P) of N numbers. Think carefully about the effect of your statements when the program is RUN.

```
5 REM***PRODUCT CALCULATED FROM A LIST OF NUMBERS
10 PRINT "YOU WANT STILL ANOTHER ENCORE? I'M FLATTERED!"
20 PRINT "I'LL COMPUTE THE PRODUCT OF A LIST OF NUMBERS."
30 PRINT
40 INPUT "HOW MANY NUMBERS IN THE LIST"; N
50 PRINT
60 PRINT "EACH TIME I TYPE 'X =?' YOU TYPE IN"
70 PRINT "ONE NUMBER AND THEN PRESS THE RETURN KEY."
80 PRINT

100 _____   ◄——— Initialize

110 _____
120 INPUT "X ="; X
130 P=P*X

140 _____
150 PRINT : PRINT "PRODUCT ="; P

RUN
YOU WANT STILL ANOTHER ENCORE? I'M FLATTERED!
I'LL COMPUTE THE PRODUCT OF A LIST OF NUMBERS.

HOW MANY NUMBERS IN THE LIST? 5

EACH TIME I TYPE 'X =?' YOU TYPE IN
ONE NUMBER AND THEN PRESS THE RETURN KEY.

X =? 7
X =? 12
X =? 4
X =? 3
X =? 19

PRODUCT = 19152
```

— — — — — — — — —

```
100 LET P=1
110 FOR K=1 TO N
140 NEXT K
```

Consider what would happen if P = 0 the first time through the loop: in line 140, P*X would be zero for the first time through the loop, *and* every time after that. No matter what value X had, zero times X would always be zero!

18. Any BASIC expression may be used to set both the initial and the maximum value of a FOR-NEXT loop control variable. The computer evaluates these expressions (that is, does the arithmetic) *before* the loop is executed the first time, and does *not* recompute these values each time through the loop.

Look at the FOR statement in this next program, and then decide whether the computer executed the loop the proper number of times.

```
10 Q=4
20 FOR P=Q TO 2*Q-1
30 PRINT P;
40 NEXT P

RUN
 4   5   6   7
```
The computer was right!

In the following program, fill in the blanks in line 20 with expressions using the variable Q, so that when the program is RUN, it will produce the printout shown below.

10 Q=4

20 FOR P=_____ TO _____

30 PRINT P;
40 NEXT P

RUN
 2 3 4 5 6 7 8 9 10 11 12

— — — — — — — — —

20 FOR P=Q/2 TO Q*3 or 20 FOR P=Q–2 TO Q+8

Note: If your answer is different and you think it is correct, try it on a computer and see if you get the same RUN that we did.

19. In the FOR-NEXT loops you have seen so far, the FOR-NEXT loop control variable takes the first value given in the FOR statement, and keeps that value until the computer comes to the NEXT statement. Then the FOR variable increases its value by one each time through the loop until it reaches the maximum value allowed by the FOR statement.

FOR X = 5 TO 10

First value of X————⌐   Maximum value for X

X = 5, then 6, then 7, then 8, then 9, and then 10

However, you can write a FOR statement that causes the value of the FOR-NEXT loop control variable to increase by multiples of other than one, or by fractional increments. You can also have the value of the FOR-NEXT variable *decrease* each time through the loop.

10 FOR X=1 TO 10 STEP 2

Tells the computer to increase the value of X by 2 every time through the FOR-NEXT loop, until X is greater than 10.

10 FOR Y-3 TO 6 STEP 1.5

Tells the computer to increase the value of Y by 1.5 every time through the FOR-NEXT loop, until Y is greater than 6.

10 FOR Z=10 TO 5 STEP −1

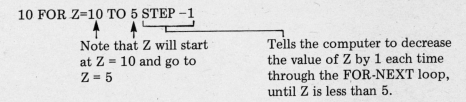

Note that Z will start at Z = 10 and go to Z = 5

Tells the computer to decrease the value of Z by 1 each time through the FOR-NEXT loop, until Z is less than 5.

Some demonstration programs will show the effects of STEP in action.

```
10 FOR B=1 TO 10 STEP 2
20 PRINT B;
30 NEXT B
40 PRINT
50 PRINT
60 PRINT "LOOP TERMINATES BECAUSE"
70 PRINT "B ="; B; ", WHICH IS GREATER THAN 10."

RUN
 1   3   5   7   9

LOOP TERMINATES BECAUSE
B = 11 , WHICH IS GREATER THAN 10.
```

The PRINT statement in line 40 "bumps" the computer off the line where it is held by the semicolon at the end of line 20. The PRINT statement in line 50 causes the space before line 60 is printed.

Note that the loop starts with the first value in the FOR statement (1) and increases by increments of 2, until the value of B = 11 which exceeds the maximum value allowed (10). At that point, the computer terminates the loop and continues running the rest of the program.

Play computer again, and fill in the RUN for this program.

```
10 D=3 : FOR F=D TO 4*D STEP D : PRINT F; : NEXT F
RUN
```

```
  3   6   9   12
```

20.   In this example, the STEP in the FOR statement is followed by a negative number. STEP may be used to decrease the value of the FOR variable in any size step, going from a large value to a smaller one.

```
10 FOR J=100 TO 10 STEP -10
20 PRINT J;
30 NEXT J
RUN
 100  90  80  70  60  50  40  30  20  10
```

Now you write one where the FOR-NEXT loop control variable E decreases in steps of 3 from 27 to 18. Show the program and the RUN.

— — — — — — — — —

```
10 FOR E = 27 TO 18 STEP -3
20 PRINT E;
30 NEXT E

RUN
 27  24  21  18
```

or

```
10 FOR E = 27 TO 18 STEP -3 : PRINT E; : NEXT E
RUN
 27  24  21  18
```

21.   As we mentioned, the steps in a FOR-NEXT loop can be fractional values, as in the following example.

```
10 FOR X = 5 TO 7.5 STEP .25
20 PRINT X;
30 NEXT X
RUN
 5   5.25   5.5   5.75   6   6.25   6.5   6.75   7   7.25   7.5
```

Show the RUN for this program if we changed line 10 to the following.

```
10 FOR X = 5 TO 7.5 STEP .5
RUN
```

— — — — — — — — —

```
RUN
 5  5.5  6  6.5  7  7.5
```

22.   Here's another useful trick. You don't *have to* use the control variable name in the NEXT statement. If no variable is used, the computer assumes you are referring to the most recent FOR statement. For example:

```
10 INPUT "HOW MANY TIMES"; T
20 FOR K=1 TO T : PRINT "*"; : NEXT
```
↑
The computer assumes NEXT K

   Write a program using a FOR-NEXT loop and all the space-saving, time-saving tricks introduced thus far in this book to print 20 random whole numbers between 1 and 50.

— — — — — — — — —

```
10 FOR X=1 TO 20 : PRINT INT(50*RND(1))+1; : NEXT
```

23.   The FOR-NEXT loop is useful for such things as repeated calculations, counting or keeping tallies, and dealing with cyclical or recurring events.

   One such recurring event is the monthly compounding of interest on a savings account or other financial investment.

   In the program on the following page, monthly interest (I) is calculated in line 170 by multiplying the initial amount of money (P for Principal) by the Rate of interest (R).

   The rate of interest is converted to a decimal fraction: R = 5 percent = 5/100 = .05

   Since 5 percent is the yearly rate of interest, only 1/12 of the calculated amount of interest is added to the principal each month.

```
100 REM***MONTHLY INTEREST COMPOUNDING
110 INPUT "PRINCIPAL"; P
120 INPUT "YEARLY INTEREST RATE (IN %)"; R
130 INPUT "HOW MANY MONTHS"; M
140 PRINT
150 PRINT "MONTH", "PRINCIPAL", "INTEREST", "PRIN. + INT."
160 FOR K=1 TO M
170 I=(P*(R/100))/12
180 PRINT K,P,I,P+I
190 P=P+I
200 NEXT K

RUN
PRINCIPAL? 200
YEARLY INTEREST RATE (IN %)? 5
HOW MANY MONTHS? 6
```

MONTH	PRINCIPAL	INTEREST	PRIN. + INT.
1	200	.833333	200.833
2	200.833	.836806	201.67
3	201.67	.840292	202.51
4	202.51	.843794	203.354
5	203.354	.847309	204.202
6	204.202	.85084	205..052

(a) Which lines are included in the FOR-NEXT loop?_____

(b) Which variable keeps track of and is used to print the number corresponding to the month for each line in the table?_____

(c) Line 150 prints the column headings for the table. The words used in the headings are separated by commas. In line 180, the values to be printed under the headings are also separated by commas, so that the spacing of headings and the numbers that go under headings match up. What would happen if the statement that prints the heading were included in the FOR-NEXT loop?_____

_____

(d) Which line keeps a running tally of Principal plus Interest?_____

— — — — — — — — — — —

(a) 160, 170, 180, 190, 200
(b) the FOR variable K
(c) The heading would be printed every time through the loop, between each line of the table.
(d) 190

Note: If you want to brush up on your business math, a useful book would be Locke, *Business Mathematics* (a Self-Teaching Guide), John Wiley & Sons, New York, 1972.

24. Can you have a FOR-NEXT *inside* another FOR-NEXT loop? Absolutely. It is called *nested* FOR-NEXT loops and is perfectly "legal" provided you follow the rule illustrated below.

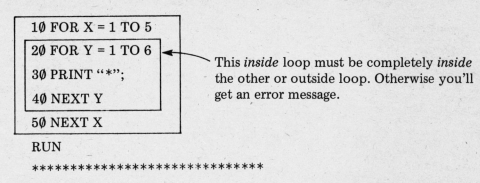

```
1Ø FOR X = 1 TO 5
2Ø FOR Y = 1 TO 6
3Ø PRINT "*";
4Ø NEXT Y
5Ø NEXT X
```

This *inside* loop must be completely *inside* the other or outside loop. Otherwise you'll get an error message.

RUN

****

Count the stars. How many are there? Do you see any relationship between the number of stars printed and the numbers 5 and 6 which appear in the two FOR statements?

A loop within a loop is called a _____ FOR-NEXT loop. The inside loop must be _____ the outside loop.

— — — — — — — — — —

nested; inside

25. Here are two programs using nested FOR-NEXT loops.

```
5 REM***PROGRAM A            5 REM***PROGRAM B
1Ø FOR N=5 TO 9             1Ø FOR N=5 TO 9
2Ø FOR L=1 TO 3             2Ø FOR L=1 TO 3
3Ø PRINT "NESTED"           3Ø PRINT "NESTED"
4Ø NEXT L                   4Ø NEXT N
5Ø PRINT "     LOOP"        5Ø PRINT "       LOOP"
6Ø NEXT N                   6Ø NEXT L
```

Which program (A or B) has correctly nested FOR-NEXT loops?_____

— — — — — — — — — —

program A

26. Program A in frame 25 produces a repeated pattern of printout. Look at the program closely and then show what the computer will print when the program is RUN.

— — — — — — — — — —

```
RUN
NESTED
NESTED
NESTED
        LOOP
NESTED
NESTED
NESTED
        LOOP
NESTED
NESTED
NESTED
        LOOP
NESTED
NESTED
NESTED
        LOOP
NESTED
NESTED
NESTED
        LOOP
```

27. Another time-saving, space-saving trick available to you is the ability to use two NEXT statements at once. In a program where nested FOR-NEXT loops end in successive statements, we would replace two NEXT statements with just one, as below.

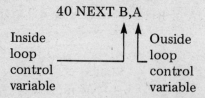

40 NEXT B,A

Inside loop control variable

Ouside loop control variable

On the following page is a program with nested loops that will print the multiplication table from 0 × 0 to 9 × 9.

```
10 FOR X=0 TO 9
20 FOR Y=0 TO 9
30 PRINT X; "X"; Y "="; X*Y,
40 NEXT Y
50 NEXT X
RUN
 0 X 0 = 0      0 X 1 = 0      0 X 2 = 0      0 X 3 = 0      0 X 4 = 0
 0 X 5 = 0      0 X 6 = 0      0 X 7 = 0      0 X 8 = 0      0 X 9 = 0
 1 X 0 = 0      1 X 1 = 1      1 X 2 = 2      1 X 3 = 3      1 X 4 = 4
 1 X 5 = 5      1 X 6 = 6      1 X 7 = 7      1 X 8 = 8      1 X 9 = 9
 2 X 0 = 0      2 X 1 = 2      2 X 2 = 4      2 X 3 = 6      2 X 4 = 8
 2 X 5 = 10     2 X 6 = 12     2 X 7 = 14     2 X 8 = 16     2 X 9 = 18
 3 X 0 = 0      3 X 1 = 3      3 X 2 = 6      3 X 3 = 9      3 X 4 = 12
 3 X 5 = 15     3 X 6 = 18     3 X 7 = 21     3 X 8 = 24     3 X 9 = 27
 4 X 0 = 0      4 X 1 = 4      4 X 2 = 8      4 X 3 = 12     4 X 4 = 16
 4 X 5 = 20     4 X 6 = 24     4 X 7 = 28     4 X 8 = 32     4 X 9 = 36
 5 X 0 = 0      5 X 1 = 5      5 X 2 = 10     5 X 3 = 15     5 X 4 = 20
 5 X 5 = 25     5 X 6 = 30     5 X 7 = 35     5 X 8 = 40     5 X 9 = 45
 6 X 0 = 0      6 X 1 = 6      6 X 2 = 12     6 X 3 = 18     6 X 4 = 24
 6 X 5 = 30     6 X 6 = 36     6 X 7 = 42     6 X 8 = 48     6 X 9 = 54
 7 X 0 = 0      7 X 1 = 7      7 X 2 = 14     7 X 3 = 21     7 X 4 = 28
 7 X 5 = 35     7 X 6 = 42     7 X 7 = 49     7 X 8 = 56     7 X 9 = 63
 8 X 0 = 0      8 X 1 = 8      8 X 2 = 16     8 X 3 = 24     8 X 4 = 32
 8 X 5 = 40     8 X 6 = 48     8 X 7 = 42     8 X 8 = 64     8 X 9 = 72
 9 X 0 = 0      9 X 1 = 9      9 X 2 = 18     9 X 3 = 27     9 X 4 = 36
 9 X 5 = 45     9 X 6 = 54     9 X 7 = 63     9 X 8 = 72     9 X 9 = 81
```

Write a single NEXT statement that will be correct for this program.

_____

— — — — — — — — — —

40 NEXT Y,X

29.   Do your kids, friends, or family hound you for arithmetic problems?
Ours sure do. On this and the following page is a little program to generate
multiplication problem *worksheets.* Fill in the blanks.

```
10 REM***PERSONALIZED MULTIPLICATION WORKSHEET
20 INPUT "WHAT IS YOUR NAME"; A$
30 INPUT "HOW MANY PROBLEMS"; T
40 INPUT "HOW MANY DIGITS IN EACH NUMBER(1,2 OR 3)"; D
50 PRINT : PRINT "MULTIPLICATION WORKSHEET FOR "; A$

60 FOR P= _____
70 FOR M=1 TO 2
80 PRINT INT (10↑D*RND(1))

90 _____
100 PRINT "-------" : PRINT : PRINT : PRINT

110 _____

RUN
WHAT IS YOUR NAME? BETTE
HOW MANY PROBLEMS? 3
HOW MANY DIGITS IN EACH NUMBER(1,2 OR 3)? 3
```

continued on next page

```
MULTIPLICATION WORKSHEET FOR BETTE
 278
 496
-------



 75Ø
 378
-------



 734
 128
-------
```

— — — — — — — — — —

60 FOR P = 1 TO T
90 NEXT (You might also have said NEXT M.)
110 NEXT P (You *must* have the P; otherwise, the computer assumes the
   most recent FOR and that was FOR M.)

29.   Look again at the program in frame 28.

(a)   Which lines contain the FOR-NEXT statements to limit the number of
      problems?_____

(b)   What does line 100 do?_____

— — — — — — — — — —

(a)   Lines 60 and 110 contain the FOR and NEXT statements. All the
      statements between are inside the loop with the control variable P.
(b)   Line 100 prints a line below which you place your answer and prints
      spaces (or does three line feeds) between problems.

30.   Sometimes our line 80 from the program in frame 28 produces random
numbers with only 2 digits when we asked for 3, or only 1 digit when we
asked for 2, as in this RUN.

```
RUN
WHAT IS YOUR NAME? MIKE
HOW MANY PROBLEMS? 2
HOW MANY DIGITS IN EACH NUMBER(1,2 OR 3)? 2

MULTIPLICATION WORKSHEET FOR MIKE
 4
 89
-------
```

continued on next page

```
 1
 5
------
```

We want you to fix our program so that won't happen, using an IF-THEN statement to check the number generated by line 80. If the number does not have the proper number of digits, direct the computer to generate another number. Notice the 10↑D in line 80. If D = 1, then 10↑1 = 10. If D = 2 then 10↑2 = 100. If D = 3 then 10↑3 = 1000. This way of using the INPUT value of D will be useful in writing the IF-THEN statement. Remember, if D = 2 we don't want 9 or less to be printed, and if D = 3 we don't want 99 or less to be used in a problem. Write your changes below.

— — — — — — — — —

Our changes:
```
80 N=INT(10↑D*RND(1)) : IF N<10↑(D-1)  THEN 80
90 PRINT N : NEXT M
```

Now a RUN always has the correct number of digits in the problem. If your answer doesn't look like ours but you think it is right, try it on a computer! You'll be seeing and using a lot more FOR-NEXT loops as you continue on in this book.

```
RUN
WHAT IS YOUR NAME? KATHY
HOW MANY PROBLEMS? 4
HOW MANY DIGITS IN EACH NUMBER(1,2 OR 3)? 2

MULTIPLICATION WORKSHEET FOR KATHY
 42
 10
-------


 28
 14
-------


 51
 76
-------


 67
 21
-------
```

SELF-TEST

Now that you have completed Chapter 6, you have acquired enough understanding of computer programming to be able to learn a lot more by experimenting at a computer terminal. As you look at our demonstration programs, you may see some possibilities that we do not specifically deal with. Build on your knowledge by trying out your own ideas.

But right now, find out if you really know how to use FOR-NEXT loops by doing the following programs.

1.   Show what will be printed if we RUN the following program.

```
10  S=0
20  FOR K=1 TO 4
30  S=S+K
40  NEXT K
50  PRINT S
RUN
```

2.   Show what will be printed if we RUN the following program.

```
10  P=1 : FOR K=1 TO 4 : P=P*K : NEXT K : PRINT P
RUN
```

3.   Examine this program. Which of the three RUNs was produced by the program? _____

```
10  N=1
20  FOR K=1 TO N
30  PRINT "*";
40  NEXT K
50  PRINT
60  N=N+1
70  IF N>10 THEN END
80  GOTO 20
```

| RUN 1 | RUN 2 | RUN 3 |

4. Write a program to print a table of N, N^2, and N^3. Use INPUT statements to indicate what list of numbers you wish included in the table. A RUN should look like this.

```
RUN
FIRST NUMBER? 4Ø
LAST NUMBER? 45

   N              N-SQUARED        N-CUBED
   4Ø               16ØØ            64ØØØ
   41               1681            68921
   42               1764            74Ø88
   43               1849            795Ø7
   44               1936            85184
   45               2Ø25            91125
```

5. Show what will be printed if we RUN the following program.

```
1Ø  S=Ø
2Ø  FOR K=1 TO 7 STEP 2
3Ø  S=S+K
4Ø  NEXT K
5Ø  PRINT S
RUN
```

6. On the following page, complete this program to print a table projecting growth rate of a population at specified intervals over a given time period (years). The formula for population growth is:

$$Q = P(1 + R/100)^N$$

where N is the number of years.

```
100 REM***REQUEST DATA AND PRINT HEADING
110 INPUT "INITIAL POPULATION"; P
120 INPUT "GROWTH RATE"; R
130 INPUT "INITIAL VALUE OF N"; A
140 INPUT "FINAL VALUE OF N"; B
150 INPUT "STEP SIZE"; H
160 PRINT : PRINT " N", "POPULATION" : PRINT
200 REM***COMPUTE AND PRINT TABLE

210 _____

220 _____

230 _____

240 _____

RUN
INITIAL POPULATION? 230
GROWTH RATE? 1
INITIAL VALUE OF N? 0
FINAL VALUE OF N? 100
STEP SIZE? 25

 N           POPULATION
 0             230
 25            294.959
 50            378.263
 75            485.095
 100           622.1

RUN
INITIAL POPULATION? 205
GROWTH RATE? 1
INITIAL VALUE OF N? 0
FINAL VALUE OF N? 100
STEP SIZE? 10
```

For U.S.A., 1970 (in millions of people).

```
 N           POPULATION
 0             205
 10            226.447
 20            250.139
 30            276.309
 40            305.217
 50            337.149
 60            372.422
 70            411.386
 80            454.426
 90            501.968
 100           554.485
```

Results are expressed in millions.

7. Write a program to compute and print the sum of whole numbers from 1 to N where the value of N is supplied in response to an INPUT statement. A RUN might look like the one on the following page.

```
RUN
GIVE ME A WHOLE NUMBER (N) AND I WILL COMPUTE
AND PRINT THE SUM OF THE WHOLE NUMBERS FROM 1 TO N.

WHAT IS N? 3
THE SUM IS 6          Because 1+2+3 = 6

WHAT IS N? 5
THE SUM IS 15         Because 1+2+3+4+5 = 15

WHAT IS N?

BREAK IN 30
```

8. Look back at the simple number guessing game in Chapter 1, frame 9. Use a FOR-NEXT loop to modify the program so that the user has only eight chances to guess the number. If he fails in eight guesses print an appropriate message before starting over again.

Answers to Self-Test

The frame numbers in parentheses refer to the frames in the chapter where the topic is discussed. You may wish to refer back to these for a quick review.

1. RUN
      10
    The answer is the *sum* of the values of K defined by the FOR statement (K = 1, 2, 3, and 4).   (frames 1-7)

2. RUN
    24

    The answer is the *product* of the values of K defined by the FOR statement (K = 1, 2, 3, and 4).   (frames 1-6, 13)

3. RUN 3. The FOR-NEXT loop (lines 20, 30, 40) causes the computer to print a *row* of N stars. The loop is done for N = 1,2,3, . . . 10. (frames 1-6, 20)

4.
```
10 INPUT "FIRST NUMBER"; A
20 INPUT "LAST NUMBER"; B
30 PRINT
40 PRINT " N", "N-SQUARED", "N-CUBED"
50 FOR N=A TO B
60 PRINT N, N↑2, N↑3
70 NEXT N
```
    (frames 9, 23)

5. RUN
    16

    Similar to question 1, but this time the values of K defined by the FOR statement are K = 1,3,5, and 7.   (frame 19)

6.
```
200 REMARK COMPUTE AND PRINT TABLE
210 FOR N=A TO B STEP H
220 LET Q=P*(1+R/100)↑N
230 PRINT N,Q
240 NEXT N
```
    (frames 19, 23)

7.
```
10 PRINT "GIVE ME A WHOLE NUMBER (N) AND I WILL COMPUTE"
20 PRINT "AND PRINT THE SUM OF THE WHOLE NUMBERS FROM 1 TO N."
30 PRINT
40 PRINT "WHAT IS N";
50 INPUT N
55 LET S=0
60 FOR W=1 TO N
70 LET S=S+W
80 NEXT W
90 PRINT "THE SUM IS";S
100 GOTO 30
```
    (frame 23)

8.
```
100 REMARK***THIS IS A SIMPLE COMPUTER GAME
110 LET X=INT .(100*RND(1))+1
120 PRINT
130 PRINT"I'M THINKING OF A NUMBER FROM 1 TO 100."
140 PRINT"GUESS MY NUMBER!!!"
150 FOR A=1 TO 8 : INPUT"YOUR GUESS";G
160 IF G<X THEN PRINT"TRY A BIGGER NUMBER" : GO TO 190
170 IF G>X THEN PRINT"TRY A SMALLER NUMBER": GO TO 190
180 IF G=X THEN PRINT"THAT'S IT!!! YOU GUESSED MY NUMBER." : GO TO 110
190 NEXT A : PRINT"TOO MANY GUESSES. THE NUMBER WAS";X : GO TO 110
```

(frames 2, 4)

CHAPTER SEVEN

Subscripted Variables

In Chapters 7 and 8 we will present another useful tool, the *subscripted variable*. First we will discuss BASIC variables with a *single* subscript.

You will learn, for example, how to count votes from a survey and how to accumulate or count dollars and assign them to different groupings. And you will get lots more practice using FOR-NEXT loops and making more attractive printed reports.

The only completely new BASIC statement is the DIMension statement, but many new programming ideas are introduced in this chapter. Read the chapter slowly and carefully. Experiment on your computer, if you have one—you will find that these new techniques give you much more range and flexibility. When you complete this chapter, you will be able to:

- recognize and use subscripted variables with a single (one) subscript;

- assign values to subscripted variables;

- use subscripted variables with variables for subscripts;

- use one-dimensional arrays to store the values of subscripted variables;

- use the DIM statement to tell the computer the maximum size of the array(s) used by a program.

1.   The concept we discuss here will require your close attention. Take it slowly, and read carefully as we enter the mysterious realm of *subscripted variables*.

Until now, we have used only *simple* BASIC variables. A simple variable consists of a letter (any letter A to Z) or a letter *followed* by a single digit (any digit 0 to 9). For example, the following are simple variables.

    P   R   K   P1   P2

Now we want to introduce a new type of variable, called a subscripted variable.

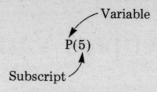

Variable

P(5)

Subscript

Say it: "P sub 5"

A subscripted variable consists of a letter (any letter A to Z) followed by a subscript enclosed in *parentheses*. P(3) is a subscripted variable; P3 is *not* a subscripted variable.

Which of the following are subscripted variables? Circle the answer(s).

X(1)   X   X1   C(23)   D

— — — — — — — — — —

X(1); C(23)

Note: X, X1, and X(1) are three distinct variables. All three can appear in the same program. They may confuse *you*, but the computer will recognize them as three different variables.

2.   A subscripted variable (like the simple variables we have been using) names a memory location inside the computer. You can think of it as a box, a place to store a number.

P(0)	
P(1)	
P(2)	
P(3)	
P(4)	
P(5)	
P(6)	
P(7)	
P(8)	

A set of subscripted variables is also called an *array*. This set of subscripted variables is a *one-way dimensional array*, also known as a vector. In Chapter 8, we will discuss two-dimensional arrays.

Pretend you are the computer, and LET P(2) = 36. In other words use your pencil or pen and write the number 36 in the box labeled P(2) in the drawing on the previous page. Then LET P(3) = 12. (Do it.) Now LET P(7) = P(2) + P(3). Check yourself by looking at our answer following the dashed line.

— — — — — — — — — — —

P(0)	
P(1)	
P(2)	36
P(3)	12
P(4)	
P(5)	
P(6)	
P(7)	48
P(8)	

3.   Subscripted variables can have variables for subscripts. The subscripted variable, Y(J), has the variable J for a subscript.

If J = 1 then Y(J) is Y(1)

If J = 2 then Y(J) is Y(2)

If J = 7 then Y(J) is Y(7)

Let us assume that the values (in the boxes on the following page) have been assigned to the corresponding variables. Note that both simple and subscripted variables are shown here.

Y(1)	4
Y(2)	−3
Y(3)	5
Y(4)	6

Z(1)	4.7
Z(2)	9.2
X(1)	2
X(2)	3

A	1
B	2
C	3
D	4

Write the value of each variable below.

$Y(1) =$ _____ $A =$ _____ $Y(A) =$ _____

$Y(2) =$ _____ $B =$ _____ $Y(B) =$ _____

$Y(C) =$ _____ $X(A) =$ _____ $X(B) =$ _____

$Z(A) =$ _____ $Z(B) =$ _____ $Y(D) =$ _____

— — — — — — — — — —

4	1	4
−3	2	−3
5	2	3
4.7	9.2	6

4.   So far we have only used single variables as subscripts. However, the subscript can be more complex. Below are two examples, still using the variables and values in the boxes in frame 3.

$$Y(A + 1) = Y(1 + 1) = Y(2) = -3$$

$$Y(2*B) = Y(2*2) = Y(4) = 6$$

Notice that the expressions inside the subscript parentheses are computed using the same rules for BASIC arithmetic as an expression in a PRINT statement, or inside a function parentheses.

Now you complete some examples as we did above, showing both the value calculated for the subscript and the value assigned to the subscripted variable with that subscript. (Refer to the boxes in frame 3.)

$Y(A + 2) =$ _____

$Y(2*A - 1) =$ _____

$Y(A + B) =$ _____

$Y(B*C - D) =$ _____

$Y(A + 3) =$ _____

Y(D − 3) = _____

Y(D − C + A) = _____

Y((C + D) − (A + B)) = _____

− − − − − − − − − −

Y(A + 2) = Y(1 + 2) = Y(3) = 5
Y(2*A − 1) = Y(2*1 − 1) = Y(2 − 1) = Y(1) = 4
Y(A + B) = Y(1 + 2) = Y(3) = 5
Y(B*C − D) = Y(2*3 − 4) = Y(6 − 4) = Y(2) = −3
Y(A + 3) = Y(1 + 3) = Y(4) = 6
Y(D − 3) = Y(4 − 3) = Y(1) = 4
Y(D − C + A) = Y(4 − 3 + 1) = Y(1 + 1) = Y(2) = −3
Y((C + D) − (A + B)) = Y((3 + 4) − (1 + 2)) = Y(7 − 3) = Y(4) = 6

5.   So how can subscripted variables contribute to the ease and versatility of programming in BASIC? One common use of subscripted variables is to store a list of numbers entered via INPUT or READ statements. This can be done with a FOR-NEXT loop. The control variable can also be used as the variable for the subscript in a subscripted variable, causing the subscript to increase by one each time through the loop. To illustrate, again we will turn to The World's Most Expensive Adding Machine.

```
100 REM***WORLD'S MOST EXPENSIVE ADDING MACHINE (AGAIN)
110 PRINT
120 INPUT "HOW MANY NUMBERS"; N
130 PRINT
140 FOR K=1 TO N
150 INPUT "X ="; X(K)        ◄─────── N Numbers are entered by the user and
160 NEXT K                            stored in X(1) through X(N)
170 T=0  ◄───────
180 FOR K=1 TO N            ─┘ First T is set to zero. Then the numbers
190 LET T=T+X(K)              in X(1) through X(N) are added to T.
200 NEXT K
210 PRINT "THE TOTAL IS"; T

RUN

HOW MANY NUMBERS? 5

X =? 37
X =? 23
X =? 46
X =? 78
X =? 59
THE TOTAL IS 243
```

    For the RUN shown, N is 5. Therefore, 5 numbers will be entered by the operator and stored in X(1) through _____.

− − − − − − − − − −

X(5)

6. Suppose the computer is running the program in frame 5. It has just completed the FOR-NEXT loop in lines 140 to 160. The numbers entered by the user are now stored as follows.

N	5
X(1)	37
X(2)	23
X(3)	46
X(4)	78
X(5)	59

The computer is ready to proceed with line 170. This statement initializes the variable T, that is, gives T its first value. Show the value of T after line 170 has been executed.

T [ ]

– – – – – – – – – –

T [0]

7. Next, the computer will execute the FOR-NEXT loop in lines 180 to 200. How many times will the FOR-NEXT loop be executed? _____

– – – – – – – – – –

5 times, because line 180 says FOR K = 1 TO N and N is equal to 5

8. The FOR-NEXT loop in lines 180 to 200 will be done 5 times, first for K = 1, then for K = 2, K = 3, K = 4, and finally for K = 5. Let's look at line 190, where K is used as a subscript.

190 LET T = T + X(K)

This statement tells the computer to add the value of X(K) to the *old* value of T and then assign the result as the *new* value of T.

What is the value of T after line 190 has been executed for K = 1?

_____ For K = 2? _____ For K = 3? _____ For K = 4? _____

For K = 5? _____

— — — — — — — — — —

37; 60; 106; 184; 243

9.   The program in frame 5 is shown the "long way" to aid your understanding of subscripted variables. Let's rewrite that program together to take advantage of BASIC's super ability to crunch a program down to size. Lines 100-130 reduce to the following.

```
100 REM***WORLD'S MOST EXPENSIVE ADDING MACHINE (AGAIN)
110 PRINT : INPUT "HOW MANY NUMBERS"; N : PRINT
```

Lines 140-160 reduce to a single line.

```
120 FOR K=1 TO N : INPUT "X ="; X(K) : NEXT K
```

Lines 170-210? Your turn.

130 _____

140 _____

— — — — — — — — — —

```
130 LET T=0 : FOR K=1 TO N : LET T=T+X(K) : NEXT K
140 PRINT "TOTAL IS"; T
```

10.   Since the use of the word LET is optional in a LET statement (also called an assignment statement), line 130 could be shortened even further. Show how it would look.

130 _____

— — — — — — — — — —

```
130 T=0 : FOR K=1 TO N : T=T+X(K) : NEXT K
```

We could also leave off the K in NEXT K to save additional time and computer memory space.

11. Let's use the World's Most Expensive Adding Machine to compute the
sum of whole numbers, 1 through 12.

```
RUN

HOW MANY NUMBERS? 12

X =? 1
X =? 2
X =? 3
X =? 4
X =? 5
X =? 6
X =? 7
X =? 8
X =? 9
X =? 1Ø
X =? 11
?BS ERROR IN 12Ø
```

This time we got an error message telling us that we had a Bad Subscript (BS). What was the largest subscript for X(K) that the computer

would accept *before* it gave us an error message? _____

— — — — — — — — — — —

10

12. The computer does not permit a subscript to be greater than 10, unless
we specify otherwise.

If subscripts greater than 10 are to be used, special instructions must
be included in the program to reserve space for a larger array of subscripted
variables. We must tell the computer the *largest* subscript it is to permit in
a subscripted variable by using a DIM statement. ("DIM" is the abbreviation
for "dimensions" of an array of subscripted variables.)

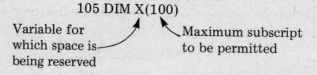

105 DIM X(100)

Variable for   Maximum subscript
which space is—   to be permitted
being reserved

The above DIM statement specifies a subscripted variable which can

have a maximum subscript of _____.

— — — — — — — — — — —

100

13. Suppose we wanted to specify that the maximum subscript is 50. Write the DIM statement.

105 _____

– – – – – – – – – –

105 DIM X(50)

14. We will add the DIM statement from frame 12 to the program from frame 9. Below is a LIST and RUN using the 12 numbers that gave us trouble before.

```
100 REM***WORLD'S MOST EXPENSIVE ADDING MACHINE (AGAIN)
105 DIM X(100)
110 PRINT : INPUT "HOW MANY NUMBERS"; N : PRINT
120 FOR K=1 TO N : INPUT "X ="; X(K) : NEXT K
130 T=0 : FOR K=1 TO N : LET T=T+X(K) : NEXT K
140 PRINT "THE TOTAL IS"; T

RUN

HOW MANY NUMBERS? 12

X =? 1
X =? 2
X =? 3
X =? 4
X =? 5
X =? 6
X =? 7
X =? 8
X =? 9
X =? 10
X =? 11
X =? 12
THE TOTAL IS 78
```

Now the program can be used to compute the sum of *at most* how many numbers? _____

– – – – – – – – – –

100. If 100 numbers are entered they will be stored in X(1) through X(100), the limit specified by the DIM statement in line 105. We can, of course, also use the program to compute the sum of fewer than 100 numbers.

15. A DIM statement may have its dimensions assigned by a variable. Look at the examples below.

DIM X(N)   DIM A$(B)   DIM D(Y+2)

This is called dynamic dimensioning, because it is done during the execution of the program. But there is a catch. An array can be dimensioned *only once* during the RUN of a program, and the computer will give you an error message and stop executing the program if it comes to a DIM statement for the same array a second time and tries to redimension the array during the same RUN.

Look at the program segment below, and the beginning of the RUN.

```
100 INPUT "HOW MANY NUMBERS"; N
110 DIM X(N) : FOR K=1 TO N : LET X(K)=0 : NEXT K
RUN
HOW MANY NUMBERS? 8
```

What will be the dimensioned size of the array during this RUN of the program? _____

— — — — — — — — — — —

8 (the value assigned to N by the INPUT statement)

16. Look at the first FOR-NEXT loop (line 120) in the program in frame 14. The first value assigned to K is 1, so the first subscripted variable X(K) is X(1). Since the array *could* start with X(0), an array dimensioned as DIM

X(100) can actually hold how many values? _____

Show how we could modify the FOR statement so that we could take advantage of every element (subscripted variable value) in the array for

storing values, provided that N = 100. _____

— — — — — — — — — — —

101
FOR K = 0 TO N

17. Instead of using an INPUT statement to get values for X(1), X(2), and so on, we can use READ and DATA statements. We'll put the value of N and the values of X(1) through X(N) in a DATA statement, as follows.

DATA 5, 37, 23, 46, 78, 59
▲ ▲ ▲ ▲ ▲ ▲
Value of N   Values of X(1) through X(5)

The program is shown on the following page.

```
100 REM***WORLD'S MOST EXPENSIVE ADDING MACHINE (AGAIN)
110 DIM X(100)
200 REM***READ N AND X(1) THROUGH X(N)
210 READ N
220 FOR J=1 TO N
230 READ X(J)
240 NEXT J
300 REM***PRINT VALUES OF N AND X(1) THROUGH X(N)
310 PRINT "N ="; N
320 PRINT "X(1) THROUGH X("; N; ") ARE:"
330 FOR K=1 TO N
340 PRINT X(K);
350 NEXT K
360 PRINT
400 REM***COMPUTE TOTAL OF X(1) TO X(N)
410 T=0
420 FOR L=1 TO N
430 T=T+X(L)
440 NEXT L
500 REM***PRINT TOTAL AND GO BACK FOR NEW DATA
510 PRINT "THE TOTAL IS"; T
520 PRINT
530 GOTO 210
900 REM***HERE ARE TWO SETS OF DATA
910 DATA 5, 37, 23, 46, 78, 59
920 DATA 12, 1, 2, 3, 4, 5, 6, 7, 8, 9, 10, 11, 12
```

In the first FOR-NEXT loop (lines 220-240), we used J as the subscript. This choice was entirely arbitrary. What subscript did we use in lines 330 to 350?_____ Lines 420 to 440?_____

— — — — — — — — — —

K; L

18. The following questions refer back to the program in frame 17.

(a) For the second set of data, which statement assigns the first item in the DATA statement to a variable? _____

(b) Which statement assigns the rest of the data to a subscripted variable?

_____

(c) Which statement prints values stored in an array instead of from the DATA statement? _____

(d) Which statement tallies or adds up all the values stored in the array?

_____

— — — — — — — — — —

(a) 210 READ N
(b) 230 READ X(J)

(c)   340 PRINT X(K);

(d)   430 T=T+X(L)

19.   If we had wanted to, could we have used J as the subscript in all three places?_____

— — — — — — — — — —

Yes. These are three separate and distinct FOR-NEXT loops. We could have used *any* variable as the subscript except N or T.

20.   Suppose we RUN the program in frame 17. Show what the RUN will look like. (Hint: Check all the PRINT statements.)

— — — — — — — — — —

```
RUN
N = 5
X( 1 ) THROUGH X( 5 ) ARE:
 37  23  46  78  59
THE TOTAL IS 243

N = 12
X( 1 ) THROUGH X( 12 ) ARE:
 1  2  3  4  5  6  7  8  9  10  11  12
THE TOTAL IS 78

?OD ERROR IN 210
```

21.   So that you can better understand and use subscripted variables in your programming, here's a little more practice at doing what a computer does when dealing with subscripted variables.

For this segment of a computer program, fill in the boxes on the following page, showing the values of D(G) at the affected locations after this FOR-NEXT loop has been run.

```
1Ø FOR G=1 TO 3
2Ø D(G)=2*G-1
3Ø NEXT G
```

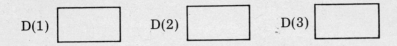

D(1) [ ]   D(2) [ ]   D(3) [ ]

— — — — — — — — — — —

D(1)	1	For G = 1, 2*G – 1 = 2*1 – 1 = 2 – 1 = 1
D(2)	3	For G = 2, 2*G – 1 = 2*2 – 1 = 4 – 1 = 3
D(3)	5	For G = 3, 2*G – 1 = 2*3 – 1 = 6 – 1 = 5

22. For the following FOR-NEXT loop, fill in the boxes showing the values in R(1) through R(4) after the loop has been carried out.

```
1Ø FOR R=1 TO 4
2Ø R(R)=R↑2
3Ø NEXT R
```

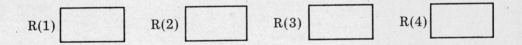

R(1) [ ]   R(2) [ ]   R(3) [ ]   R(4) [ ]

— — — — — — — — — —

R(1)	1	For R = 1, R↑2 = 1↑2 = 1
R(2)	4	For R = 2, R↑2 = 2↑2 = 4
R(3)	9	For R = 3, R↑2 = 3↑2 = 9
R(4)	16	For R = 4, R↑2 = 4↑2 = 16

23.   Let's do one more of these. Show what values will be in the boxes after this FOR-NEXT loop has been executed.

```
1Ø FOR N=1 TO 6
2Ø P(N)=2↑N
3Ø NEXT N
```

P(1) [   ]   P(2) [   ]   P(3) [   ]

P(4) [   ]   P(5) [   ]   P(6) [   ]

— — — — — — — — — —

P(1) [2]   P(2) [4]   P(3) [8]

P(4) [16]   P(5) [32]   P(6) [64]

24. Next, assume that numbers are stored in C(1) through C(5), as follows:

C(1) [18]   C(2) [34]   C(3) [12]

C(4) [20]   C(5) [17]

What will be printed if the following FOR-NEXT loop is carried out?

```
45 FOR A=1 TO 5
53 PRINT C(A);
67 NEXT A
```

RUN

_____

— — — — — — — — — —

```
RUN
  18   34   12   2Ø   17
```

25. Suppose numbers are stored in C(1) through C(5) as shown in frame 24. What will be printed if the following FOR-NEXT loop is carried out?

```
45 FOR A=5 TO 1 STEP -1
53 PRINT C(A);
67 NEXT A
RUN
```

_____

— — — — — — — — — —

RUN
  17 20 12 34 18

The values are printed in reverse order. If you missed this, review Chapter 6, frames 19 and 20.

26. Assume that an election is approaching and you have conducted a poll among your friends, using the following questionnaire.

> Who will you vote for in the coming election? Circle the number to the left of your choice.
> 1. Sam Smoothe
> 2. Gabby Gruff

Let's write a program to count the votes each candidate received in the poll. You have 35 responses to your questionnaire, each response being either a "1" or a "2". First, record the votes in a DATA statement.

```
910 DATA 1,1,2,2,2,1,1,2,2,2,1,1,1,2,1,2,1,1
920 DATA 2,2,1,1,1,2,1,2,2,2,1,1,2,1,1,2,1,-1
```

End-of-data flag (not a vote)

How many votes did Sam Smoothe receive? _____

— — — — — — — — — — —

19

27. How many votes did Gabby Gruff receive? _____ (Do your answers total 35?)

— — — — — — — — — — —

16

28. To answer those last two questions, you probably counted the 1's in the DATA statements to find out how many votes Sam Smoothe received. Then you counted the 2's to find out how many votes Gabby Gruff received.

Your computer can count votes by using subscripted variables to keep a running total of the 1's and 2's read from the DATA statements. When it comes to the end-of-data flag (-1) it stops counting and prints the results. On the following page is a program to count the votes.

```
100 REM***VOTE COUNTING PROGRAM
110 REM***INITIALIZE
120 DIM C(2) : C(1)=0 : C(2)=0
200 REM***READ AND COUNT VOTES
210 READ V
220 IF V=-1 THEN 310
230 C(V)=C(V)+1  ◄──────── Crucial vote-counting statement.
240 GOTO 210
300 REM***PRINT RESULTS
310 PRINT "SAM SMOOTHE:"; C(1)
320 PRINT "GABBY GRUFF:"; C(2)
910 DATA 1,1,2,2,2,1,1,2,2,2,1,1,1,2,1,2,1,1
920 DATA 2,2,1,1,1,2,1,2,2,2,1,1,2,1,1,2,1,-1

RUN
SAM SMOOTHE: 19
GABBY GRUFF: 16
```

Is the DIM statement really necessary? Why or why not? _____

_____

_____

— — — — — — — — — — —

No, since only C(1) and C(2) are involved, no subscript exceeds 10. However, we feel it is good practice *always* to use a DIM statement.

29.   After the computer executes line 120, what are the values of C(1) and C(2)?

C(1) ⬚

C(2) ⬚

— — — — — — — — — — —

Both have a value of 0. These are the initial values prior to counting votes. We call the process *initializing* as shown in the REMark statement in line 110.

30.   The entire line 120 is unnecessary for this particular program. It is good programming practice to include it anyway and a good habit for you to practice. Although our BASIC sets variables to zero if no other assignment is made, you should get in the habit of including the initializing process so the next user of your program, on whatever computer, will be able to "see" the procedure from your program. When your programs get so long

that they start exceeding the computer's memory capacity, delete the initializing process (and REMarks) to save memory space.

To save memory space, which statements could be deleted from the program and still have it RUN as shown in frame 28? _____

— — — — — — — — — — —

100, 110, 120, 200, and 300

31. Look again at the crucial vote-counting statement from frame 28.

230 LET C(V) = C(V)+1

It is the subscripted variable equivalent of a similar statement which has been used in earlier programs to keep count.

LET N = N+1

Note how the variable *subscript* of C is used to determine whether either the value of C(1) is increased by one, or the value of C(2) is increased by one. Since V can have only two values, either 1 or 2, line 230 is actually a double-purpose line. Depending on the value of V, line 230 is actually equivalent to:

LET C(1) = C(1)+1, or LET C(2) = C(2)+1

When the preceding program is RUN, what values will the computer have stored for C(1) and C(2) after the *first* vote has been read and processed? (That is, lines 210 through 230 have been done for the first vote in the first DATA statement.)

C(1) [   ]   C(2) [   ]

What values will be stored for C(1) and C(2) after the *second* vote has been read and processed?

C(1) [   ]   C(2) [   ]

What values will be stored in C(1) and C(2) after the third vote has been read and processed?

C(1) [   ]   C(2) [   ]

— — — — — — — — — — —

C(1)	1		C(2)	0

C(1)	2		C(2)	0

C(1)	2		C(2)	1

32. In the program we have been discussing (frame 28), line 220 checks for the end-of-data flag with the following statement.

IF V = −1 THEN 310

If we switch lines 220 and 230, this section of the program would look like this:

```
210 READ V
220 LET C(V)=C(V)+1
230 IF V=-1 THEN 310
240 GOTO 210
```

(a) What would be the last value assigned to V from the DATA statement?

_____

(b) If the computer used this value for V in line 220, what would the subscripted variable look like? _____

(c) Since negative subscripts are not allowed, what error message would our computer print? _____

− − − − − − − − − −

(a) −1
(b) C(−1)
(c) BS ERROR—a bad subscript. Moral: Beware of *where* you place the test for the end-of-data flag. The best place is usually right after the READ or INPUT statement where the flag might appear.

33. Suppose the following poll is conducted.

> Which candidate will you vote for in
> the coming election? Circle the num-
> ber to the left of your choice.
>   1. Sam Smoothe
>   2. Gabby Gruff
>   3. No opinion

The results of this poll are shown below.

2,2,2,1,2,1,1,2,1,1,3,2,1,3,2,1
1,3,1,3,2,2,1,1,3,2,1,3,1,1,2,1,2,1,1

Modify the vote-counting program from frame 28 to process this data.
You will have to add a line to set C(3) to zero and a PRINT statement to
print the NO OPINION total. You will also have to change the DATA statements for the new data, as well as the DIM statement. Here is how it should
RUN.

```
RUN
SAM SMOOTHE: 17
GABBY GRUFF: 12
NO OPINION: 6
```

Write your program below.

— — — — — — — — — —

Here are the modifications.

```
120 DIM C(3) : C(1)=Ø : C(2)=Ø : C(3)=Ø
330 PRINT "NO OPINION:"; C(3)
910 DATA 2,2,2,1,2,1,1,2,1,1,3,2,1,3,2,1
920 DATA 1,3,1,3,2,2,1,1,3,2,1,3,1,1,2,1,2,1,1,-1
```

Did you remember the flag?

The complete program now looks like this.

```
100 REM***VOTE COUNTING PROGRAM
110 REM***INITIALIZE
120 DIM C(3) : C(1)=0 : C(2)=0 : C(3)=0
200 REM***READ AND COUNT VOTES
210 READ V
220 IF V=-1 THEN 310
230 C(V)=C(V)+1
240 GOTO 210
300 REM***PRINT RESULTS
310 PRINT "SAM SMOOTHE:"; C(1)
320 PRINT "GABBY GRUFF:"; C(2)
330 PRINT "NO OPINION:"; C(3)
910 DATA 2,2,2,1,2,1,1,2,1,1,3,2,1,3,2,1
920 DATA 1,3,1,3,2,2,1,1,3,2,1,3,1,1,2,1,2,1,1,-1
```

34. Suppose we have a questionnaire with 4 possible answers, or 5 or 6. Instead of writing a separate program for each, let's write one program to count votes for a questionnaire with N possible answers. The value of N will appear in a DATA statement prior to the actual answers, or votes. For example, the data for the questionnaire in frame 26 would look like this.

```
900 REM***THE DATA
901 REM***FIRST DATA STATEMENT TELLS NUMBER OF POSSIBLE ANSWERS
910 DATA 2
919 REM***THE VOTES AND THE FLAG (-1)
920 DATA 1,1,2,2,2,1,1,2,2,2,1,1,1,2,1,2,1,1
930 DATA 2,2,1,1,1,2,1,2,2,2,1,1,2,1,1,2,1,-1
```

Line 910 is the value of N. In this case, N is 2 and possible votes are 1 or 2. How would the data for the questionnaire in frame 33 be placed in DATA statements?

```
900 REM***THE DATA
901 REM***FIRST DATA STATEMENT TELLS NUMBER OF POSSIBLE ANSWERS

910 DATA _____
919 REM***THE VOTES AND THE FLAG (-1)

920 _____

930 _____
```

— — — — — — — — — —

```
910 DATA 3
920 DATA 2,2,2,1,2,1,1,2,1,1,3,2,1,3,2,1
930 DATA 1,3,1,3,2,2,1,1,3,2,1,3,1,1,2,1,2,1,1,-1
```

This time N = 3 (line 910) and possible votes are 1, 2, or 3.

35. Your turn. Write a program to read and count votes for a questionnaire with N different possible answers (votes), where N is less than or equal to 20. You will have to do the following things.

(1) DIMension for the *maximum* subscript for C. Remember, we said N is less than or equal to 20.
(2) Read the value of N.
(3) Set C(1) through C(N) to zero. (Use a FOR-NEXT loop.)
(4) Read and count votes until a flag is read.
(5) Print the results, as shown in the sample runs below.

Example: N = 2

```
RUN
ANSWER # 1 : 19
ANSWER # 2 : 16
```

Example: N = 5

```
RUN
ANSWER # 1 : 12
ANSWER # 2 : 7
ANSWER # 3 : 9
ANSWER # 4 : 9
ANSWER # 5 : 10
```

Here's a good opportunity to practice writing multiple statements per line. Our sample runs above were produced using these two sets of data.

```
900 REM***THE DATA
901 REM***FIRST DATA STATEMENT TELLS NUMBER OF POSSIBLE ANSWERS
910 DATA 2
919 REM***THE VOTES AND THE FLAG (-1)
920 DATA 1,1,2,2,2,1,1,2,2,2,1,1,1,2,1,2,1,1
930 DATA 2,2,1,1,1,2,1,2,2,2,1,1,2,1,1,2,1,-1
```

```
900 REM***THE DATA
901 REM***FIRST DATA STATEMENT TELLS NUMBER OF POSSIBLE ANSWERS
910 DATA 5
919 REM***THE VOTES AND THE FLAG (-1)
920 DATA 4,3,4,2,4,1,1,5,5,3,5,4,5,1,3,2,5,5,4,4,5,1,2,3
930 DATA 3,3,5,2,2,3,1,5,4,1,1,1,2,3,1,4,1,5,1,2,3,4,1,-1
```

Write your program below. (You need not show the DATA statements.)

— — — — — — — — —

```
100 REM***VOTE COUNTING PROGRAM
110 REM***INITIALIZE
120 DIM C(20) : READ N : FOR K=1 TO N : C(K)=0 : NEXT K
200 REM***READ AND COUNT VOTES
210 READ V : IF V <> -1 THEN LET C(V)=C(V)+1 : GOTO 210
300 REM***PRINT RESULTS
310 FOR K=1 TO N : PRINT "ANSWER #"; K; ":"; C(K) : NEXT K
```

Note: DATA statements are omitted here. There are many ways you could have done this. Another example is:

```
210 READ V
220 IF V = -1 THEN 310
230 C(V)=C(V)+1
240 GOTO 210
```

36.   The problems in frames 26-35 dealt with counting votes. Each time through the loop that reads data (a data loop) you added one (1) to an array element (LET C(V) = C(V)+1). Almost any vote counting application you might want to try is going to be similar to the solutions in frame 35. Now you can volunteer to be the official ballot counter for all the elections in your community—PTA, computer club, school class offices, church groups, ad infinitum.

On to more serious business. A similar, but not identical application of simple one-dimension arrays deals with counting things or money, instead of votes.

Let's set the stage. You are the sponsor for the neighborhood computer club for eight local kids. The kids want to buy a new superduper color graphics terminal for the neighborhood computer system. It's only $1200 in kit form. Raising funds is the problem. The kids agree to sell milk chocolate candy bars for $1.00 each to raise money. (The club makes 55¢ profit per sale, not bad!). But you must do the recordkeeping. You assign each kid a number. Whenever a kid comes by for candy bars, you identify the kid, by number, and note how many bars were taken. The money will be turned in later.

Here are the ID numbers assigned to each club member.

1.	Jerry	5.	Karl
2.	Bobby	6.	Mimi
3.	Mary	7.	Doug
4.	Danny	8.	Scott

When Danny first takes 6 bars you note it as 4,6. The 4 is Danny's ID number for the computer, and 6 is the number of candy bars he took. When Doug takes 12 bars, your note is _____, _____. When Mary takes 6, the note is _____,_____.

— — — — — — — — — —

7,12; 3,6

37.   After a few weeks of this, you've accumulated quite a pile of notes. It's time to tally and see how much money you've raised thus far. The information from your notes will be placed into DATA statements. (You could enter the information using INPUT, but it could take much too long!) Start

at line 910 (a good place to put DATA assuming the rest of the program won't have line numbers past 900.)

```
900 REM***KID ID NUMBER FOLLOWED BY QUANTITY. FLAG:-1,-1
910 DATA 4,6,7,12,3,6,1,8,4,5,5,3,8,20
```

This shows that Danny took *another* five candy bars.

```
920 2,4,3.8,6,6,5,10,7,12,8,4,1,3
```

Mary took *another* 8.

```
930 DATA -1,-1
```

(a)   Each item of data has (how many?) _____ numbers.

(b)   DATA 6,6 means _____.

(c)   The end-of-data flag has (how many?) _____ numbers. Why?_____

_____

— — — — — — — — — —

(a)   two
(b)   Mimi took 6 bars
(c)   Two. Each data element has two numbers. Two values will be read with one READ statement. An OD ERROR would result if there were only one (flag) value for the two variables in the READ statement.

38.   Just as you complete entering the DATA, Bobby shows up to take another six bars. Show how you could add this data without changing any of the existing DATA statements. Use the highest line number permissible and still have the end-of-data flags as the last values read by the program.

_____

— — — — — — — — — —

929 DATA 2,6

The line number cannot be larger than 929, or the flags in line 930 will not be the *last* data item read by the program. Moral: Be careful *where* you add DATA into an existing program.

39.   We need an array with eight elements. That means we need a subscripted variable with subscripts from 1 to 8, to represent the eight members of the club. The *value* added to each element (or subscripted variable) in the array will be the number of candy bars each kid took. But first, initialize the array

by writing one multiple-statement line that will dimension the array and assign a zero to each element. We will call this the A array and use A(X) for the subscripted variable.

```
100 REM***CANDY BAR COUNTER
110 REM***INITIALIZE

120 _____
```

— — — — — — — — — —

```
120 DIM A(8) : FOR X=1 TO 8 : LET A(X)=0 : NEXT X
```

You could omit the LET, and the X after NEXT. You could omit the DIM statement since BASIC allows up to 10 elements in an array automatically, but we consider that a poor programming practice. For that matter, you could omit the whole line in MICROSOFT™ BASIC and many other versions of BASIC, as the computer will consider *any* variable it comes upon to have a value of zero if it has not been assigned a value earlier in the program. But we consider it good programming practice to initialize the program as shown.

40.   Now let's read the *data in pairs* (two items at a time). Use K for kid and Q for quantity of candy bars, and test for end of DATA, all on one line. If we run out of data, have the program branch to line 310.

```
200 REM***READ DATA, TEST FOR FLAG, AND ACCUMULATE (TALLY)

210 _____
```

— — — — — — — — — —

```
210 READ K,Q : IF K=-1 THEN 310
```

41.   Now the hard one! We must accumulate the number of bars in the correct array element corresponding to the kid who took them. Think of the subscript K in the subscripted variable A(K) as the kid's ID code.

220 LET A(K)=A(K)+Q : GOTO 210

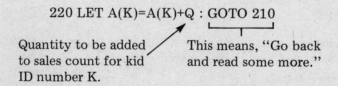

Quantity to be added
to sales count for kid
ID number K.

This means, "Go back
and read some more."

If K (for kid) is 2 and Q (quantity) is 4, then line 220 will cause array element A(___) to increase by _____.

— — — — — — — — — —

A(2); 4

42.   If the array elements look like those on the left *before*, how will they look *after* reading and adding the additional DATA given here?

920 DATA 4,6, 3,8, 6,6, 7,2, 4,3

	Before			After
A(1) =	8		A(1) =	
(2) =	4		(2) =	
(3) =	6		(3) =	
(4) =	4		(4) =	
(5) =	3		(5) =	
(6) =	2		(6) =	
(7) =	12		(7) =	
(8) =	7		(8) =	

_ _ _ _ _ _ _ _ _ _

A(1) =	8
(2) =	4
(3) =	14
(4) =	13
(5) =	3
(6) =	8
(7) =	14
(8) =	7

43. Here's our program so far.

```
100 REM***CANDY BAR COUNTER
110 REM***INITIALIZE
120 DIM A(8) : FOR X=1 TO 8 : LET A(X)=0 : NEXT X
200 REM***READ DATA, TEST FOR FLAG, AND ACCUMULATE (TALLY)
210 READ K,Q : IF K=-1 THEN 310
220 LET A(K)=A(K)+Q : GOTO 210
900 REM***KID ID NO. FOLLOWED BY QUANTITY. FLAG:-1,-1
910 DATA 4,6,7,12,3,6,1,8,4,5,5,3,8,20
920 DATA 2,4,3,8,6,6,5,10,7,12,8,4,1,3
929 DATA 1,6
930 DATA -1,-1
```

It starts and it accumulates. Before it stops, we must have it print our report. Let's start the report with a heading.

```
300 REM***PRINT THE REPORT
310 PRINT "KID ID NO.", "QUANTITY"
```

Now we print the results using a FOR-NEXT loop.

```
320 FOR X=1 TO 8
330 PRINT X, A(X)
340 NEXT X
```

or

```
320 FOR X=1 TO 8 : PRINT X, A(X) : NEXT X
```

Using the data in the DATA statement, show below how the report will look after running our program.

— — — — — — — — — —

```
RUN
KID ID NO.      QUANTITY
  1               17
  2               4
  3               14
  4               11
  5               13
  6               6
  7               24
  8               24
```

44.   So far our report shows us who has what but doesn't give us names or totals or profits. With some help, the computer can do all those things.

Let's start with the total. In MICROSOFT™ BASIC and most others, each array has an element we haven't used yet. It's the zero (0) element. Remember, when you DIMension an array of eight elements with a DIM statement, DIM A(8), you really get 9: 0, 1, 2, 3, 4, 5, 6, 7, and 8.

Since we haven't assigned any kid the ID number 0 (zero), the "A array" element with the subscript 0 has not been used or assigned a value. So the A(0) element can be used for accumulating totals, although we could use some other variable. Look at statement 410, which accumulates the total number of bars sold in A(0).

```
400 REM***ACCUMULATE TOTAL AND PRINT RESULT
410 FOR X=1 TO 8 : LET A(Ø)=A(Ø)+A(X) : NEXT X
```

If the A array starts at zero, we must remember to change the FOR statement in the initializing routine to start assigning zeros at A(0). Replace (rewrite) the initializing line for this program so that all the array elements are given the initial value of zero.

120 _____

— — — — — — — — — —

```
12Ø DIM A(8) : FOR X=Ø TO 8 : A(X)=Ø : NEXT X
```

45.   The statement that tallies up all the candy sold by the club uses the A(0) element in the A array to accumulate the value stored in A(1) through A(8).

If the array looks as it did in frame 42 (after reading data), then what value will be stored in A(0) after one time through the loop in line 410?

_____ After three times through the loop in 410? _____

— — — — — — — — — —

8; 26

46.   Write a line 420 to print the total and the profit (55¢ on each bar). Here is what we want line 420 to print:

    TOTAL IS 113
    PROFIT IS 62.15

420 _____

— — — — — — — — — —

```
42Ø PRINT "TOTAL IS"; A(Ø) : PRINT "PROFIT IS"; A(Ø)*.55
```

47.   Here is a complete list and run so far.

```
100 REM***CANDY BAR COUNTER
110 REM***INITIALIZE
120 DIM A(8) : FOR X=0 TO 8 : A(X)=0 : NEXT X
200 REM***READ DATA, TEST FOR FLAG, AND ACCUMULATE (TALLY)
210 READ K,Q : IF K=-1 THEN 310
220 LET A(K)=A(K)+Q : GOTO 210
300 REM***PRINT THE REPORT
310 PRINT "KID ID NO.", "QUANTITY"
320 FOR X=1 TO 8 : PRINT X, A(X) : NEXT X
400 REM***ACCUMULATE TOTAL AND PRINT RESULT
410 FOR X=1 TO 8 : LET A(0)=A(0)+A(X) : NEXT
420 PRINT "TOTAL IS"; A(0) : PRINT "PROFIT IS"; A(0)*.55
900 REM***KID ID NO. FOLLOWED BY QUANTITY. FLAG:-1,-1
910 DATA 4,6,7,12,3,6,1,8,4,5,5,3,8,20
920 DATA 2,4,3,8,6,6,5,10,7,12,8,4,1,3
929 DATA 1,6
930 DATA -1,-1

RUN
KID ID NO.     QUANTITY
  1               17
  2                4
  3               14
  4               11
  5               13
  6                6
  7               24
  8               24
TOTAL IS 113
PROFIT IS 62.15
```

That's a nice report . . . but wait! In this day of impersonalization, wouldn't it be nice to print each kid's name instead of a number? How can we do it? Easily. We can have the computer READ the names from DATA statements into another array, and then print elements from that array in the appropriate places. To do this, we use the subscripted *string* variable.

Arrays that store strings follow all the same rules as arrays that store numerical values. As before, the subscript identifies a particular element or box in the array, and the subscripted string variable can be used like any other variable in READ, LET, INPUT, and PRINT statements.

Subscripted string variables must be DIMensioned, just as an array storing numerical values instead of strings. You can use one DIM statement to dimension all the arrays in your program, whether numerical or string. Just don't forget the properly placed $ that identifies a string variable. You may prefer to DIMension each array in the same multiple-statement line where the array is first used or initialized.

Write a DIM statement to initialize N$(X) for string array N$ that will be enough to store the names of the members of the computer club.

130 _____

— — — — — — — — —

```
130 DIM N$(8)
```

We would accept DIM N$(7) as an answer, since many versions of BASIC allow string array elements to start numbering at zero, just as we showed for numeric arrays.

48. Let's say that we have placed the club members' names in a DATA statement, in the same order as their ID numbers.

```
DATA JERRY,BOBBY,MARY,DANNY,KARL,MIMI,DOUG,SCOTT
```

Write a FOR-NEXT loop on the same line as the DIM statement that will read the names in the DATA statement into the elements or "boxes" in array N$.

```
130 DIM N$(8) : _____
```

— — — — — — — — — —

```
130 DIM N$(8) : FOR X=1 TO 8 : READ N$(X) : NEXT X
```

49. After executing line 130, what will we find stored in N$(1)?_____
In N$(4)?_____

— — — — — — — — — —

JERRY; DANNY

50. Here is a listing of the program.

```
100 REM***CANDY BAR COUNTER
110 REM***INITIALIZE
120 DIM A(8) : FOR X=0 TO 8 : A(X)=0 : NEXT X
130 DIM N$(8) : FOR X=1 TO 8 : READ N$(X) : NEXT X
200 REM***READ DATA, TEST FOR FLAG, AND ACCUMULATE (TALLY)
210 READ K,Q : IF K=-1 THEN 310
220 LET A(K)=A(K)+Q : GOTO 210
300 REM***PRINT THE REPORT
310 PRINT "KID ID NO.", "QUANTITY"
320 FOR X=1 TO 8 : PRINT X, A(X) : NEXT X
400 REM***ACCUMULATE TOTAL AND PRINT RESULT
410 FOR X=1 TO 8 : LET A(0)=A(0)+A(X) : NEXT X
420 PRINT "TOTAL IS"; A(0) : PRINT "PROFIT IS"; A(0)*.55
900 REM***KID ID NO. FOLLOWED BY QUANTITY. FLAG:-1,-1
910 DATA 4,6,7,12,3,6,1,8,4,5,5,3,8,20
920 DATA 2,4,3,8,6,6,5,10,7,12,8,4,1,3
929 DATA 1,6
930 DATA -1,-1
```

There is now the touchy problem of *where* to place the DATA statement that contains the club members' names. Keep in mind that we want to avoid an error message just because a READ statement with a numeric variable came upon a DATA statement containing strings!

What line numbers in the program would the DATA statements have?

_____

— — — — — — — — — —

901 to 909 (or any place *before* line 910)

51. One final change is needed in line 320 in the report printing section. Line 320 looks like this.

```
320 FOR X=1 TO 8 : PRINT X, A(X) : NEXT X
```

Change the line so it will cause the name to be printed instead of the kid number. While you're at it, change the heading line (310) to print NAME and QUANTITY.

310 _____

320 _____

— — — — — — — — — —

```
310 PRINT "NAME", "QUANTITY"
320 FOR X=1 TO 8 : PRINT N$(X), A(X) : NEXT X
```

52. Now here is the real test of your understanding. Ready to play computer? Show what a RUN of this program would look like.

```
100 REM***CANDY BAR COUNTER
110 REM***INITIALIZE
120 DIM A(8) : FOR X=0 TO 8 : A(X)=0 : NEXT X
130 DIM N$(8) : FOR X=1 TO 8 : READ N$(X) : NEXT X
200 REM***READ DATA, TEST FOR FLAG, AND ACCUMULATE (TALLY)
210 READ K,Q : IF K=-1 THEN 310
220 LET A(K)=A(K)+Q : GOTO 210
300 REM***PRINT THE REPORT
310 PRINT "NAME", "QUANTITY"
320 FOR X=1 TO 8 : PRINT N$(X), A(X) : NEXT X
400 REM***ACCUMULATE TOTAL AND PRINT RESULT
410 FOR X=1 TO 8 : LET A(0)=A(0)+A(X) : NEXT X
420 PRINT "TOTAL IS"; A(0) : PRINT "PROFIT IS"; A(0)*.55
900 REM***DATA: NAMES, AND ID NUMBER FOLLOWED BY QUANTITY. FLAG: -1,-1
909 DATA JERRY,BOBBY,MARY,DANNY,KARL,MIMI,DOUG,SCOTT
910 DATA 4,6,7,12,3,6,1,8,4,5,5,3,8,20
920 DATA 2,4,3,8,6,6,5,10,7,12,8,4,1,3
929 DATA 1,6
930 DATA -1,-1
```

— — — — — — — — — —

```
RUN
NAME            QUANTITY
JERRY            17
BOBBY            -4
MARY             14
DANNY            11
KARL             13
MIMI             6
DOUG             24
SCOTT            24
TOTAL IS 113
PROFIT IS 62.15
```

53.   Let's look at one other application of singly-subscripted variables. This one neither counts votes nor accumulates anything.

No doubt you've read about computer dating. Ever wonder how it works? You answer a series of questions that are then stored in the computer; other people who wish to be matched do likewise. Then the responses are compared to test for "compatibility." Let's do a simplified version of a computer dating program which you can alter for your own uses.

We'll use a multiple-choice questionnaire with only five questions. (Ask anything you'd like!) Responses will be stored in DATA statements, with the name first, and the five responses following. My responses appear in line 910 below.

```
900 REM***QUESTIONNAIRE RESPONSES. NAME THEN ANSWERS.
909 REM***LINE 910: 'HIS' REPONSES
910 DATA LEROY,3,3,4,2,1
```

Now, you create DATA statements in lines 920-970 for these respondents, plus an end-of-data flag.

	Q1	Q2	Q3	Q4	Q5
JOAN	1	4	2	2	1
TONI	2	2	2	3	3
LAURA	2	3	3	1	2
MARY	3	3	4	2	1
IRENE	3	1	4	2	1

920 _____

930 _____

940 _____

950 _____

960 _____

970 _____

— — — — — — — — — —

```
920 DATA JOAN,1,4,2,2,1
930 DATA TONI,2,2,2,3,3
940 DATA LAURA,2,3,3,1,2
950 DATA MARY,3,3,4,2,1
960 DATA IRENE,3,1,4,2,1
970 DATA END
```

54.   Now, you write the rest of the program with some gentle supervision. First, you will need a DIM statement that will allow the program to compare "his" responses (stored in array C), with "her" responses (stored in array A).

```
100 REM***COMPUTER DATING SIMULATION
105 REM***INITIALIZE
```

110 _____

— — — — — — — — — —

```
110 DIM C(5), A(5)
```

Note: You can DIMension more than one array in one DIM statement.

55.   Next, READ the first data statement which contains "his" name, and READ "his" five responses. The responses should be read directly into array C. Then print "his" name and responses all on one line, so that later you can compare them with "hers."

```
200 REM***READ AND PRINT 'HIS' NAME & REPONSES
```

210 _____

220 _____

— — — — — — — — — —

```
210 READ N$ : FOR X=1 TO 5 : READ C(X) : NEXT
220 PRINT N$, : FOR X=1 TO 5 : PRINT C(X); : NEXT X : PRINT
```

Did you remember this carriage-returning PRINT statement?

56. Next, READ *one* set of "her" names and responses into array A, and print "her" responses so you can visually compare the "his" responses with "her" responses. After you read "her" name in line 310, check to see if it is the end-of-data flag (the word END). Use the string comparison IF H\$ = "END" THEN END. The output we want so far should look like this.

```
                    RUN
                    LEROY      3 3 4 2 1
                    JOAN       1 4 2 2 1
```

Complete the program segment to produce this output or printout.

300 REM***READ AND PRINT 'HER' NAMES AND RESPONSES

310 _____

320 _____

330 _____

999 _____

— — — — — — — — — —

```
310 READ H$ : IF H$="END" THEN END
320 FOR X=1 TO 5 : READ A(X) : NEXT X
330 PRINT H$, : FOR X=1 TO 5 : PRINT A(X); : NEXT X : PRINT
999 END
```

57. Now comes the crucial part. This is where you compare the contents of array C with the contents of array A and add the number of matches into variable M. Think about that and complete the program below, so that a RUN of the complete program looks like the one here.

```
RUN
LEROY        3   3   4   2   1
JOAN         1   4   2   2   1
  2 MATCHES

TONI         2   2   2   3   3
  Ø MATCHES

LAURA        2   3   3   1   2
  1 MATCHES

MARY         3   3   4   2   1
  5 MATCHES

IRENE        3   1   4   2   1
  4 MATCHES
```

400 REM***COMPARE RESPONSES & PRINT NUMBER OF 'MATCHES'
410 M=0
420 FOR X=1 TO 5

430 IF _____ THEN 450◄— Compare

440 LET M= _____ ◄——————— Add matches

450 _____ ◄——————— Close the loop to compare another

460 PRINT _____ "MATCHES"

470 PRINT

480 GOTO _____ ◄——————— Read another set of responses

— — — — — — — — — —

```
400 REM***COMPARE RESPONSES & PRINT NUMBER OF 'MATCHES'
410 M=0
420 FOR X=1 TO 5
430 IF C(X)<>A(X) THEN 450
440 LET M=M+1
450 NEXT X
460 PRINT M; "MATCHES"
470 PRINT
480 GOTO 310
```

Following is a complete listing and RUN of our computer dating program.

```
100 REM***COMPUTER DATING SIMULATION
105 REM***INITIALIZE
110 DIM C(5), A(5)
200 REM***READ AND PRINT 'HIS' NAME & RESPONSES
210 READ N$ : FOR X=1 TO 5 : READ C(X); : NEXT
220 PRINT N$, : FOR X=1 TO 5 : PRINT C(X); : NEXT X : PRINT
300 REM***READ AND PRINT 'HER' NAMES AND RESPONSES
310 READ H$ : IF H$="END" THEN END
320 FOR X=1 TO 5 : READ A(X) : NEXT X
330 PRINT H$, : FOR X=1 TO 5 : PRINT A(X); : NEXT X : PRINT
400 REM***COMPARE RESPONSES & PRINT NUMBER OF 'MATCHES'
410 M=0
420 FOR X=1 TO 5
430 IF C(X)<>A(X) THEN 450
440 LET M=M+1
450 NEXT X
460 PRINT M; "MATCHES"
470 PRINT
480 GOTO 310
900 REM***QUESTIONNAIRE RESPONSES. NAME THEN ANSWERS.
909 REM***LINE 910 : 'HIS' REPONSES
910 DATA LEROY,3,3,4,2,1
920 DATA JOAN,1,4,2,2,1
930 DATA TONI,2,2,2,3,3
940 DATA LAURA,2,3,3,1,2
950 DATA MARY,3,3,4,2,1
960 DATA IRENE,3,1,4,2,1
970 DATA END
```

```
RUN
LEROY          3   3   4   2   1
JOAN           1   4   2   2   1
 2 MATCHES


TONI           2   2   2   3   3
 0 MATCHES


LAURA          2   3   3   1   2
 1 MATCHES


MARY           3   3   4   2   1
 5 MATCHES


IRENE          3   1   4   2   1
 4 MATCHES
```

SELF-TEST

If you can complete the Self-Test on subscripted variables, you will be ready for the next chapter, which will expand your programming ability to include the use of more complex subscripted variables. Therefore, it is important that you have the information in this chapter well in hand.

1. Indicate which of the following are legal BASIC subscripted variables.

    _____ (a) X   _____ (b) X2   _____ (c) X(2)

    _____ (d) 2(X)   _____ (e) XX(2)   _____ (f) X(K)

    _____ (g) X_2 _____ (h) X(I–J)

2. Assume that values have been assigned to variables as shown below. Note that both simple and subscripted variables are shown.

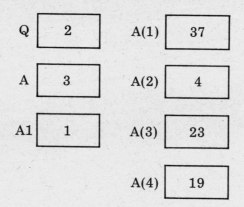

Q `2`   A(1) `37`

A `3`   A(2) `4`

A1 `1`   A(3) `23`

                A(4) `19`

    Remember, A, A1, and A(1) are distinct variables. Write the value of each variable below.

    (a)   A(Q) _____

    (b)   A(A) _____

    (c)   A(A1) _____

    (d)   A(A(2)) _____

    (e)   A(A(Q)) _____

    (f)   A(A–Q) _____

    (g)   A(A+A1) _____

    (h)   A(2*Q) _____

3. What will be printed if we RUN the following program?

```
100 REMARK MYSTERY PROGRAM
110 READ N
120 FOR K=1 TO N
130 READ X(K)
140 NEXT K
150 FOR K=1 TO N
160 IF X(K)<0 THEN 180
170 PRINT X(K);
180 NEXT K
900 REMARK VALUES OF N AND X(1) THRU X(N)
910 DATA 7
920 DATA 23,-44,37,0,-12,-58,87
```

4. There is no DIM statement in the preceding program of question 3.
Therefore, what is the largest value of N for which the program can be
used? _____ What would happen if we tried to RUN the program
using the following DATA?

```
910 DATA 12
920 DATA 3,6,-2,0,9,0,7,3,-5,4,-1,7
```

5. Modify the vote-counting program of frame 28 so that the total votes
(for both candidates) are also printed. The printout might look like
this.

```
RUN

SAM SMOOTHE:  19
GABBY GRUFF:   16

TOTAL VOTES:  35
```

6. Modify the vote-counting program of frame 28 so that the printout is
% of total votes, rounded to the nearest *whole number %*.

```
RUN

SAM SMOOTHE: 54%
GABBY GRUFF 46%
```

7. You are selected chairman of the United Collection in your neighborhood. You have 5 people who collect money door-to-door and turn in
the money to you at the end of each day. You record their names and
dollar amounts collected on a form. This data is then entered into your
computer for further processing. Write a BASIC program that will accumulate the current amount each person has collected and the total
amount collected by all 5 people. Your report should show the names
of each collector with the amounts collected.

```
RUN

NAME            AMOUNT COLLECTED
FRED            125
JOANN           205
MARYJO          100
JERRY           100
BOB             200
TOTAL 730
```

8. Your computer club kids decide they want to find out who is the best
programmer in their group. As club sponsor, you decide to give them a
multiple choice test on programming concepts and correct the test
using the computer. The multiple choice answers will be the numbers
1, 2, 3, 4, or 5. There are 10 questions on the test. You enter the 10
correct answers in the first DATA statement in the program. These are
read into array K. In subsequent DATA statements, you first enter the

name of the club member, followed by the 10 answers that person gave
for the test. (Enter in array R.) Your task is to write a BASIC program
that will correct the tests and print a report that looks similar to the
one below.

```
RUN
NAME            SCORE
DANNY            5
KARL             5
MIRIAM           4
SCOTT            7
```

9.   Are you curious about your chances of winning at any game using
      dice? If you developed a program to simulate the rolling of one die and
      counted how many times each side appeared, you would get a better
      idea of your chances of winning.
           Write a BASIC program to simulate the roll of one die, 1000 times
      (or make that an input variable). After each simulated roll, accumulate
      or add to the correct array element one appearance or "vote." After
      1000 rolls, print the contents of your array in report form showing
      how many times each die side appeared during the computer simula-
      tion. Your report should look like the one below. There is room to
      write your program on the next page.

```
RUN
HOW MANY SIMULATED ROLLS? 1000
DICE ROLL     NO. OF OCCURENCES
   1              159
   2              152
   3              173
   4              142
   5              189
   6              185
```

Answers to Self-Test

The frame numbers in parentheses refer to the frames in the chapter where the topic is discussed. You may wish to refer back to these for quick review.

1.   (c), (f), and (h) are legal subscripted variables. Longer variable names such as item (e) may be legal on *your* computer. Check the reference manual for your computer.   (frame 1)

2.   (a)   4
     (b)   23
     (c)   37
     (d)   19 $A(A(2)) = A(4) = 19$
     (e)   19 $A(A(Q)) = A(A(2)) = A(4) = 19$
     (f)   37 $A(3-2) = A(1) = 37$
     (g)   19 $A(3+1) = A(4) = 19$
     (h)   19 $A(2+2) = A(4) = 19$
     (frame 4)

3.   RUN

       23   37   Ø   87

     (frames 7-8)

4.   10
     The computer would print an error message. Our computer printed:

     BS ERROR AT LINE 130

     (frames 11-12)

5.   Add the following statements.

```
33Ø PRINT
34Ø PRINT "TOTAL VOTES:";C(1)+C(2)
```

     (frames 45-46)

6. Beginning at line 310, make these changes.

```
310 LET T=C(1)+C(2)
320 LET S=INT(100*C(1)/T + .5)
330 LET G=INT(100*C(2)/T + .5)
340 PRINT "SAM SMOOTHE:";S;"%"
350 PRINT "GABBY GRUFF:";G;"%"
```

(frame 28 and Chapter 4)

7.
```
10 REMARK***UNITED COLLECTION ANALYSIS
15 REM INITIALIZE
20 DIM N$(5),T(5) : G=0 : FOR X=1 TO 5 : LET T(X)=0 : NEXT X
25 REM READ NAMES
30 FOR N=1 TO 5 : READ N$(N) : NEXT N
35 REM READ AND ACCUMULATE DATA
40 READ P,D : IF P=-1 THEN 60
50 LET T(P)=T(P)+D : G=G+D : GO TO 40
55 REM PRINT REPORT
60 PRINT"NAME","AMOUNT COLLECTED"
70 FOR P=1 TO 5 : PRINT N$(P),T(P) : NEXT P
80 PRINT "TOTAL";G
90 REM NAMES OF COLLECTORS
100 DATA FRED, JOANN, MARYJO, JERRY, BOB
110 REM DATA BY PERSON BY AMOUNT
120 DATA 2,45,1,75,3,25,4,100,3,25,5,125
130 DATA 3,50,1,50,2,120,2,40,5,75,-1,-1
```

(frames 36-52)

8.
```
10 REMARK***TEST CORRECTOR
15 REM INITIALIZE
20 DIM K(10),R(10) : PRINT"NAME","SCORE"
25 REM READ CORRECT ANSWERS
30 FOR X=1 TO 10 : READ K(X) : NEXT X
35 REM READ STUDENT RESPONSE
40 READ N$ : IF N$="END"THEN END
50 FOR X=1 TO 10 : READ R(X) : NEXT X : LET S=0
55 REM CORRECT TESTS
60 FOR X=1 TO 10 : IF K(X)<>R(X) THEN 70
65 LET S=S+1
70 NEXT X : PRINT N$,S : GO TO 40
90 REM TEST ANSWERS
100 DATA 3,4,3,3,5,1,2,3,2,1
110 REM TEST RESPONSES
120 DATA DANNY,1,2,3,4,5,1,2,3,4,5
130 DATA KARL,1,3,2,4,4,1,2,3,2,1
140 DATA MIRIAM,3,2,2,1,4,1,2,3,1,2
150 DATA SCOTT,1,2,3,3,5,1,2,3,2,2
160 DATA END
```

(frames 53-57)

9.
```
10 REMARK***DICE SIMULATION
20 DIM D(6) : FOR X=1 TO 6 : LET D(X)=Ø : NEXT X
30 INPUT "HOW MANY SIMULATED ROLLS";R
40 FOR X=1 TO R : LET N=INT(6*RND(1))+1 : LET D(N)=D(N)+1 : NEXT X
50 PRINT"DICE ROLL","NO. OF OCCURENCES"
55 REM PRINT REPORT
60 FOR X=1 TO 6 : PRINT X,D(X) : NEXT X
```

(frames 26-31)

CHAPTER EIGHT

Double Subscripts

In Chapter 7 you were introduced to singly-subscripted variables and their many applications. The only *new* statement was DIM. There are no new statements in this chapter, just some new uses and variations of what you already know.

In this chapter we'll extend your use of MICROSOFT™ BASIC to variables with *two* subscripts, which we call doubly-subscripted variables. Doubly-subscripted variables are used with arrays of numbers which might require several columns and rows, such as in complex voter analysis problems, detailed dollar analysis problems, and a whole host of board game applications. When you complete this chapter, you will be able to:

- use variables with two subscripts;

- assign values to doubly-subscripted variables in a two-dimensional array (also called a table or matrix);

- use the DIM statement to tell the computer the dimensions of two-dimensional arrays.

1. In Chapter 7, we described subscripted variables such as X(7) and T(K). These are *singly-subscripted* variables. That is, each variable has exactly *one* subscript.

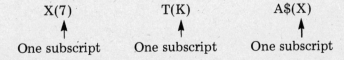

$$X(7) \qquad\qquad T(K) \qquad\qquad A\$(X)$$

One subscript   One subscript   One subscript

In this chapter, we will use *doubly-subscripted* variables, variables that have *two* subscripts.

$$T(2,3)$$

Two subscripts,
separated by a comma

$T(3)$ is a subscripted variable with how many subscripts? _____

$T(7,5)$ is a subscripted variable with how many subscripts? _____

— — — — — — — — — — —

1; 2

2.　It is convenient to think of doubly-subscripted variables arranged in an *array* of *rows* and *columns*, as shown below.

	Column 1	Column 2	Column 3	Column 4
Row 1	A(1,1) [ ]	A(1,2) [ ]	A(1,3) [ ]	A(1,4) [ ]
Row 2	A(2,1) [ ]	A(2,2) [ ]	A(2,3) [ ]	A(2,4) [ ]
Row 3	A(3,1) [ ]	A(3,2) [ ]	A(3,3) [ ]	A(3,4) [ ]

The above array has _____ rows and _____ columns.

— — — — — — — — — — —

3; 4

3.　With the arrangement shown in frame 2, we can relate subscripts to
particular places (locations, or "boxes" for values) in rows and columns.
These are called the *elements* in the array. For example:

$$A(2,3)$$

Row
Column

$A(1,1)$ is in row 1, column 1. $A(1,2)$ is in row 1, column 2. What subscripted
variable is in row 3, column 2? _____

— — — — — — — — — —

A(3,2)

4.   The rectangular arrangement of doubly-subscripted variables shown in frame 2 is called a *table, matrix,* or *two-dimensional array.*

In Chapter 7 we described arrays of singly-subscripted variables which are also called *lists, vectors,* or *one-dimensional arrays.*

This is a *list*:	X(1)	X(2)	X(3)
This is a *table:*	C(1,1)	C(1,2)	C(1,3)
	C(2,1)	C(2,2)	C(2,3)
	C(3,1)	C(3,2)	C(3,3)

(a)   A list is also called a _____ or a _____.

(b)   A table is also called a _____ or a _____.

_ _ _ _ _ _ _ _ _ _

(a)   vector, one-dimensional array (one subscript)
(b)   matrix, two-dimensional array (two subscripts)

5.   A doubly-subscripted variable is simply the name of a location in the computer. As with any other variable, you can think of it as the name for a box, a place to store a number. Here is a table of doubly-subscripted variables.

B(1,1) [   ]   B(1,2) [   ]   B(1,3) [   ]

B(2,1) [   ]   B(2,2) [   ]   B(2,3) [   ]

Pretend you are the computer and assign the value of 73 to variable B(2,1). In other words, take pencil in hand and write the number 73 in the box labeled B(2,1). Then do the same for the following.

```
LET B(1,3)=0
LET B(1,1)=49
LET B(2,3)=B(2,1) - B(1,1)
LET B(1,2)=2*B(2,1)
LET B(2,2)=INT(B(2,1)/B(2,3))
```

_ _ _ _ _ _ _ _ _ _

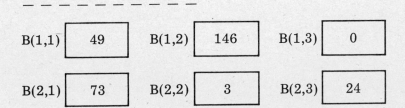

B(1,1) [49]   B(1,2) [146]   B(1,3) [0]

B(2,1) [73]   B(2,2) [3]   B(2,3) [24]

6.   As we learned in Chapter 7, subscripts can be variables. The subscripted variable P(R,C) has variable subscripts.

If R = 1 and C = 2, then P(R,C) is P(1,2).

If R = 4 and C = 3, then P(R,C) is P(4,3).

If R = 7 and C = 5, then P(R,C) is _____.

— — — — — — — — — —

P(7,5)

7.   Let's assume that the following values (in the boxes) have been assigned to the corresponding variables. Note that there are both simple and subscripted variables.

R	2		T(1,1)	7		T(1,2)	0		T(1,3)	−12
C	3		T(2,1)	9		T(2,2)	5		T(2,3)	8
A	1		T(3,1)	16		T(3,2)	13		T(3,3)	10
B	2									

Write the value of each variable below, and the value of subscripts.

T(2,3) = _____   T(1,1) = _____

R = _____   A = _____

C = _____   T(A,A) = _____

T(R,C) = _____   T(B,R) = _____

T(A,B) = _____   T(R,A) = _____

            T(R+1,C−2) = _____

— — — — — — — — — —

8   7
2   1
3   7
8   5
0   9
    16 T(R+1,C−2) = T(2+1,3−2) = T(3,1)

8.   Election time again. (Before starting on this, you may wish to review the vote-counting application in Chapter 7.) The questionnaire below requires two answers.

> Q1. Who will you vote for in the coming election?
>   Circle the number to the left of your choice.
>   1. Sam Smoothe
>   2. Gabby Gruff
>   3. No opinion
> Q2. What age group are you in? Circle the number
>   to the left of your age group.
>   1. Under 30
>   2. 30 or over

Since there are two questions, each reply consists of two numbers: the answer to question 1 and the answer to question 2. We will use V (for Vote) to represent the answer to question 1 and A (for Age) to represent the answer to question 2.

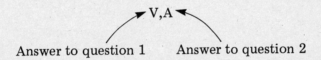

Answer to question 1   Answer to question 2

The possible values of V are 1, 2, or 3. What are the possible values of

A?_____

— — — — — — — — — — — —

1 or 2

9.   We sent out some questionnaires. Some typical replies are shown below.

Reply	Meaning
1,1	one vote for Sam Smoothe, voter is under 30
1,2	one vote for Sam Smoothe, voter 30 or over
3,1	no opinion, voter is under 30

What does the reply 2,2 mean? _____

— — — — — — — — — — —

one vote for Gabby Gruff, voter is 30 or over

10.   We want to write a program to summarize data for a two-question questionnaire. We will use subscripted variables to count votes as shown on the following page.

	Under 30		30 or over
Sam Smoothe	C(1,1)	C(1,2)	
Gabby Gruff	C(2,1)	C(2,2)	
No opinion	C(3,1)	C(3,2)	

In other words, C(1,1) will hold the count for Sam Smoothe by people under 30. C(1,2) will hold the total for Sam Smoothe by people 30 or over. C(2,1) will hold the total for _____ by people

_____.

What subscripted variable will hold the No opinion count for people 30 or over?_____

— — — — — — — — — — —

Gabby Gruff; under 30; C(3,2)

11.   Here are 29 replies to our questionnaire. Remember, each reply is a *pair* of numbers and represents *one* vote. The first number of each pair is the answer to question 1. The second number of each pair is the answer to question 2.

3,1	2,2	3,2	1,2	1,2	2,1
2,2	1,1	1,2	3,1	3,2	2,2
3,1	2,1	2,2	1,1	1,1	1,2
1,1	2,1	2,1	1,2	2,1	3,1
2,1	3,1	2,1	3,1	2,2	

Write the appropriate count in each box below.

	Under 30		30 or over
Sam Smoothe	C(1,1)		C(1,2)
Gabby Gruff	C(2,1)		C(2,2)
No opinion	C(3,1)		C(3,2)

- - - - - - - - - -

C(1,1)	4	C(1,2)	5
C(2,1)	7	C(2,2)	5
C(3,1)	6	C(3,2)	2

12. Naturally, we want the computer to do the counting. Below is the beginning of our program.

```
100 REM***VOTE COUNTING, TWO QUESTIONS
110 DIM C(3,2)
```

The DIM statement (line 110) defines an array with at most 3 rows and 2 columns. That is, the DIM statement defines an array of doubly-subscripted variables in which the maximum value of the first subscript is 3 and the maximum value of the second subscript is 2. You must always DIM doubly-subscripted arrays or you'll get an error message.

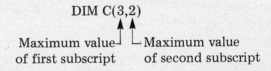

DIM C(3,2)

Maximum value—⌐ ⌐—Maximum value
of first subscript   of second subscript

Next, we want to set all counts to zero. That is, we want to assign zero to C(1,1), C(1,2), and so on up to C(3,2). Even though other versions of BASIC might do this automatically, it is good programming practice to initialize every program. *You* complete this part of the program.

```
200 REM***INITIALIZE: SET ALL COUNTS TO ZERO
```

— — — — — — — — —

Here are four ways to do it!

Method 1

```
210 LET C(1,1)=0
220 LET C(1,2)=0
230 LET C(2,1)=0
240 LET C(2,2)=0
250 LET C(3,1)=0
260 LET C(3,2)=0
```

Method 2

```
210 FOR K=1 TO 3
220 LET C(K,1)=0
230 LET C(K,2)=0
240 NEXT K
```

Method 3

```
210 FOR K=1 TO 3
220 FOR L=1 TO 2
230 LET C(K,L)=0
240 NEXT L
250 NEXT K
```

Method 4

```
210 FOR K=1 TO 3 : FOR L=1 TO 2 : LET C(K,L)=0 : NEXT L,K
```

We will use Methods 3 and 4 because they are easily generalized to arrays of different sizes. Using Method 3, we can add more rows by changing line 210, more columns by changing line 220. (Of course, we would also have to change the DIM statement.)

13.   The array is now set up. Let's READ and count the votes.

```
300 REM***READ AND COUNT VOTES
310 READ V,A : IF V=-1 THEN 410
320 LET C(V,A)=C(V,A)+1 : GOTO 310
```

Line 320 is the crucial vote-counting statement. It adds 1 (vote) to the array element specified by V and A. Suppose this is the array before executing lines 310 and 320.

C(1,1)	0		C(1,2)	4
C(2,1)	2		C(2,2)	7
C(3,1)	5		C(3,2)	0

Show how the array would look after this additional data was processed.

910 DATA 3, 1, 2, 2, 3, 2, 1, 2

C(1,1)		C(1,2)	
C(2,1)		C(2,2)	
C(3,1)		C(3,2)	

– – – – – – – – – –

C(1,1)	0	C(1,2)	5
C(2,1)	2	C(2,2)	8
C(3,1)	6	C(3,2)	1

14. Since line 310 is a READ statement, some DATA statements must be given somewhere. Here they are, featuring the data from frame 11.

```
900 REM***VOTE AND AGE GROUP DATA IN PAIRS. FLAGS=-1,-1
910 DATA 3,1, 2,2, 3,2, 1,2, 1,2, 2,1
920 DATA 2,2, 1,1, 1,2, 3,1, 3,2, 2,2
930 DATA 3,1, 2,1, 2,2, 1,1, 1,1, 1,2
940 DATA 1,1, 2,1, 2,1, 1,2, 2,1, 3,1
950 DATA 2,1, 3,1, 2,1, 3,1, 2,2, -1,-1
```

Remember, each reply is a *pair* of numbers representing *one* vote. To emphasize this, we have typed a space after each reply (pair of values) in the

DATA statements above. Why is the flag −1,−1 instead of just −1? _____

_____

_____

– – – – – – – – – –

If the computer could not find a value for READ variable A as well as variable V in line 310, it would print a data error message and stop.

15. Only one task remains—print the results! For the data shown in frame 14, the results should look like the one on the following page when the program is RUN.

```
RUN
CANDIDATE        UNDER 30      30 OR OVER

SAM SMOOTHE      4             5
GABBY GRUFF      7             5
NO OPINION       6             2
```

You do it. Complete the program segment to print the results—C(1,1), C(1,2), and so on—as shown above.

```
400 REM***PRINT THE RESULTS
```

— — — — — — — — — —

We did it like this.

```
400 REM***PRINT THE RESULTS
410 PRINT "CANDIDATE", "UNDER 30", "30 OR OVER"
420 PRINT
430 PRINT "SAM SMOOTHE", C(1,1), C(1,2)
440 PRINT "GABBY GRUFF", C(2,1), C(2,2)
450 PRINT "NO OPINION", C(3,1), C(3,2)
```

16. Here is a listing of the complete vote-counting program.

```
100 REM***VOTE COUNTING, TWO QUESTIONS
110 DIM C(3,2)
200 REM***INITIALIZE: SET ALL COUNTS TO ZERO
210 FOR K=1 TO 3 : FOR L=1 TO 2 : LET C(K,L)=0 : NEXT L,K
300 REM***READ AND COUNT VOTES
310 READ V,A : IF V=-1 THEN 410
320 LET C(V,A)=C(V,A)+1 : GOTO 310
400 REM***PRINT THE RESULTS
410 PRINT "CANDIDATE", "UNDER 30", "30 OR OVER"
420 PRINT
430 PRINT "SAM SMOOTHE", C(1,1), C(1,2)
440 PRINT "GABBY GRUFF", C(2,1), C(2,2)
450 PRINT "NO OPINION", C(3,1), C(3,2)
900 REM***VOTE AND AGE GROUP DATA IN PAIRS. FLAGS=-1,-1
910 DATA 3,1, 2,2, 3,2, 1,2, 1,2, 2,1
920 DATA 2,2, 1,1, 1,2, 3,1, 3,2, 2,2
930 DATA 3,1, 2,1, 2,2, 1,1, 1,1, 1,2
940 DATA 1,1, 2,1, 2,1, 1,2, 2,1, 3,1
950 DATA 2,1, 3,1, 2,1, 3,1, 2,2, -1,-1
```

Suppose the questionnaire had been the following.

> Q1. Who will you vote for in the coming election?
> Circle the number to the left of your choice.
> 1. Sam Smoothe
> 2. Gabby Gruff
> 3. No opinion
> Q2. What is your political affiliation? Circle the
> number to the left of your answer.
> 1. Democrat
> 2. Republican
> 3. Other

Modify the vote-counting program so that answers are counted as follows.

	Democrat	Republican	Other
Sam Smoothe	C(1,1)	C(1,2)	C(1,3)
Gabby Gruff	C(2,1)	C(2,2)	C(2,3)
No opinion	C(3,1)	C(3,2)	C(3,3)

You will have to change lines 110, 210, 410, 430, 440, and 450.

110 _____

210 _____

410 _____

430 _____

440 _____

450 _____

— — — — — — — — —

```
110 DIM (3,3)
210 FOR K=1 TO 3 : FOR L=1 TO 3 : LET C(K,L)=0 : NEXT L,K
410 PRINT "CANDIDATE", "DEMOCRAT", "REPUBLICAN", "OTHER"
430 PRINT "SAM SMOOTHE", C(1,1), C(1,2), C(1,3)
440 PRINT "GABBY GRUFF", C(2,1), C(2,2), C(2,3)
450 PRINT "NO OPINION", C(3,1) C(3,2), C(3,3)
```

Note: Even though we changed the questionnaire, we didn't have to change the crucial vote-counting statement in line 320.

17. On the following page is a LISTing of the modified program and new DATA statements for the questionnaire in frame 16. You be the computer and print the output for the program when it is RUN.

```
100 REM***VOTE COUNTING, TWO QUESTIONS
110 DIM C(3,3)
200 REM***INITIALIZE: SET ALL COUNTS TO ZERO
210 FOR K=1 TO 3 : FOR L=1 TO 3 : LET C(K,L)=0 : NEXT L,K
300 REM***READ AND COUNT VOTES
310 READ V,A : IF V=-1 THEN 410
320 LET C(V,A)=C(V,A)+1 : GOTO 310
400 REM***PRINT THE RESULTS
410 PRINT "CANDIDATE", "DEMOCRAT", "REPUBLICAN", "OTHER"
420 PRINT
430 PRINT "SAM SMOOTHE", C(1,1), C(1,2), C(1,3)
440 PRINT "GABBY GRUFF", C(2,1), C(2,2), C(2,3)
450 PRINT "NO OPINION", C(3,1), C(3,2), C(3,3)
900 REM***VOTE AND POLITICAL AFFILIATION. FLAGS=-1,-1
910 DATA 1,3, 1,2, 2,1, 2,3, 3,3, 3,3, 3,2, 3,3, 1,3
920 DATA 2,1, 3,1, 1,3, 2,2, 3,1, 3,1, 2,1, 2,3, 3,2
930 DATA 1,3, 1,1, 1,1, 2,3, 3,2, 3,2, 2,2, 2,1, 1,3
940 DATA 3,3, 3,1, 2,3, 1,2, 2,1, 1,2, 1,2, 3,1, 1,1
950 DATA 3,1, 2,3, 3,3, 1,2, 1,1, 2,2, 2,1, 3,2, -1,-1

RUN
```

————————————

```
RUN
CANDIDATE        DEMOCRAT        REPUBLICAN      OTHER

SAM SMOOTHE      4               5               5
GABBY GRUFF      6               3               5
NO OPINION       6               5               5
```

18. Look at this section of the program.

```
430 PRINT "SAM SMOOTHE", C(1,1), C(1,2), C(1,3)
440 PRINT "GABBY GRUFF", C(2,1), C(2,2), C(2,3)
450 PRINT "NO OPINION", C(3,1), C(3,2), C(3,3)
```

We have used the subscripted variables with the actual numerical values for the subscripts. Instead, we could have used a FOR-NEXT loop to print the results for each candidate and no opinion, and could do this using just three multiple-statement lines. Think about it carefully, then rewrite lines 430, 440, and 450 so that FOR-NEXT loops are used to print the values stored in the C array. The RUN should look exactly as it did before.

430 _____

440 _____

450 _____

————————————

```
430 PRINT "SAM SMOOTHE", : FOR X=1 TO 3 : PRINT C(1,X), : NEXT: PRINT
440 PRINT "GABBY GRUFF", : FOR X=1 TO 3 : PRINT C(2,X), : NEXT: PRINT
450 PRINT "NO OPINION", : FOR X=1 TO 3 : PRINT C(3,X), : NEXT
```

Note that a PRINT statement must end lines 430 and 440. Since only four standard print positions are used in the report, you must use PRINT to tell the computer to start a new line.

19.   Just as for one-dimensional arrays, the subscripts for variables that identify elements in a two-dimensional array can start at zero. Our current version of the program uses four of the five standard print positions in the report. Let's add another column to the report that gives the total votes for each candidate, with those totals printed from $C(1,0)$, $C(2,0)$, and $C(3,0)$. You should look carefully through the program to be sure you make all changes necessary to accomplish this. (Hints: Initialize all elements of the array, accumulate the votes for each candidate regardless of political affiliation in the section or subroutine called READ AND COUNT VOTES, and make the necessary changes in the routine that prints the report.) Shown below is how it should RUN.

```
RUN
CANDIDATE      TOTAL        DEMOCRAT     REPUBLICAN     OTHER

SAM SMOOTHE    14           4            5              5
GABBY GRUFF    14           6            3              5
NO OPINION     16           6            5              5
```

— — — — — — — — — —

The listing below (DATA statements omitted) has the modified or added lines checkmarked.

```
 100 REM***VOTE COUNTING, TWO QUESTIONS
 110 DIM C(3,3)
 200 REM***INITIALIZE: SET ALL COUNTS TO ZERO
✓210 FOR K=0 TO 3 : FOR L=0 TO 3 : LET C(K,L)=0 : NEXT L,K
 300 REM***READ AND COUNT VOTES
✓310 READ V,A : IF V=-1 THEN 330
 320 LET C(V,A)=C(V,A)+1 : GOTO 310
✓330 FOR K=1 TO 3 : FOR L=1 TO 3 : LET C(K,0)=C(K,0)+C(K,L) : NEXT L,K
 400 REM***PRINT THE RESULTS
✓410 PRINT "CANDIDATE", "TOTAL", "DEMOCRAT", "REPUBLICAN", "OTHER"
 420 PRINT
✓430 PRINT "SAM SMOOTHE", : FOR X=0 TO 3 : PRINT C(1,X), : NEXT
✓440 PRINT "GABBY GRUFF", : FOR X=0 TO 3 : PRINT C(2,X), : NEXT
✓450 PRINT "NO OPINION", : FOR X=0 TO 3 : PRINT C(3,X), : NEXT
```

Note to people using CRT terminals with less than 72 print positions per line: Check the Appendix for the TAB function, which may help you write PRINT statements to fit this report in lines with less than 72 characters.

20. Do you remember the problem on counting candy bars? You might want to review it in Chapter 7, frames 36 to 52 before we go on.

Before, we were selling one chocolate candy bar for $1.00, on which the profit was $.55. Now let's add another product—a bag of jelly beans which sells for $.50, on which we profit $.30. Our job is to re-program our computer to tabulate individual sales and overall profits. Here's the report we'd like to produce.

```
RUN
KID ID NO.      TOTAL $        CHOCOLATE      JELLY BEANS
  1               Ø               Ø               Ø
  2               3               3               Ø
  3               Ø               Ø               Ø
  4               6               3               6
  5              1Ø               6               8
  6               Ø               Ø               Ø
  7               Ø               Ø               Ø
  8              12               6              12

TOTALS:          31              18              26

PROFITS:        17.7             9.9             7.8
```

(a) From the report above, who had the greatest overall dollar sales?_____

(b) Who sold the most chocolate bars? _____

(c) The most jelly beans? _____

(d) Can you tell who made us the most profit? _____

– — — — — — — — — — —

(a) 8
(b) 5 and 8
(c) 8
(d) not directly from the report. (It's number 8.)

21. For recordkeeping purposes we will prepare some preprinted forms to keep track of who takes what. Now, when one of the kids asks for candy we fill in a form like the one on the following page.

```
Name        Danny
ID No.        4
   1.  Milk Chocolate    3
   2.  Jelly Beans       6
```

This shows that Danny (number 4) took 3 chocolate bars and 6 bags of jelly beans. When we convert that into computer data we use the following format.

kid number, candy number (1 or 2), quantity

Thus, to show the data on this one slip requires 6 data items.

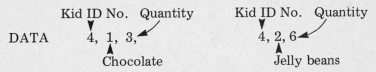

(Notice how we designed the form to conform to our system of data entry!)

From the three forms below, complete the DATA statements. Include end-of-data flags.

```
ID No. 5          ID No. 2          ID No. 8
1.      6          1.      3          1.      6
2.      8          2.      0          2.      12
```

```
900 REM***KID´ID NUMBER, CANDY ID NUMBER, QUANTITY
910 DATA 4,1,3, 4,2,6

920 _____

930 _____
```

— — — — — — — — — — —

This data is not even necessary, since this kid didn't take any jelly beans to sell.

```
920 DATA 5,1,6, 5,2,8, 2,1,3, 2,2,Ø, 8,1,6, 8,2,12
930 DATA -1,-1,-1 ◄──── End-of-data flag
```

22.   Our array will look like this.

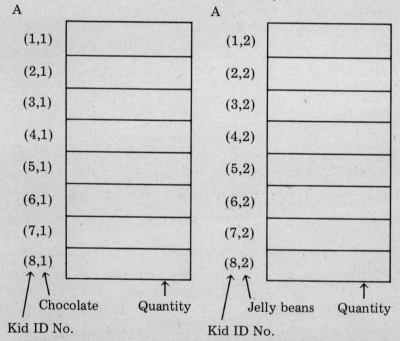

Here is another way to visualize the same A-array.

Your first task is to write the statement(s) to initialize the array and zero it out, that is, set the dimensions and set the values for all the variables to zero.

```
100 REM***CANDY BAR & JELLY BEAN COUNTER
110 REM***INITIALIZE

120 _____
```

— — — — — — — — — —

```
120 DIM A(8,2) : FOR X=1 TO 8 : FOR Y=1 TO 2 : A(X,Y)=0 : NEXT Y,X
```

23. Now READ a set of data (K,C,Q) and test for the end-of-data condition. When you encounter the end-of-data flag, jump to 410.

```
200 REM***READ DATA AND TEST FOR FLAG

210 _____
```

— — — — — — — — — —

```
210 READ K,C,Q : IF K=-1 THEN 410
```

24. The heart of this program is found in line 220, where the "accumulation" takes place.

```
220 A(K,C)=A(K,C)+Q : GOTO 210
```
⬆ _____ Go back and read some more.

K is the kid ID number, C is the candy number (1 = chocolate, 2 = jelly beans), and Q is the quantity. Assume we have the following DATA.

910 DATA 4, 1, 3

(a) The value of what array element (subscripted variable) will be increased?

_____

(b) By how much will it be increased? _____

— — — — — — — — — —

(a) A(4,1)
(b) 3

25. If the array looked like this before:

A

(1,1)	7
(2,1)	0
(3,1)	6
(4,1)	5
(5,1)	3
(6,1)	6
(7,1)	8
(8,1)	3

Kid ID No. ↑↑ Chocolate   Quantity ↑

A

(1,2)	10
(2,2)	0
(3,2)	8
(4,2)	12
(5,2)	0
(6,2)	8
(7,2)	9
(8,2)	10

Kid ID No. ↑↑ Jelly beans   Quantity ↑

How will it look *after* accumulating the data in these DATA statements?

```
910 DATA 4,1,3,  4,2,6
920 DATA 5,1,6,  5,2,8,  2,1,3,  2,2,0,  8,1,6,  8,2,12
```

A

(1,1)	
(2,1)	
(3,1)	
(4,1)	
(5,1)	
(6,1)	
(7,1)	
(8,1)	

A

(1,2)	
(2,2)	
(3,2)	
(4,2)	
(5,2)	
(6,2)	
(7,2)	
(8,2)	

A   A

(1,1)	7		(1,2)	10
(2,1)	3		(2,2)	0
(3,1)	6		(3,2)	8
(4,1)	8		(4,2)	18
(5,1)	9		(5,2)	8
(6,1)	6		(6,2)	8
(7,1)	8		(7,2)	9
(8,1)	9		(8,2)	22

26. Here is our program, so far.

```
100 REM***CANDY BAR & JELLY BEAN COUNTER
110 REM***INITIALIZE
120 DIM A(8,2) : FOR X=1 TO 8 : FOR Y=1 TO 2 : A(X,Y)=0 : NEXT Y,X
200 REM***READ DATA AND TEST FOR FLAG
210 READ K,C,Q : IF K=-1 THEN 410
220 A(K,C)=A(K,C)+Q : GOTO 210
900 REM***KID ID NUMBER, CANDY ID NUMBER, QUANTITY
910 DATA 4,1,3, 4,2,6
920 DATA 5,1,6, 5,2,8, 2,1,3, 2,2,0, 8,1,6, 8,2,12
930 DATA -1,-1,-1
```

Now let's print a preliminary report like the one in frame 20, but without any totals. You fill in the blanks in the program on the following page. This is how the report should look when the program is RUN.

```
RUN
KID ID NO.      CHOCOLATE      JELLY BEANS
  1                0               0
  2                3               0
  3                0               0
  4                3               6
  5                6               8
  6                0               0
  7                0               0
  8                6              12
```

```
400 REM***REPORT #1
410 PRINT "KID ID NO.", _____
420 FOR K=1 TO 8
430 PRINT K,  ◄──────── The comma is important.
440 FOR C=1 TO _____
450 PRINT _____,  ◄──────── The comma is important.
460 NEXT C
470 PRINT
480 NEXT _____
```

— — — — — — — — — —

```
410 PRINT  KID ID NO.", "CHOCOLATE", "JELLY BEANS"
440 FOR C=1 TO 2
450 PRINT A(K,C),
480 NEXT K  ◄──────── The K is optional, but not the NEXT.
```

27. In frame 26, why are the commas placed at the end of lines 430 and 450? _____

— — — — — — — — — —

to suppress the normal carriage return after the PRINT (that is, to keep the computer output on the same line)

28. Why did we include line 470 PRINT where we did? _____

_____

_____

— — — — — — — — — —

to force a carriage return (start a new line of printout), so the next KID ID No. will be printed in the correct place or position when line 420 is executed again

29. Running our program now gives these results.

```
RUN
KID ID NO.     CHOCOLATE      JELLY BEANS
  1               Ø               Ø
  2               3               Ø
  3               Ø               Ø
  4               3               6
  5               6               8
  6               Ø               Ø
  7               Ø               Ø
  8               6              12
```

Now, let's complete the program so it will print everything shown in frame 20.

When we DIMensioned our array DIM (8,2) it included the 0,0 elements shown below. We are going to use these zero elements to accumulate totals.

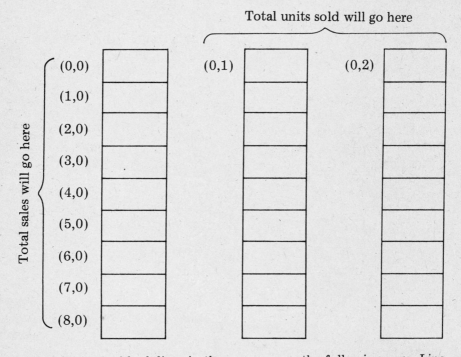

Total units sold will go here

Total sales will go here

You fill in the blank lines in the program on the following page. Line 120 is fixed to set all array elements (boxes) to zero, starting at the 0,0 element. Line 320 adds the total sales per kid (remember, jelly beans sell for $.50 per bag). And line 350 adds units sold.

```
120 DIM A(8,2) : FOR X=Ø TO 8 : FOR Y=Ø TO 2 : A(X,Y)=Ø : NEXT Y,X
210 READ K,C,Q : IF K=-1 THEN 310
220 LET A(K)=A(K)+Q : GOTO 210
300 REM***TOTAL OF UNITS SOLD AND TOTAL SALES IN DOLLARS

310 FOR K=1 TO _____
320 A(K,Ø)=A(K,1)*1.ØØ+A(K,2)*.5Ø   .
330 A(Ø,Ø)=A(Ø,Ø)+A(K,Ø)

340 FOR C= _____

350 A(Ø,C)=A(Ø,C)+A(K,_____)
360 NEXT C

370 _____
380 REM***CALCULATE PROFITS

390 P1=A(Ø,1)*.55 : P2=_____ : P=P1+P2
```

— — — — — — — — — — —

```
310 FOR K=1 TO 8
340 FOR C=1 TO 2
350 A(Ø,C)=A(Ø,C)+A(K,C)
370 NEXT K
390 P1=A(Ø,1)*.55 : P2=A(Ø,2)*.3Ø : P=P1+P2
```

30. Did you understand what went on in lines 320, 330, and 350? If not, go back and review the problem a little more. These statements are *crucial* to your complete understanding of this type of problem.

Write the *line numbers* in the labeled boxes below to show which lines generate values for those boxes.

(0,0) ☐   (0,1) ☐   (0,2) ☐
(1,0) ☐
(2,0) ☐
(3,0) ☐
(4,0) ☐
(5,0) ☐
(6,0) ☐
(7,0) ☐
(8,0) ☐

— — — — — — — — — — —

(0,0)	330	(0,1)	350	(0,2)	350
(1,0)	320				
(2,0)	320				
(3,0)	320				
(4,0)	320				
(5,0)	320				
(6,0)	320				
(7,0)	320				
(8,0)	320				

31.   In frame 29, what does line 330 do?

```
330 A(0,0)=A(0,0)+A(K,0)
```

— — — — — — — — — —

accumulate grand total sales in A(0,0)

32.   In line 390, how would you describe what the statement P = P1+P2 accomplishes?

```
390 P1=A(0,1)*.55 : P2=A(0,2)*.30 : P=P1+P2
```

— — — — — — — — — —

computes total profits and assigns them to variable P

33.   Time to redo our report printing section to update *everything* shown in the RUN on the following page (the same RUN as in frame 20). Fill in the blanks.

```
RUN
KID ID NO.        TOTAL $          CHOCOLATE        JELLY BEANS
    1               Ø                  Ø                Ø
    2               3                  3                Ø
    3               Ø                  Ø                Ø
    4               6                  3                6
    5              1Ø                  6                8
    6               Ø                  Ø                Ø
    7               Ø                  Ø                Ø
    8              12                  6               12

TOTALS:          31                  18               26

PROFITS:         17.7                9.9              7.8
```

```
4ØØ REM***REPORT VERSION #2

41Ø PRINT "KID ID NO." _____
42Ø FOR K=1 TO 8

43Ø PRINT _____

44Ø FOR C= _____

45Ø PRINT A _____
46Ø NEXT C

47Ø _____

48Ø _____
49Ø PRINT

5ØØ PRINT "TOTALS:", _____
51Ø PRINT

52Ø PRINT "PROFITS:" _____
```

— — — — — — — — — —

```
41Ø PRINT "KID ID NO.", "TOTAL $", "CHOCOLATE", "JELLY BEANS"
43Ø PRINT K,
44Ø FOR C=Ø TO 2
45Ø PRINT A(K,C),
47Ø PRINT
48Ø NEXT K
5ØØ PRINT "TOTALS:", A(Ø,Ø), A(Ø,1), A(Ø,2)
52Ø PRINT "PROFITS:", P, P1, P2
```

Now the program is done and the RUN should look just like the one above.
On the following page is a complete listing of the program.

```
100 REM***CANDY BAR & JELLY BEAN COUNTER
110 REM***INITIALIZE
120 DIM A(8,2) : FOR X=0 TO 8 : FOR Y=0 TO 2 : A(X,Y)=0 NEXT Y,X
200 REM***READ DATA AND TEST FOR FLAG
210 READ K,C,Q : IF K=-1 THEN 310
220 A(K,C)=A(K,C)+Q : GOTO 210
300 REM***TOTAL OF UNITS SOLD AND TOTAL OF SALES IN DOLLARS
310 FOR K=1 TO 8
320 A(K,0)=A(K,1)*1.00 +A(K,2)*.50
330 A(0,0)=A(0,0)+A(K,0)
340 FOR C=1 TO 2
350 A(0,C)=A(0,C)+A(K,C)
360 NEXT C
370 NEXT K
380 REM***CALCULATE PROFITS
390 P1=A(0,1)*.55 : P2=A(0,2)*.30 : P=P1+P2
400 REM***REPORT VERSION #2
410 PRINT "KID ID NO", "TOTAL $", "CHOCOLATE", "JELLY BEANS"
420 FOR K=1 TO 8
430 PRINT K,
440 FOR C=0 TO 2
450 PRINT A(K,C),
460 NEXT C
470 PRINT
480 NEXT K
490 PRINT
500 PRINT "TOTALS:", A(0,0), A(0,1), A(0,2)
510 PRINT
520 PRINT "PROFITS:", P, P1, P2
900 REM*** KID ID NUMBER, CANDY ID NUMBER, QUANTITY
910 DATA 4,1,3, 4,2,6
920 DATA 5,1,6, 5,2,8, 2,1,3, 2,2,0, 8,1,6, 8,2,12
930 DATA -1,-1,-1
```

33. Here is one final double array application. In a small class of 8 students, each student has taken 4 quizzes. The scores are shown below.

	Quiz 1	Quiz 2	Quiz 3	Quiz 4
Student 1	65	57	71	75
Student 2	80	90	91	88
Student 3	78	82	77	86
Student 4	45	38	44	46
Student 5	83	82	79	85
Student 6	70	68	83	59
Student 7	98	92	100	97
Student 8	85	73	80	77

Let $S(B,J)$ be the score obtained by student B on quiz J. $S(5,2)$ is the score obtained by student _____ on quiz _____. What is the value of $S(5,2)$? _____

— — — — — — — — —

5; 2; 82

34. Another class might have 30 students and 5 quizzes per student. Still another class might have 23 students and 7 quizzes per student, and so on. Let's begin a program to read scores for N students and Q quizzes per student.

```
100 REM***QUIZ-SCORE PROGRAM
110 DIM S(50,10)
```

The DIM statement permits up to _____ students and up to _____ quizzes.

— — — — — — — — — —

50; 10

35. Next, we want to read the values of N and Q for a particular set of scores—in this case, the scores shown in frame 33. For this set of scores the value of N (number of students) is _____ and the value of Q (number of quizzes) is _____.

— — — — — — — — — —

8; 4

36. We will put the values of N and Q and the scores in DATA statements. Now the program looks like this.

```
100 REMARK QUIZ-SCORE PROGRAM
110 DIM S(50,10)

900 REMARK VALUES OF N AND Q FOLLOWED BY SCORES
905 DATA 8,4  ◄──────────────────────────── Values of N,Q
911 DATA 65,57,71,75 ⎤
912 DATA 80,90,91,88 ⎥
913 DATA 78,82,77,86 ⎥
914 DATA 45,38,44,46 ⎥
915 DATA 83,82,79,85 ⎬──── N by Q array of quiz scores from frame 33
916 DATA 70,68,83,59 ⎥
917 DATA 98,92,100,97 ⎥
918 DATA 85,73,80,77 ⎦
```

Your turn. Complete line 120, below, to READ the values of N and Q.

120 _____

— — — — — — — — — —

120 READ N,Q (That's all there is to it!)

37. The values of N and Q read by line 120 (in frame 36) will be read from which DATA statement? Line _____.

— — — — — — — — — —

905

38. Now let's read the N by Q array of scores using FOR-NEXT loops. Fill in the blanks.

130 FOR X=1 TO N: FOR Y=_____:READ_____NEXT Y:NEXT X

— — — — — — — — — — —

130 FOR X=1 TO N: FOR Y=1 TO Q: READ S(X,Y): NEXT Y: NEXT X

39. The numerical values read by line 130 are stored in the DATA statements, lines _____ through _____.

— — — — — — — — —

911; 918

40. Now that we have the array in the computer, what shall we do with it? One thing someone might want is the average score for each student. Let's do it, beginning at line 200.

```
200 REMARK COMPUTE AND PRINT AVERAGES FOR EACH STUDENT
210 PRINT "STUDENT #","AVERAGE"
220 FOR B=1 TO N
230 LET T=0
240 FOR J=1 TO Q        — Compute total of quiz scores for student B
250 LET T=T+S(B,J)
260 NEXT J
270 LET A=T/Q        Compute average for student B
280 PRINT B,A        Print student number and average
290 NEXT B        Go back and compute scores for next student
```

Lines 230 through 280 are done for each student. That is, for B=1, then B=2, and so on up to B=N. For B=1, what is the value of T computed by lines 230 through 260? T=_____.

— — — — — — — — — —

268. This is the sum of the 4 scores for student 1. Remember, Q=4. Therefore, line 250 will be done for J=1, J=2, J=3, and J=4.

41. For B=1, what is the value of A computed by line 270?

A = T/Q = _____.

— — — — — — — — — —

67. A = T/Q = 268/4 = 67.

42. Here is the complete program and a RUN.

```
100 REMARK QUIZ-SCORE PROGRAM
110 DIM S(50,10)
120 READ N,Q
130 FOR X=1 TO N : FOR Y=1 TO Q : READS (X,Y) : NEXT Y : NEXT X
200 REMARK COMPUTE AND PRINT AVERAGES FOR EACH STUDENT
210 PRINT "STUDENT #","AVERAGE"
220 FOR B=1 TO N
230 LET T=0
240 FOR J=1 TO Q
250 LET T=T+S(B,J)
260 NEXT J
270 LET A=T/Q
280 PRINT B,A
290 NEXT B
900 REMARK VALUES OF N AND Q FOLLOWED BY SCORES
905 DATA 8,4
911 DATA 65,57,71,75
912 DATA 80,90,91,88
913 DATA 78,82,77,86
914 DATA 45,38,44,46
915 DATA 83,82,79,85
916 DATA 70,68,83,59
917 DATA 98,92,100,97
918 DATA 85,73,80,77
RUN
STUDENT #      AVERAGE
  1              67
  2              87.25
  3              80.75
  4              43.25
  5              82.25
  6              70
  7              96.75
  8              78.75
```

Your turn. Beginning with line 300, write a program segment to compute and print the average score for each quiz. For the data used in the program, the results might look like this.

```
RUN
QUIZ #         AVERAGE
  1              75.5
  2              72.75
  3              78.125
  4              76.625
```

— — — — — — — — —

```
300 REMARK COMPUTE AND PRINT AVERAGE OF EACH QUIZ
310 PRINT "QUIZ #","AVERAGE"
320 FOR J=1 TO Q
330 LET T=0
340 FOR B=1 TO N
350 LET T=T+S(B,J)
360 NEXT B
370 LET A=T/N
380 PRINT J,A
390 NEXT J
```

43. Suppose some students take a multiple-choice quiz, 10 questions with 4 possible answers per question. We want to know how many students gave answer number 1 to question number 1, how many gave answer number 2 to question number 1, and so on.

Here are the answers given by 7 students. Each set of answers is in a DATA statement. The last DATA statement is a "fictitious student" and really means "end of data."

```
911 DATA 2,3,1,1,1,2,4,3,4,1
912 DATA 2,3,2,4,1,2,4,2,1,1
913 DATA 2,3,3,1,1,4,3,3,4,1
914 DATA 3,2,4,1,1,2,3,3,4,1
915 DATA 2,3,4,1,1,3,4,3,4,1
916 DATA 2,1,2,3,1,2,4,3,4,2
917 DATA 3,4,1,1,1,4,3,1,4,2
918 DATA -1,0,0,0,0,0,0,0,0,0
```

In each line of data, the first number is the answer to question 1, the second number is the answer to question 2, and so on.

"Fictitious student"

Student 1 (line 911) gave answer 1 to question 3. Student 5 (line 915) gave answer _____ to question 9. Student 7 (line 917) gave answer _____ to question 1.

— — — — — — — — —

4; 3

44. Complete the following table showing the number of students giving each answer (1, 2, 3, or 4) to questions 1, 2, and 3.

	Answer 1	Answer 2	Answer 3	Answer 4
Question 1	0	5	2	0
Question 2	1	1	_____	_____
Question 3	_____	_____	_____	_____

— — — — — — — — — —

```
        4   1
2   2   1   2
```

45. In frame 44, with your help, we have shown how the 7 students answered the first 3 questions. The totals look like a 3 by 4 array. If we had continued for all 10 questions the totals would have looked like a

_____ by 4 array.

— — — — — — — — — —

10

46. Let's define an array T with 10 rows and 4 columns to hold the totals. Complete the following DIM statement.

```
100 REM***QUIZ ANALYSIS PROGRAM

110 DIM _____
```

— — — — — — — — — —

110 DIM T(10,4)

47. For each student there are 10 answers. Let's define a *list* of answers A(1) through A(10). Complete the following DIM statement.

```
120 DIM _____
```

— — — — — — — — — —

120 DIM A(10)

48. We can save space by *combining* the two DIM statements into one DIM statement.

```
110 DIM T(10,4),A(10)
```

The above DIM statement defines a _____ called T with at most 10 rows and 4 columns, and a _____ called A with at most 10 members.

— — — — — — — — — —

two-dimensional array, matrix, or table
one-dimensional array, list, or vector

Note that a comma is used to separate T(10,4) and A(10).

49. Here is the beginning of a program to read the students' answers and compute the totals array.

```
100 REM***QUIZ ANALYSIS PROGRAM
110 DIM T(10,4),A(10)
```

Next, we want to initialize the totals array. That is, we want it to be a *zero* array. You do it.

```
120 REM***SET ALL TOTALS TO ZERO

130 _____
```

— — — — — — — — — —

130 FOR X=1 TO 10 : FOR Y=1 TO 4 : LET T(X,Y)=0 : NEXT X : NEXT Y

50. Write a statement to read the *list* A of answers for one student.

```
140 REM***READ ONE SET OF ANSWERS

150 _____
```

— — — — — — — — — —

150 FOR X=1 TO 10 : READ A(X) : NEXT X

51. Now, is this a real student or a fictitious student? Recall that a fictitious student signals the end of data. If this is the case we want to print the

answers, beginning with line 310. Complete the IF-THEN statement.

```
16Ø REM***CHECK FOR END OF DATA

17Ø IF _____ THEN 31Ø
```

— — — — — — — — — — —

A(1)=−1

52.   If the data are for a real student, we want to update the running tally in the T array. We did it this way.

```
18Ø REM***UPDATE THE TOTALS ARRAY
19Ø FOR Q=1 TO 1Ø
2ØØ LET T(Q,A(Q))=T(Q,A(Q))+1
21Ø NEXT Q
```

Here are the answers for one student. These are the values of A(1) through A(10).

2,3,1,1,1,2,4,3,4,1

Suppose Q = 1. Then A(Q)=_____ and T(Q,A(Q)) is T(_____,_____).

— — — — — — — — — — —

2; T(1,2) (since Q=1 and A(Q)=2)

53.   In the above case (frame 52), what happens when the computer obeys line 200?_____

— — — — — — — — — '— — —

The total in T(1,2) is increased by one. (It's just like counting votes!)

54.   Since line 200 is in a FOR-NEXT loop, it will be done for each value of Q specified by the FOR statement. That is, it will be done for A = 1, 2, 3, 4, 5, 6, 7, 8, 9, and 10. When Q = 10, which element of the T matrix is increased by one? T(_____,_____).

— — — — — — — — — —

T(10,A(10)) or T(10,1) for the data in frame 52.

55. Let's move on. After tallying the answers for one student, we want the computer to return to line 150 and read another set of answers. (See frame 50.)

```
220 REM***GO BACK FOR ANOTHER SET OF ANSWERS
230 GO TO 150
```

Then the IF-THEN statement (frame 51) is encountered again. The IF-THEN statement causes the computer to go to line 310 if a fictitious student has been read. In that case, we want to print the headings and results, then stop.

```
300 REM***PRINT THE TOTALS ARRAY
310 PRINT "QUESTION #","NUMBER OF STUDENTS WHO CHOSE ANSWER #"
320 PRINT, 1, 2, 3, 4  : PRINT
```

330 _____

340 _____

350 _____

— — — — — — — — — —


```
330 FOR X=1 TO 10 : PRINT X,
340 FOR Y=1 TO 4 : PRINT T(X,Y),
350 NEXT Y,X
```

Note: The comma following PRINT in line 320 will cause the computer to tab over to standard print position number 2. Some BASICs will give an error message; in that case, substitute the following PRINT statement.

```
320 PRINT " ", 1, 2, 3, 4 : PRINT
```

Here is a complete LIST and RUN.

```
LIST
100 REM***QUIZ ANALYSIS PROGRAM
110 DIM T(10,4)
120 REM***SET ALL TOTALS TO ZERO
130 FOR X=1 TO 10 : FOR Y=1 TO 4 : T(X,Y)=0 : NEXT Y,X
140 REM***READ ONE SET OF ANSWERS
150 FOR X=1 TO 10 : READ A(X) : NEXT X
160 REM***CHECK FOR END OF DATA
170 IF A(1)=-1 THEN 310
180 REM***UPDATE THE TOTALS ARRAY
190 FOR Q=1 TO 10
200 T(Q,A(Q))=T(Q,A(Q))+1
210 NEXT Q
220 REM***GO BACK FOR ANOTHER SET OF ANSWERS
230 GOTO 150
300 REM***PRINT THE TOTALS ARRAY
310 PRINT "QUESTION #", "NUMBER OF STUDENTS WHO CHOSE ANSWER #"
320 PRINT, 1, 2, 3, 4 : PRINT
330 FOR X=1 TO 10 : PRINT X,
340 FOR Y=1 TO 4 : PRINT T(X,Y),
350 NEXT Y,X
900 REM***STUDENT ANSWERS TO MULTIPLE CHOICE QUIZ
911 DATA 2,3,1,1,1,2,4,3,4,1
912 DATA 2,3,2,4,1,2,4,2,1,1
913 DATA 2,3,2,4,1,2,4,2,1,1
914 DATA 3,2,4,1,1,2,3,3,4,1
915 DATA 2,3,4,1,1,3,4,3,4,1
916 DATA 2,1,2,3,1,2,4,3,4,2
917 DATA 3,4,1,1,1,4,3,1,4,2
918 DATA -1,0,0,0,0,0,0,0,0,0
RUN
```

QUESTION #	NUMBER OF STUDENTS WHO CHOSE ANSWER #			
	1	2	3	4
1	0	5	2	0
2	1	1	4	1
3	2	3	0	2
4	4	0	1	2
5	7	0	0	0
6	0	5	1	1
7	0	0	2	5
8	1	2	4	0
9	2	0	0	5
10	5	2	0	0

SELF-TEST

Good for you! You have reached the Chapter 8 Self-Test. These problems will help you review the BASIC instructions you have learned for dealing with arrays of numbers, using variables with double subscripts.

1. Indicate which of the following are legal BASIC doubly-subscripted variables.

    _____ (a) X(2+2)   _____ (b) X(5,5)

    _____ (c) X1(100,100)   _____ (d) X(A+B,C)

    _____ (e) X(X(1,2),X(2,1))   _____ (f) X(A,A)

Questions 2 through 7 refer to the following array, A.

	Column 1	Column 2
Row 1	1	2
Row 2	3	4
Row 3	5	6

2. What are the dimensions of A? _____,_____

3. Write a DIMension statement for A, using line number 100.

    100 _____

4. What variable locates the "box" in row 3, column 2 of A? _____

5. What is the value of the following?

    (a) A(1,1) _____   (b) A(3,1) _____

6. Let X = 2, Y = 3. What is the value of:

    (a) A(X,X) _____   (b) A(X+1,Y−1) _____

7. What is the value of A(A(1,2),A(2,1)−1)? _____

8. Write a program which uses two FOR-NEXT loops to fill a 10 by 10 array (M) with zeros.

9. Your city officials seek to conduct a census of the citizenry. Among other things, they want to analyze the age and sex breakdown of the community. They ask you to program your home computer to take data from the form below and prepare a report like the RUN shown.

CITY CENSUS REPORT
DATA FORM
(check one box for each question)

Question one — Age Group

- 1. less than 10
- 2. 10-15
- 3. 16-21
- 4. 22-30
- 5. 31-40
- 6. 41-50
- 7. 51-65
- 8. over 65

Question two — Sex

- 1. male
- 2. female

Use the following DATA statements in your program.

```
100 REM DATA BY AGE GROUP, SEX GROUP
110 DATA 1,2,2,1,3,2,4,1,5,2,6,2,7,2,8,1
120 DATA 1,2,1,1,2,1,2,2,3,1,3,1,3,2,3,1,3,2,4,1,4,2
130 DATA 5,1,5,1,5,2,5,2,6,1,6,1,6,2,7,1,7,2,7,2,7,2
140 DATA 8,1,8,1,8,2,8,2,3,1,4,2,5,2,6,1,6,1,7,1,8,2
150 DATA -1,-1
160 DATA  <10,10-15,16-21,22-30,31-40,41-50,51-65,>65
```

```
RUN
AGE           TOTAL        MALE          FEMALE
<10            3            1             2
10-15          3            2             1
16-21          7            4             3
22-30          4            2             2
31-40          6            2             4
41-50          6            4             2
51-65          6            2             4
>65            6            3             3

TOTALS        41           20            21
```

10. Your brother-in-law owns the local "jeans" store. He carries a large inventory with tremendous variety but now finds he must cut back. The question is *which* items to cut back. He asks you to use your computer to analyze his sales and help him make the "which-item" decisions. He wants to analyze sales of children's pants first. He carries 10 styles in children's pants, each style with 3 colors. For your program, you should number the styles 1 through 10 and the colors 1 through 3, so that each piece of data will look like that below.

DATA　　1,　　2,　　12.50

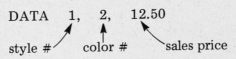

style #　　　color #　　　sales price

Write a program to analyze the sales and prepare a report like the one below. Use the following DATA statements in your program.

```
100 REM DATA STYLE, COLOR, DOLLAR SALES
120 DATA 1,1,12,1,2,13,1,3,14,2,1,22,2,2,10,2,3,12
130 DATA 3,1,45,3,2,14,3,3,32,4,1,13,4,2,10,4,3,15
140 DATA 5,1,12,5,2,13,5,3,12,6,1,12,6,2,12,6,3,12
150 DATA 7,1,13,7,2,13,7,3,13,8,1,14,8,2,14,8,3,14
160 DATA 9,1,15,9,2,15,9,3,15,10,1,14,10,2,14,10,3,14
170 DATA 3,2,35,5,1,50,6,1,36,10,3,30,9,3,12,10,2,28
180 DATA 2,3,40,5,1,24,3,3,14,4,1,48,1,1,12,2,1,12,3,1,13
190 DATA -1,-1,-1
```

```
RUN
STYLE #          TOTAL          COLOR 1          COLOR 2          COLOR 3
   1              51              24               13               14
   2              96              34               10               52
   3             153              58               49               46
   4              86              61               10               15
   5             111              86               13               12
   6              72              48               12               12
   7              39              13               13               13
   8              42              14               14               14
   9              57              15               15               27
  10             100              14               42               44

TOTALS          807             367              191              249
```

11. In an effort to save some of your monthly budget dollars, you decide to "shop around" for some of the staple goods you use at home. There are four different stores nearby. You decide to shop the following six items in each store and then compare prices on your home computer: toothpaste, paper towels, paper napkins, laundry soap, flour, tissues.

Write a program that will prepare a report like the one shown below. The easiest way to enter your data is using DATA statements with the prices for all six items from one store in one DATA statement. (Be sure the six are in the same order for all four stores.)

```
RUN
ITEM           STORE 1        STORE 2        STORE 3        STORE 4
TOOTHPASTE      .89            .95            .85            .83
PAPER TOWELS    .49            .55            .53            .47
NAPKINS         .85            .8             .79            .75
SOAP            .95            .93            .99            .9
FLOUR           .79            .85            .89            .75
TISSUES         .39            .45            .49            .39

TOTALS         4.36           4.53           4.54           4.09
```

Answers to Self-Test

The frame numbers in parentheses refer to the frames in the chapter where the topic is discussed. You may wish to refer back to these for quick review.

1. (b), (d), (e), and (f) are legal (Longer variable names such as item (c) may be legal on *your* computer. Check the reference manual for your computer.)   (frames 5-7)

2. 3,2 meaning 3 rows, 2 columns   (frames 2-4)

3. 100 DIM A(3,2)   (frame 12)

4. A(3,2)   (frames 9-11)

5. (a) 1; (b) 5   (frame 11)

6. (a) 4; (b) 6   (frame 11)

7. 4   (frame 11)

8.
```
10 DIM M(10,10)
20 FOR R=1 TO 10
30 FOR C=1 TO 10
40 M(R,C)=0
50 NEXT C
60 NEXT R
```
(frame 12)

9.
```
LIST
10 REMARK***POPULATION AGE/SEX ANALYSIS
15 REM INITIALIZE
20 DIM V(8,2):FOR A=0 TO 8:FOR S=0 TO 2:LET V(A,S)=0:NEXT S:NEXT A
25 REM READ DATA, TEST, ACCUMULATE
30 READ A,S : IF A=-1 THEN 60
40 LET V(A,S)=V(A,S)+1 : LET V(0,0)=V(0,0)+1
50 LET V(0,S)=V(0,S)+1 : LET V(A,0)=V(A,0)+1 : GO TO 30
55 REM PRINT REPORT
60 PRINT"AGE","TOTAL","MALE","FEMALE"
70 FOR A=1 TO 8 : READ A$ : PRINT A$,V(A,0),
80 FOR S=1 TO 2 : PRINT V(A,S), : NEXT S : PRINT
90 NEXT A : PRINT : PRINT "TOTALS",V(0,0),V(0,1),V(0,2)
100 REM DATA BY AGE GROUP, SEX GROUP
110 DATA 1,2,2,1,3,2,4,1,5,2,6,2,7,2,8,1
120 DATA 1,2,1,1,2,1,2,2,3,1,3,1,3,2,3,1,3,2,4,1,4,2
130 DATA 5,1,5,1,5,2,5,2,6,1,6,1,6,2,7,1,7,2,7,2,7,2
140 DATA 8,1,8,1,8,2,8,2,3,1,4,2,5,2,6,1,6,1,7,1,8,2
150 DATA -1,-1
160 DATA <10,10-15,16-21,22-30,31-40,41-50,51-65,>65
```
(frame 19)

10.
```
LIST
10 REMARK***SALES ANALYSIS
15 REM INITIALIZE
20 DIM T(10,3):FOR S=0 TO 10:FOR C=0 TO 3:LET T(S,C)=0:NEXT S
25 REM READ, TEST, ACCUMULATE
30 READ S,C,D : IF S=-1 THEN 60
40 LET T(S,C)=T(S,C)+D : LET T(0,0)=T(0,0)+D
50 LET T(0,C)=T(0,C)+D : LET T(S,0)=T(S,0)+D : GO TO 30
55 REM PRINT REPORT
60 PRINT"STYLE #","TOTAL","COLOR 1","COLOR 2","COLOR 3"
70 FOR S=1 TO 10 : PRINT S,T(S,0),
80 FOR C=1 TO 3 : PRINT T(S,C), : NEXT C
90 NEXT S : PRINT : PRINT"TOTALS", : FOR X=0 TO 3 : PRINT T(0,X), : NEXT
100 REM DATA STYLE, COLOR, DOLLAR SALES
120 DATA 1,1,12,1,2,13,1,3,14,2,1,22,2,2,10,2,3,12
130 DATA 3,1,45,3,2,14,3,3,32,4,1,13,4,2,10,4,3,15
140 DATA 5,1,12,5,2,13,5,3,12,6,1,10,6,2,12,6,3,12
150 DATA 7,1,13,7,2,13,7,3,13,8,1,14,8,2,14,8,3,14
160 DATA 9,1,15,9,2,15,9,3,15,10,1,14,10,2,14,10,3,14
170 DATA 3,2,35,5,1,50,6,1,36,10,3,30,9,3,12,10,2,28
180 DATA 2,3,40,5,1,24,3,3,14,4,1,48,1,1,12,2,1,12,3,1,13
190 DATA -1,-1,-1
```

(frame 33)

11.
```
LIST
10 REMARK***STORE PRICE COMPARISON
15 REM INITIALIZE
20 DIM P(6,4)
30 FOR S=0 TO 4 : FOR I=0 TO 6 : READ P(I,S) : NEXT I : NEXT S
35 REM ACCUMULATE STORE TOTALS
40 FOR S=1 TO 4
50 FOR I=1 TO 6 : LET P(0,S)=P(0,S)+P(I,S) : NEXT I
60 NEXT S
65 REM PRINT REPORT
70 PRINT "ITEM","STORE 1","STORE 2","STORE 3","STORE 4"
80 FOR I=1 TO 6 : READ I$ : PRINT I$,
90 FOR S=1 TO 4 : PRINT P(I,S), : NEXT S
100 NEXT I : PRINT : PRINT"TOTALS",
110 FOR S=1 TO 4 : PRINT P(0,S), : NEXT S
120 REM PRICES BY STORE
130 DATA .89,.49,.85,.95,.79,.39
140 DATA .95,.55,.80,.93,.85,.45
150 DATA .85,.53,.79,.99,.89,.49
160 DATA .83,.47,.75,.90,.75,.39
170 DATA TOOTHPASTE,PAPER TOWELS,NAPKINS,SOAP,FLOUR,TISSUES
```

(frame 42)

CHAPTER NINE

String Variables
and String Functions

In Chapter 3, we showed you a few ways to use alphanumeric string variables. We also used string variables in the chapters that followed as we introduced new programming concepts. In this chapter we will review what you already know about string variables and introduce you to some new goodies, as well. Generally you will find that there is as wide a range of manipulation for string variables as for a numeric variable.

When you have completed this chapter you will be able to use the RESTORE statement with READ and DATA statements. You will also be able to use the following string functions with the string variables you will learn about in this chapter.

VAL
STR$
CHR$
ASC
MID$
LEFT$
RIGHT$
LEN
INSTR

1.   So far, our use of alphanumeric (mixed alphabetic and numeric) phrases has mostly been limited to the use of strings in PRINT statements such as the following.

```
1Ø PRINT "THIS IS A STRING"
```

Now we can add a new feature to BASIC, the string variable.

```
10 LET T$="STRING FOR THE STRING VARIABLE T$"
```

This is a string variable.

You identify a string variable by using any legal variable name followed by a dollar sign ($). String variables permit you to manipulate alphanumeric data with greater ease. String variable instructions include LET, PRINT, IN-PUT, READ, DATA, and IF-THEN, plus special string functions.

A string variable may be any size up to 255 characters. How many characters in the string variable T$ above? _____ (Did you count blank spaces?)

— — — — — — — — — —

33 characters

2.   As you know, you can assign values to a string variable using an INPUT statement that asks for one or more string variables to be entered by the user.

```
10 INPUT "WHAT IS YOUR NAME"; N$
10 INPUT "YOUR NAME AND SUN SIGN"; N$,S$
10 INPUT "YOUR NAME, CITY, AND STATE YOU LIVE IN"; N$,C$,S$
```

You may also assign numeric and string variables in the same INPUT statement as shown here.

```
10 INPUT "WHAT IS YOUR NAME AND AGE"; N$,A
```

If, however, you want to INPUT a string variable with an imbedded comma (a comma included as part of the string) or if you want leading or trailing space(s) in the string, you must enter the string variable enclosed in quotes.

Show how you would respond to this computer prompt.

ENTER YOUR NAME, LAST NAME FIRST? _____

— — — — — — — — — —

"BROWNSTONE, IRENE" (your name inside quotes)

3.   Write a program to enter and print an auto license plate that has a 3-letter alphabetic string and a 3-digit number (such as SAM 123). Enter the letters as a string variable and the number as a numeric variable.

— — — — — — — — — —

```
10 INPUT A$,B
20 PRINT A$;B

RUN
? SAM,123
SAM 123

RUN
? MAX,-456
MAX-456
```

Where did the space come from? Remember, BASIC reserves a place for the sign of the number (see example below).

If you enter a negative number (which you normally wouldn't for this problem) it will look like this.

4.   You can also enter string variables by using READ and DATA statements.

```
1 REMARK***STRING READ/DATA COURSE LIST
10 PRINT "COURSE","HOURS","GRADE"
20 READ A$,B,C$
30 PRINT A$,B,C$
40 GOTO 20
50 DATA ENGLISH 1A,3,B,SOC 130,3,A
60 DATA BUS ADM 1A,4,B,STAT 10,3,C
70 DATA HUMANITIES,3,A,HISTORY 17A,3,B
80 DATA CALCULUS 3A,4,C
```

```
RUN
COURSE            HOURS           GRADE
ENGLISH 1A          3               B
SOC 130             3               A
BUS ADM 1A          4               B
STAT 10             3               C
HUMANITIES          3               A
HISTORY 17A         3               B
CALCULUS 3A         4               C
?OD ERROR IN 20
```

Look at the output produced by line 30 in the program above. What is the function of the comma in a string variable PRINT statement? _____

_____

_____

— — — — — — — — — —

The comma causes the output to be printed in up to five columns across the page, (though here we only used three columns), just as with numeric variables.

Note: If the string variable size is greater than 15 characters, the print column sequence will *not* be followed, but will skip to the next available print position.

5.   The string LET assigns a particular string to a string variable. Note that you must enclose the string in quotes as in these two examples.

```
20 LET A$=" GOOD EXAMPLE"
30 LET B$=" THIS IS A "

20 LET A$="YES"
30 LET B$="NO"
40 LET C$=A$ ◄——————— C$ now contains "YES"
```

Write a string LET statement that assigns the book name BASIC FOR HOME COMPUTERS to the variable S$.

— — — — — — — — —

```
10 LET S$="BASIC FOR HOME COMPUTERS"
```

6.   Now, write a program similar to the one in frame 4. Instead of courses and grades, the data should be books contained in your home library. Your DATA should include author, title, and number of pages. Your RUN should look like this (with your books, of course).

```
RUN
TITLE                          AUTHOR         PAGES
BASIC FOR HOME COMPUTERS        ALBRECHT        300
YOUR HOME COMPUTER             WHITE           225
BASIC PROGRAMMING              KEMENY          150
INTRO TO MICROCOMPUTERS        OSBORNE         384
COMPUTER LIB/DREAM MACHINES    NELSON          186
101 BASIC GAMES                AHL             180
GAMES FOR THE POCKET CALC      THIAGI           54
```

— — — — — — — — —

```
10 REMARK***STRING/DATA HOME LIBRARY LIST
15 PRINT "TITLE"," ","AUTHOR","PAGES"
20 READ A$,T$,P : IF A$="END"THEN STOP
30 PRINT T$,A$,P : GOTO 20
40 REM AUTHOR,TITLE,PAGES
50 DATA ALBRECHT, BASIC FOR HOME COMPUTERS,300
60 DATA WHITE, YOUR HOME COMPUTER,225
70 DATA KEMENY, BASIC PROGRAMMING,150
80 DATA OSBORNE, INTRO TO MICROCOMPUTERS,384
90 DATA NELSON, COMPUTER LIB/DREAM MACHINES,186
100 DATA AHL, 101 BASIC GAMES,180
110 DATA THIAGI, GAMES FOR THE POCKET CALC,54
120 DATA END, END,1
```

7.   Modify the program you just wrote for frame 6 so that it will only print those books with fewer than 200 pages. Our RUN looked like this.

```
RUN
TITLE                             AUTHOR        PAGES
BASIC PROGRAMMING                 KEMENY          150
COMPUTER LIB/DREAM MACHINES NELSON               186
101 BASIC GAMES                   AHL             180
GAMES FOR THE POCKET CALC   THIAGI               54
```

_ _ _ _ _ _ _ _ _

```
25 IF P >= 200 THEN 20
```

8.   The string IF-THEN allows you to compare the contents of two string variables.

```
15 LET B$ = "NO"
20 INPUT "DO YOU WANT INSTRUCTIONS? YES OR NO"; A$
30 IF A$ = B$ THEN 140
40 PRINT "THIS SIMULATION PERMITS YOU TO REGULATE . . ."
```

Line 30 compares the contents of the string variable A$ (YES) to the contents of string variable B$ (NO). If you responded YES to the INPUT statement, A$ and B$ are not equal (they do not have the same contents), the computer will execute the next statement, line 40, which in this case will print the instructions. If you respond NO to line 20 above, the program would branch to line 140 and continue execution there.

The comparison in line 30 is between _____.

_ _ _ _ _ _ _ _ _

the contents of two string variables, A$ and B$

9.   You can compare the contents of a string variable to a string enclosed in quotes.

```
10 INPUT "DO YOU WANT INSTRUCTIONS? YES OR NO"; A$
20 IF A$="NO" THEN 140
30 PRINT "THIS SIMULATION PERMITS YOU TO REGULATE . . ."
```

The comparison in line 20 above is between a _____

and a _____.

— — — — — — — — — —

string assigned to a string variable (the contents of a string variable) and a
string enclosed in quotes

10.　You *cannot* compare a numeric variable to a string variable.

```
11Ø IF A$ = B THEN 14Ø
```
◄─────── This is not permitted.

But you *can* change a string variable into its numeric equivalent using the
VAL($) function. In the above example, if A$ contained a number (entered
as a string variable) you could compare it with numeric variable B by changing line 110 to read as follows.

```
11Ø IF VAL(A$) = B THEN 14Ø
```

　　　When BASIC converts a numeric string to a numeric value with the
VAL function, you must consider the leading space that is included in a
numeric value (the space reserved for the sign of the number). To aid your
understanding, look at this demonstration.

```
1Ø LET S$="3.14159"
2Ø PRINT S$
3Ø LET S=VAL(S$)
4Ø PRINT S

RUN
3.14159
 3.14159
```

Notice that no leading space was included when the *string* was printed. However, a leading space *is* included in the printed *numeric* value of 3.14159.
(Remember, a positive number has the implied sign +.)

Here is another demonstration program. Circle the correct RUN for the program.

```
10 LET A$="32" : LET B$="1.115" : LET C$="-10"
20 PRINT A$ : PRINT VAL(A$)
30 PRINT B$ : PRINT VAL(B$)
40 PRINT C$ : PRINT VAL(C$)
```

```
RUN            RUN            RUN
32             32             32
32              32              32
1.115          1.115          1.115
1.115           1.115          1.115
-10            -10            -10
-10            -10             -10
```

— — — — — — — — — —

The middle RUN is correct.

11.   Using the STR$ function, you can convert a numeric variable to a string or place a numeric variable into a string variable.

```
10 PRINT STR$(X) ◄———————    Will print the string equivalent of the nu-
                             meric content of variable X.
20 LET A$ = STR$(X)◄———————  Will place into string variable A$ the nu-
                             meric content of variable X.
```

When you convert a positive numeric variable to a string or string variable, the result *will include* the leading space reserved for the sign of the number. Circle the correct RUN for this demonstration program.

```
10 V = 112 : PRINT V : PRINT STR$(V)
```

```
RUN            RUN            RUN            RUN
112             112           112             112
112            112            112             112
```

— — — — — — — — — —

The fourth RUN (on the right) is the correct one. Both the numeric value of 112 and the string value of 112 were printed with a leading space.

12.   In a string IF-THEN, the comparison is made one character at a time. For example, if a space is introduced in the wrong place, it may cause a comparison other than what you expect.

```
10 INPUT A$
20 IF A$ = "MCGEE" THEN 140
```

If the user enters MC GEE in response to the computer's prompt during the RUN, the comparison will not be equal. Why will this comparison not be equal? _____

_____

— — — — — — — — — — —

The space between C and G is a character which is not present in "MCGEE."

13.   You can compare strings using the same symbols you used earlier: <>, <, >, <=, >=, and =. It's a little tricky so you should use caution with these comparisons. The comparison is still made one character at a time from left to right. The *first* difference found determines the relationship. The relationship is based on position in the alphabet; C is "less than" S; T is "greater than" M.

```
10 LET A$ = "SMITH"
20 LET B$ = "SMYTH"
30 IF A$ < B$ THEN 100
```

In line 30 above, will the program branch to line 100 or continue to the next statement in sequence? _____

— — — — — — — — — — —

Jump to line 100. The first difference is the third character and since I is "less than" Y, the IF-THEN condition is TRUE.

14.   Here is another example.

```
120 LET D$ = "COMPUTE"
130 LET E$ = "COMPUTER"
140 IF D$ < E$ THEN 180
150 PRINT D$
  :
  :
180 PRINT E$
```

Which statement will be executed after the comparison in line 140? _____

— — — — — — — — — — —

Line 180. D$ is "less than" E$. It is smaller in size, therefore "less than" E$.

15.   Change line 140 in frame 14 to read as follows.

```
140 IF D$ = E$ THEN 180
```

Now which statement will be executed after the comparison of line 140?

_____

— — — — — — — — — —

Line 150. D$ is not equal to E$.

16. In frame 14 change line 140 to read as follows.

```
140 IF E$ > D$ THEN 180
```

Which statement will be executed after the comparison? _____

— — — — — — — — — —

Line 180. E$ is "greater than" D$.

17. To expand your understanding of string comparisons, we would like to introduce you to the ASCII (pronounced ASKEE) code. Who's ASCII, you ask? ASCII stands for the American Standard Code for Information Interchange. For each character you type on the keyboard, an ASCII code number for that character is sent to the computer. The computer sends back an ASCII code number for each character that appears on your printer or screen. That's the "information interchange" referred to by ASCII.

The version of BASIC we are using allows us to enter ASCII code numbers instead of keyboard characters with the use of the CHR$ function and allows us to convert a character into its ASCII code number using the ASC function.

CHR$(X)   The ASCII number to be converted is placed in X before you use this function. Or you can place the number directly into the parentheses instead of X, as in CHR$(65).

ASC(X$)   The string character to be converted to ASCII code is placed in X$ before execution.

For example, the uppercase letters we use in BASIC correspond to ASCII code numbers 65 to 90 inclusive: A = 65, B = 66, C = 67, . . . X = 88, Y = 89, Z = 90. Check your reference manual to see how your version of BASIC converts ASCII numbers to characters and vice versa. A complete table of ASCII code numbers and the characters they represent can be found in the Appendix, page 333.

The little program on the following page prints a quotation from John Wayne that is found in the DATA statement in ASCII code numbers.

```
10 READ X : IF X = -1 THEN END
20 PRINT CHR$(X); : GOTO 10
30 DATA 89,85,80,-1

RUN
YUP
```

Referring to that table of ASCII code numbers, tell what the following program will print when RUN.

```
10 READ A : IF A = -1 THEN END
20 PRINT CHR$(A); : GOTO 10
30 DATA 72,65,80,80,89,32,67,79,77,80,85,84,73,78,71,-1
```

— — — — — — — — — —

```
RUN
HAPPY COMPUTING
```

18.   Using the ASC function you can find out the ASCII code number for a string character. Here's a demonstration.

```
10 LET X$ = "A" : LET Y$ = "B" : LET Z$ = "C"
20 PRINT "A ="; ASC(X$), "B ="; ASC(Y$), "C ="; ASC(Z$)

RUN
A = 65          B = 66          C = 67
```

Write a program using the ASC function to provide you with the ASCII code for the following characters, so that the RUN looks like this.

```
RUN
CHARACTER       ASCII CODE

$                   36
=                   61
?                   63
```

— — — — — — — — — —

Here are two possible solutions.

```
10 A$ = "$" : B$ = "=" : C$ = "?"
20 PRINT "CHARACTER", "ASCII CODE" : PRINT
30 PRINT A$, ASC(A$)
40 PRINT B$, ASC(B$)
50 PRINT C$, ASC(C$)

10 PRINT "CHARACTER", "ASCII CODE" : PRINT
20 PRINT "$", ASC("$")
30 PRINT "=", ASC("=")
40 PRINT "?", ASC("?")
```

19.   Now, let's return to string comparisons using the IF-THEN statement. Strings are compared using a character by character process and the computer uses ASCII code numbers to do the comparing. For example, in frame 12, we saw this program segment.

```
10  INPUT A$
20  IF A$ = "MCGEE" THEN 140
```

When the program is RUN and the user enters MC GEE, the computer compares ASCII code numbers as follows.

<table>
<tr><td>"MCGEE"</td><td>A$ (user-entered)</td></tr>
<tr><td>M = 77 ——————</td><td>M = 77</td></tr>
<tr><td>C = 67 ——————</td><td>C = 67</td></tr>
<tr><td>G = 71 ——————</td><td>space = 32</td></tr>
<tr><td>E = 69 ——————</td><td>G = 71</td></tr>
<tr><td>E = 69 ——————</td><td>E = 69</td></tr>
<tr><td></td><td>E = 69</td></tr>
</table>

The computer finds the two strings equal for the first two characters, but the third character comparison is unequal (71 *vs.* 32).

Show how the computer, using ASCII codes, will compare the strings in the following segment.

```
10  INPUT "DO YOU WANT INSTRUCTIONS? YES OR NO"; A$
20  IF A$ = "NO" THEN 140

RUN
DO YOU WANT INSTRUCTIONS? YES OR NO? YES.
```

A$ "NO"

Is the comparison true or false? _____

— — — — — — — — — — —

A$ "NO"
Y = 89   N = 78
E = 69   O = 79
S = 83
The comparison is false.

20.   Before you proceed, we need to introduce the RESTORE statement and its use in connection with READ and DATA statements. A READ statement causes the next item(s) of data to be read from the DATA statements. You may find that you want the program to read through the data from the beginning again. To do so, use a RESTORE statement which causes the next

DATA item to be READ to be the first piece of data in the *first* DATA statement. See line 15 below.

Now that you have seen how to use string variable comparisons, you can understand this simple information retrieval program that permits retrieving information from DATA statements.

The program in frame 4 prints courses, hours, and grades. The program below permits the operator to enter the course: the computer will then print the course, hour, and grade.

```
1 REMARK***STRING COURSE INFO RETRIEVAL
10 INPUT "ENTER COURSE NAME"; D$
15 RESTORE
20 READ A$, B, C$ : IF A$=D$ THEN 40
30 GOTO 20
40 PRINT A$, B, C$ : PRINT : GOTO 10
50 DATA ENGLISH 1A,3,B, SOC 130,3,A
60 DATA BUS ADM 1A,4,B, STAT 10,3,C
70 DATA HUMANITIES,3,A, HISTORY 17A,3,B
80 DATA CALCULUS 3A,4,C

RUN
ENTER COURSE NAME? HUMANITIES
HUMANITIES     3               A

ENTER COURSE NAME? STAT 10
STAT 10        3               C

ENTER COURSE NAME? ECON 1A ◄───────
?OD ERROR IN 20
```

Whoops, no such course. The computer read through all the data and found no such course; therefore, it printed this error message.

Let's look at another RUN of the program.

```
RUN
ENTER COURSE NAME? SOC130
?OD ERROR IN 20
```

Why did we get an error message this time? _____

— — — — — — — — — —

The course name is stored SOC 130, but the user typed SOC130 without a space between SOC and 130.

21. Refer back to the program in frame 20.

(a) What is the purpose of this part of line 20?

   ... IF A\$ = D\$ THEN 40

_____

(b) Under what conditions will line 30 be executed? 30 GOTO 20

_____

— — — — — — — — — —

(a) to test whether or not the course read from the DATA statement is the course requested in the INPUT statement
(b) when the course READ is not the course requested in the INPUT statement

22. Modify the program in frame 20 so it will print the message "NO SUCH COURSE" instead of the data error message, indicating that the course entered by the user does not exist in the computer's information system. You might try putting a flag at the end of the regular data.

— — — — — — — — — —

Add these statements (or ones similar to them).

```
25 IF A$ = "END" THEN PRINT "NO SUCH COURSE" : GOTO 1Ø
9Ø DATA END,Ø,END
```

Remember, the end-of-data signal must contain a string, followed by a numeric value, followed by a string, because the READ statement calls for three variables at once.

23. It's your turn. Write a program that contains the names and phone numbers of your friends and business associates that you would like to "retrieve" using your computer. When you type in a name, the computer should respond with the correct phone number, as shown below.

```
NAME? ADAM OZ

ADAM OZ        415-555-2222

NAME? JUDY WIL

JUDY WIL       112-555-ØØ75

NAME? JERRY
NAME NOT IN FILE
```

— — — — — — — — — —

```
1 REMARK***STRING TELEPHONE RETRIEVAL SYSTEM
10 INPUT "NAME"; N$
20 RESTORE
30 READ D$,T$ : IF N$ = D$ THEN PRINT : PRINT D$,T$ : PRINT : GOTO 10
35 IF D$ = "END" THEN PRINT "NAME NOT IN FILE" : GOTO 10
40 GOTO 30
50 DATA TONY BOD, 415-555-8117
60 DATA MARY JAY, 213-555-0144
70 DATA MARY MMM, 213-555-1212
80 DATA JUDY WIL, 112-555-0075
90 DATA ADAM OZ, 415-555-2222
100 DATA BOBBY ALL, 312-555-1667
110 DATA END, END
```

24.   Next, we will show you some new functions that allow you to manipulate and examine parts of strings, called *substrings*. The rules for these functions get a little complicated so we suggest that you do all the exercises in
this section but don't worry about memorizing the rules. Once you have a
good general idea about how they work, you can always look back to this
section to recall the exact rules.

The MID$ function will cause the computer to produce part of a string
beginning with a specified character. Thus, MID$(A$,N) will give you that
part of the string A$ beginning with character number N and continuing to
the end of the string. For example, if A$ is HELLO, then H is character 1,
E is character 2, and so on. If N is 4, then the statement PRINT MID$(A$,N)
tells the computer to print the substring starting with character 4 and continuing to the end of the string. In this case the computer will print LO.

Here is a demonstration program. Remember, a space is counted as one
character.

```
10 LET A$ = "MY HUMAN UNDERSTANDS ME"
20 PRINT MID$(A$,10)

RUN
UNDERSTANDS ME
```

Replace line 20 with PRINT MID$(A$,15). What will be printed when the
new line 20 is RUN?_____

— — — — — — — — — —

STANDS ME

25.   Now let's look at some more examples of the MID$ function. To iso-
late one character, you need to use two values in the MID$ function. The
first numeric value in the parentheses tells the computer where to start the
substring, just as before. The second numeric value tells the computer how
many characters beyond the starting point to include in the substring. Thus,
to isolate and print just one character in a substring, the second numeric
value in the parentheses would be one (1). Here's a sample program and
RUN.

```
10 LET A$ = "MY HUMAN UNDERSTANDS ME"
20 PRINT MID$(A$,4,1)

RUN
H
```

In the example below, we print a substring that starts at character 1 and continues through character 8 (inclusive).

```
10 LET A$ = "MY HUMAN UNDERSTANDS ME"
20 PRINT MID$(A$,1,8)

RUN
MY HUMAN
```

Suppose we change line 20 above to read 20 PRINT MID$(A$,4,8). What
will be printed when the new line 20 is executed? _____

— — — — — — — — — — —

HUMAN

26.   What will be printed by the following program?

```
20 LET A$ = "GAMES COMPUTERS PLAY"
30 PRINT MID$(A$,7,9), MID$(A$,17), MID$(A$,1,5)

RUN
```

_____

— — — — — — — — — —

```
RUN

COMPUTERS      PLAY           GAMES
```

Notice that the second MID$ function in the program does not specify how
many characters to print, because it will automatically print to the end of
the string A$.

27. Here are parts of a program to PRINT the string variable A$ backwards, one character at a time. Fill in the blanks and show the RUN.

```
10 LET A$ = "ABCDEFGHIJKLMNOPQRSTUVWXYZ"
20 FOR X = _____ TO _____ STEP −1
30 PRINT MID$(A$, _____, _____);
40 _____
```

— — — — — — — — —

```
20 FOR X = 26 TO 1 STEP −1
30 PRINT MID$(A$,X,1);
40 NEXT X
RUN
ZYXWVUTSRQPONMLKJIHGFEDCBA
```

28. Let's go all the way back to frame 9 of Chapter 1 and change our number guessing game to a *letter* guessing game. Here's the old program. All its logic should still apply.

```
100 REMARK***THIS IS A SIMPLE COMPUTER GAME
110 LET X = INT(100*RND(1))+1
120 PRINT
130 PRINT "I'M THINKING OF A NUMBER FROM 1 TO 100."
140 PRINT "GUESS MY NUMBER!!!"
150 PRINT : INPUT "YOUR GUESS"; G
160 IF G<X THEN PRINT "TRY A BIGGER NUMBER" : GOTO 150
170 IF G>X THEN PRINT "TRY A SMALLER NUMBER" : GOTO 150
180 IF G=X THEN PRINT "THAT'S IT!!! YOU GUESSED MY NUMBER." : GOTO 110
```

We should first add line 105, a LET statement with all the letters of the alphabet.

105 _____

— — — — — — — — —

```
105 LET A$ = "ABCDEFGHIJKLMNOPQRSTUVWXYZ"
```

29. Now change line 110 to randomly select a number between 1 and 26.

110 _____

— — — — — — — — —

```
110 LET X = INT(26*RND(1))+1
```

30. Let's place our selected choice into X\$.

115 LET X\$ = _____

— — — — — — — — — —

```
115 LET X$ = MID$(A$,X,1)
```

31. You complete lines 140 and 150.

130 PRINT "I'M THINKING OF A LETTER FROM A TO Z"

140 _____

150 _____

— — — — — — — — — —

```
140 PRINT "GUESS MY LETTER!!!"
150 PRINT : INPUT "YOUR GUESS"; G$
```

32. Change lines 160, 170, and 180 as necessary. RUN your new game.

160 _____

170 _____

180 _____

— — — — — — — — — —

Here's the entire LIST and on the following page is a RUN.

```
100 REMARK***THIS IS A SIMPLE COMPUTER GAME
105 LET A$ = "ABCDEFGHIJKLMNOPQRSTUVWXYZ"
110 LET X = INT(26*RND(1))+1
115 LET X$ = MID$(A$,X,1)
120 PRINT
130 PRINT "I'M THINKING OF A LETTER FROM A TO Z"
140 PRINT "GUESS MY LETTER!!!"
150 PRINT : INPUT"YOUR GUESS"; G$
160 IF G$<X$ THEN PRINT "TRY A BIGGER LETTER." : GOTO 150
170 IF G$>X$ THEN PRINT "TRY A SMALLER LETTER." : GOTO 150
180 IF G$=X$ THEN PRINT "THAT'S IT!!! YOU GUESSED MY LETTER." : GOTO 110
```

```
RUN
I'M THINKING OF A LETTER FROM A TO Z
GUESS MY LETTER!!!

YOUR GUESS? L
TRY A SMALLER LETTER.

YOUR GUESS? G
TRY A BIGGER LETTER.

YOUR GUESS? H
TRY A BIGGER LETTER.

YOUR GUESS? K
TRY A SMALLER LETTER.

YOUR GUESS? I
TRY A BIGGER LETTER.

YOUR GUESS? J
THAT'S IT!!! YOU GUESSED MY LETTER.
```

33. You can manipulate the left and right portion of a string using the LEFT\$ and RIGHT\$ functions. It's really not all that complicated. Complete the RUN below.

```
10 LET A$ = "ABCDEFGHIJKLMNOPQRSTUVWXYZ"
20 PRINT LEFT$(A$,5) ◄─────── Print the leftmost 5 characters of A$.
30 PRINT RIGHT$(A$,5) ◄─────── Print the rightmost 5 characters of A$.
RUN

ABCDE
```

————————————————————————

— — — — — — — — — —

VWXYZ (In practice we have found many more uses for MID\$ than for LEFT\$ and RIGHT\$.)

34. Using the data from the program in frame 23, write a program that will print a list of phone numbers of people whose first name begins with the letter M.

```
RUN
MARY JAY       213-555-0144
MARY MMM       213-555-1212
?OD ERROR IN 30
```

— — — — — — — — — —

```
1 REMARK***STRING TELEPHONE DIRECTORY
20 RESTORE
30 READ D$,T$ : IF LEFT$(D$,1) = "M" THEN PRINT D$,T$ : GOTO 30
40 GOTO 30
50 DATA TONY BOD,415-555-8117
60 DATA MARY JAY,213-555-0144
70 DATA MARY MMM,213-555-1212
80 DATA JUDY WIL,112-555-0075
90 DATA ADAM OZ,415-555-2222
100 DATA BOBBY ALL,312-555-1667
110 DATA END,999
```

35. Modify your program in frame 34 so that the computer will print telephone numbers and names located in area code 415 (you are going there for a visit and want to call old friends).

```
RUN
415-555-8117   TONY BOD
415-555-2222   ADAM OZ
?OD ERROR IN 30
```

— — — — — — — — — —

```
1 REMARK***STRING TELEPHONE DIRECTORY
20 RESTORE
30 READ D$,T$ : IF LEFT$(T$,3) <> "415" THEN 30
40 PRINT T$,D$ : GOTO 30
50 DATA TONY BOD,415-555-8117
60 DATA MARY JAY,213-555-0144
70 DATA MARY MMM,213-555-1212
80 DATA JUDY WIL,112-555-0075
90 DATA ADAM OZ,415-555-2222
100 DATA BOBBY ALL,312-555-1667
110 DATA END,999
```

36. On some, but not all, home computers, you will be able to use the INSTR function (normally called IN STRING). The INSTR function is used to search for the location of one substring within a string. For example, if we wanted to find the word UNDER in the sentence MY COMPUTER UNDERSTANDS ME, we could use the program on the following page.

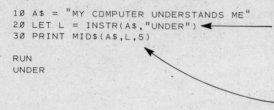

```
10 A$ = "MY COMPUTER UNDERSTANDS ME"
20 LET L = INSTR(A$,"UNDER")
30 PRINT MID$(A$,L,5)

RUN
UNDER
```

Search the contents of string variable A$ for the substring found in quotes. Place the beginning character location in variable L.

Print contents of A$ beginning with character number L.

What if UNDER did not exist in string variable A$? The computer would place the number zero (0) into variable L indicating the substring was not found. Add line 25 to the program above to test to see if L equals 0. If yes, the program should print CANNOT FIND WORD and stop, rather than continue to line 30 which would print the wrong information.

25 _____

— — — — — — — — — —

```
25 IF L = 0 THEN PRINT "CANNOT FIND WORD" : STOP
```

37.   The INSTR function can also search one string variable attempting to match the contents of another string variable. Here is an example.

```
10 LET A$ = "MY COMPUTER UNDERSTANDS ME"
20 LET B$ = "STAND"
30 LET T = INSTR(A$,B$)         B$ used instead of "STAND"
40 IF T = 0 THEN END
50 PRINT MID$(A$,T,5)

RUN
STAND
```

Examine this program carefully. What will be printed?

```
10 LET A$ = "MY COMPUTER UNDERSTANDS ME"
20 LET B$ = "U"
30 LET T = INSTR(A$,B$)
40 IF T = 0 THEN END
50 PRINT MID$(A$,T,11)

RUN
```

_____

— — — — — — — — — —

UTER UNDERS (The INSTR function seeks the *first* match. User beware . . . .)

38.   You can use the INSTR function for checking answers to questions, to "edit" responses, and a host of other things. Here is a testing program for

you to complete. The program asks a question, requests a user response, and then checks the answer and makes an appropriate remark. Fill in the missing parts.

```
10 REMARK***US HISTORY TEST
20 INPUT "WHO WAS THE FIRST PRESIDENT OF THE US"; A$

30 LET A = INSTR(_____, _____)

40 IF A = _____ THEN PRINT "YOUR ANSWER IS WRONG" : END
50 PRINT "CORRECT"
```

— — — — — — — — — —

```
30 LET A = INSTR(A$,"WASHINGTON")
40 IF A = Ø THEN PRINT "YOUR ANSWER IS WRONG" : END
```

39. Using the answers for frame 38, if the user answered WASHINGTON IRVING to the question, what will the computer print? _____

— — — — — — — — — —

CORRECT (We only tested for WASHINGTON. Think of what might happen if we only tested for WASH—even WASHING MACHINE would qualify for a correct answer!)

40. Sometimes we need to know the length of the contents of a string variable (how many characters). And, of course, BASIC has a special function, LEN, to help you find the answer. LEN(A$) will tell you the number of characters including blanks in the string A$. Here are some examples.

```
10 LET A = LEN(A$)
20 PRINT LEN(C$)
30 IF LEN(A$)<>LEN(B$) . . .
```

If your computer does not have the INSTR function, you can use the MID$ and LEN($) functions to accomplish the same purpose. Using the problem from frame 39, here's the same activity without INSTR.

```
20 INPUT "WHO WAS THE FIRST PRESIDENT OF THE US"; A$
30 FOR X = 1 TO LEN(A$)-9
40 IF MID$(A$,X,10) = "WASHINGTON" THEN PRINT "CORRECT" : END
50 NEXT X
60 PRINT "YOUR ANSWER IS WRONG"
```

How will *this* program respond to the answer WASHINGTON IRVING?

_____

— — — — — — — — — —

CORRECT (Again! We didn't solve that problem.)

41. The LEN function can be used to "edit" data entered by users that might have to be a certain size, and no bigger because of forms you use or because of the size of your computer memory. Examine the example below and answer the questions which follow.

```
10 INPUT "ENTER YOUR NAME"; N$
20 IF LEN(N$)>20 THEN PRINT "LIMIT YOUR NAME TO 20 CHARACTERS PLEASE":GOTO 10
30 INPUT "ENTER YOUR ADDRESS"; A$
40 IF LEN(A$)>15 THEN PRINT "PLEASE ABBREVIATE YOUR ADDRESS":GOTO 30
```

How many characters are allowed for name? _____ For address? _____

— — — — — — — — — —

20; 15

SELF-TEST

Try this Self-Test, so you can evaluate how much you have learned so far.

1. Write a program to permit INPUT of a 5-letter word and then print the word backwards.

2. Write a program to read a series of 4-letter words from DATA statements and print only those words that begin with the letter A.

3. Modify the program in question 2 to print only words that begin with A and end with S.

4. Some years ago, the auto industry was hard-pressed to come up with names for new cars. They used a computer to generate a series of 5-letter words. Write a program to generate 100 5-letter words with randomly selected consonants in the first and third and fifth places and randomly selected vowels in the second and fourth places.

5. You have the following DATA statements containing names in last-name-first order. Write a program to print these names first-name-first without the comma.

```
9000 DATA "BUTLER, LINDA", "OLIVER, RACHELLE"
9010 DATA "DANIELS, JAMES", "JOHNSON, DIANE"
9020 DATA "CASH, BETTY", END
```

Answers to Self-Test

The frame numbers in parentheses refer to the frames in the chapter where the topic is discussed. You may wish to refer back to these for quick review.

1.
```
10 REMARK STRING SELF-TEST 9-1
20 INPUT A$
30 FOR X = 5 TO 1 STEP -1 : PRINT MID$(A$,X,1); : NEXT X
40 PRINT : GOTO 20
```

(frames 25-27)

2.
```
10 REMARK STRING SELF-TEST 9-2
20 READ A$ : IF LEFT$(A$,1) <> "A" THEN 20
30 PRINT A$ : GOTO 20
40 DATA ANTS,GNATS,LOVE,BALD,APES
50 DATA BAKE,MIKE,KARL,BARD,ALAS
```

(frame 33)

3.
```
20 READ A$ : IF RIGHT$(A$,1) <> "S" THEN 20
25 IF LEFT$(A$,1) <> "A" THEN 20
```
(frame 33)

4.
```
1 REMARK STRING SELF-TEST 9-4
10 LET A$ = "AEIOU"
20 LET B$ = "BCDFGHJKLMNPQRSTVWXYZ"
25 FOR X = 1 TO 100
30 FOR Z = 1 TO 2
40 LET B = INT(21*RND(1))+1
50 PRINT MID$(B$,B,1);
60 LET A = INT(5*RND(1))+1
70 PRINT MID$(A$,A,1);
75 NEXT Z
80 LET B = INT(21*RND(1))+1
90 PRINT MID$(B$,B,1),
95 NEXT X
```

(frames 25 and 33)

5.
```
1 REMARK STRING SELF-TEST 9-5
20 READ N$ : IF N$ = "END" THEN END
30 FOR X = 1 TO 20 : IF MID$(N$,X,1) = "," THEN 40
35 NEXT X : GOTO 20
40 PRINT MID$(N$,X+1),LEFT$(N$,X-1)
50 GOTO 20
9000 DATA "BUTLER,LINDA","OLIVER, RACHELLE"
9010 DATA "DANIELS, JAMES","JOHNSON, DIANE"
9020 DATA "CASH, BETTY",END

RUN
 LINDA       BUTLER
 RACHELLE    OLIVER
 JAMES       DANIELS
 DIANE       JOHNSON
 BETTY       CASH

BREAK IN 20
```

(frames 25 and 33)

CHAPTER TEN

Subroutines

We're heading down the home stretch. This chapter deals with things that you can live without but are sure nice to have when you need them. We're about to enter the realm of programs within programs, called *subroutines*. Subroutines let you organize computer programs for easy use by breaking them down into functional parts that may be reused in other programs when needed.

When you complete this chapter, you will be able to design programs in subroutine format, write appropriate main programs to access subroutines, and be able to use the following BASIC statements.

    GOSUB
    RETURN
    STOP

1.   In this book we have worked with two computer program building processes. The first method was analogous to remodeling: the modification of an existing program. The second was building a program from the ground up. Now let us try building with prefabricated parts. This technique is handy for organizing a program according to the function performed by a group of one or more statements.

The prefabricated sections, or groups of statements, are called *subroutines*. The statement that tells a computer to go to a subroutine is, appropriately enough, the GOSUB statement. Like the GOTO statement, it is followed by a line number that corresponds to the first statement in the subroutine.

    20 GOSUB 100   means skip to the subroutine in this program that
                    has 100 as the line number of its first statement

The last statement in a subroutine is the RETURN statement. It automatically causes the computer to RETURN to the main program, that is, to the line number immediately following the GOSUB statement that originally "called up" the subroutine. For example, the subroutine at line 100 in the following program was "called" by line 20. After executing the subroutine, the last statement the computer encounters is 130 RETURN. This tells the computer to return to line 30, the line after the statement that originally called the subroutine. Look at this demonstration program to see how GOSUB and RETURN statements work.

```
5 REMARK HOW GOSUB AND RETURN WORK
10 REMARK MAIN PROGRAM
20 GOSUB 100
30 GOSUB 200
40 GOSUB 300
50 PRINT "THIS IS THE END OF THE MAIN PROGRAM."
60 STOP

100 REMARK SUBROUTINE #1 STARTS HERE
110 PRINT "THIS IS SUBROUTINE #1 (OR 100)."
120 PRINT
130 RETURN

200 REMARK SUBROUTINE #2 STARTS HERE
210 PRINT "THIS LINE COURTESY OF SUBROUTINE #2 (OR 200)."
220 PRINT
230 RETURN

300 REMARK SUBROUTINE #3 STARTS HERE
310 PRINT "SUBROUTINE #3 (OR 300 IF YOU PREFER) AT YOUR SERVICE."
320 PRINT
330 RETURN

RUN
THIS IS SUBROUTINE #1 (OR 100).

THIS LINE COURTESY OF SUBROUTINE #2 (OR 200).

SUBROUTINE #3 (OR 300 IF YOU PREFER) AT YOUR SERVICE.

THIS IS THE END OF THE MAIN PROGRAM.
```

Examine the program and the RUN. To demonstrate your understanding of how the computer goes from the main program (lines 5 to 60) to the subroutine and back again to the main program, list the line numbers in the order in which the computer executes them in running this program.

_____

_____

— — — — — — — — — —

5, 10, 20, 100, 110, 120, 130, 30, 200, 210, 220, 230, 40, 300, 310, 320, 330, 50, 60

2.   There are two helpful statements that may be used in conjunction with GOSUB and RETURN. These are the STOP and END statements. Either may be used at the end of a main program. If you use STOP in our version

of BASIC, the computer tells you the line number where it encountered the STOP with the message BREAK IN 60. If you use END, the computer merely gives you the message OK to indicate that it has finished the RUN.

If we did not have a STOP or END statement as the last statement in the main program in frame 1, what would the computer execute next after

RETURNing from the last subroutine called? _____

_____

– – – – – – – – – –

The computer would execute line 100 and the rest of the subroutine in line number order on through the program, or terminate with an error message when it encountered a RETURN and did not know where to RETURN to.

3. Below, we have modified a portion of just the main program of the program in frame 1. (No subroutines are changed.) Notice how these modifications change the printout of the RUN.

```
20 GOSUB 300
30 GOSUB 100
40 GOSUB 200

RUN
SUBROUTINE #3 (OR 300 IF YOU PREFER) AT YOUR SERVICE.

THIS IS SUBROUTINE #1 (OR 100).

THIS LINE COURTESY OF SUBROUTINE #2 (OR 200).

THIS IS THE END OF THE MAIN PROGRAM.
```

Here is another modification of the main program. (Subroutines remain as they were in frame 1.) What will the computer type when the program is RUN?

```
5 REMARK HOW GOSUB AND RETURN WORK
10 REMARK MAIN PROGRAM
20 GOSUB 100
50 PRINT "THIS IS THE END OF THE MAIN PROGRAM"
60 STOP

RUN
```

– – – – – – – – – –

```
RUN
THIS IS SUBROUTINE #1 (OR 100).

THIS IS THE END OF THE MAIN PROGRAM.
```

4.   Now try this one. What will the computer print when the program is RUN? (Subroutines remain as they were in frame 1.)

```
5 REMARK HOW GOSUB AND RETURN WORK
10 REMARK MAIN PROGRAM
20 GOSUB 100
30 GOSUB 100
40 GOSUB 100
50 PRINT "THIS IS THE END OF THE MAIN PROGRAM."
60 STOP

RUN
```

— — — — — — — — —

```
RUN
THIS IS SUBROUTINE #1 (OR 100).

THIS IS SUBROUTINE #1 (OR 100).

THIS IS SUBROUTINE #1 (OR 100).

THIS IS THE END OF THE MAIN PROGRAM.
```

5.   Below is a listing of the CANDY BAR & JELLY BEAN COUNTER program which you developed in Chapters 7 and 8.

```
100 REM***CANDY BAR & JELLY BEAN COUNTER
110 REM***INITIALIZE
120 DIM A(8,2) : FOR X=0 TO 8. : FOR Y=0 TO 2 : A(X,Y)=0 : NEXT Y,X
200 REM***READ DATA AND TEST FOR FLAG
210 READ K,C,Q : IF K=-1 THEN 310
220 A(K,C)=A(K,C)+Q : GOTO 210
300 REM***TOTAL OF UNITS SOLD AND TOTAL OF SALES IN DOLLARS
310 FOR K=1 TO 8
320 A(K,0) = A(K,1)*1.00 + A(K,2)*.50
330 A(0,0) = A(0,0)+A(K,0)
340 FOR C=1 TO 2
350 A(0,C) = A(0,C) + A(K,C)
360 NEXT C
370 NEXT K
380 REM***CALCULATE PROFITS
390 P1=A(0,1)*.55 : P2=A(0,2)*.30 : P=P1+P2
400 REM***REPORT VERSION #2
410 PRINT "KID ID NO.", "TOTAL $", "CHOCOLATE", "JELLY BEANS"
420 FOR K=1 TO 8
430 PRINT K,
440 FOR C=0 TO 2
450 PRINT A(K,C),
460 NEXT C
470 PRINT
480 NEXT K
490 PRINT
500 PRINT "TOTALS:", A(0,0), A(0,1), A(0,2)
510 PRINT
520 PRINT "PROFITS:", P, P1, P2
900 REM***KID ID NUMBER, CANDY ID NUMBER, QUANTITY
910 DATA 4,1,3, 4,2,6
920 DATA 5,1,6, 5,2,8, 2,1,3, 2,2,0, 8,1,6, 8,2,12
930 DATA -1,-1,-1
```

(a) How many times is the section beginning at line 200 processed when the program is RUN? _____

(b) How many times are the sections beginning at line 300 and 400 processed when the program is RUN? _____

— — — — — — — — — —

(a) nine times, once for each set of data. However, once the computer has finished reading all the data, it does not return to this section of the program again during the same RUN.

(b) once each

6.   As an exercise in the use of GOSUBs, modify the program in frame 5 to subroutine format. All subroutines should be "called up" by statements in the *main program only*. Show your modifications on the following page.

Note: Checkmarks indicate added or modified lines. A RUN is included just to convince you that the program functions properly.

```
 100 REM***CANDY BAR & JELLY BEAN COUNTER
✓101 GOSUB 110
✓102 GOSUB 200
✓103 GOSUB 300
✓104 GOSUB 400
✓105 END
 110 REM***INITIALIZE
 120 DIM A(8,2) : FOR X=0 TO 8 : FOR Y=0 TO 2 : A(X,Y)=0 : NEXT Y,X
✓130 RETURN
 200 REM***READ DATA AND TEST FOR FLAG
✓210 READ K,C,Q : IF K=-1 THEN RETURN
 220 LET A(K,C) = A(K,C)+Q : GOTO 210
 300 REM***TOTAL OF UNITS SOLD AND TOTAL OF SALES IN DOLLARS
 310 FOR K=1 TO 8
 320 LET A(K,0) = A(K,1)*1.00 + A(K,2)*.50
 330 LET A(0,0) = A(0,0) + A(K,0)
 340 FOR C=1 TO 2
 350 LET A(0,C) = A(0,C) + A(K,C)
 360 NEXT C
 370 NEXT K
 380 REM***CALCULATE PROFITS
✓390 LET P1 = A(0,1)*.55 : LET P2 = A(0,2)*.30 : P=P1+P2 : RETURN
 400 REM***REPORT VERSION #2
 410 PRINT "KID ID NO.", "TOTAL $", "CHOCOLATE", "JELLY BEANS"
 420 FOR K=1 TO 8
 430 PRINT K,
 440 FOR C=0 TO 2
 450 PRINT A(K,C),
 460 NEXT C
 470 PRINT
 480 NEXT K
 490 PRINT
 500 PRINT "TOTALS:", A(0,0), A(0,1), A(0,2)
 510 PRINT
 520 PRINT "PROFITS:", P, P1, P2
✓530 RETURN
 900 REM***KID ID NUMBER, CANDY ID NUMBER, QUANTITY
 910 DATA 4,1,3, 4,2,6
 920 DATA 5,1,6, 5,2,8, 2,1,3, 2,2,0, 8,1,6, 8,2,12
 930 DATA -1,-1,-1

RUN
```

KID ID NO.	TOTAL $	CHOCOLATE	JELLY BEANS
1	0	0	0
2	3	3	0
3	0	0	0
4	6	3	6
5	10	6	8
6	0	0	0
7	0	0	0
8	12	6	12
TOTALS:	31	18	26
PROFITS:	17.7	9.9	7.8

7. Here is a good practical problem that lends itself well to using subroutines. It's a number sorting process. We want to sort a series of numbers. For demonstration purposes, let's limit the number of values to be sorted to

50. You may want to increase the number of values to be sorted for your purposes; the exact size limit possible will depend on your computer's memory size. Our first subroutine should ask the user how many numbers are to be sorted and then initialize an array of that size (don't forget to DIMension the array). Here's a RUN of the first subroutine.

```
RUN
HOW MANY NUMBERS IN THE TEST TO BE SORTED? 8
```

The main program begins like this.

```
100 REM***NUMBER SORTING PROGRAM
110 GOSUB 400
```

Complete the subroutine below:

400 REM***INITIALIZING SUBROUTINE

— — — — — — — — — —

```
400 REM***INITIALIZING SUBROUTINE
410 INPUT "HOW MANY NUMBERS IN THE TEST TO BE SORTED"; N
420 DIM X(N) : FOR Z=1 TO N : LET X(Z) = 0 : NEXT Z
430 RETURN
```

8.   Next, we need a subroutine to enter N numbers into array X. You may want to use INPUT, or READ from DATA statements, that's up to you. For our demonstration program, we have decided to use randomly generated integer numbers between 1 and 100. Here is the main program so far.

```
100 REM***NUMBER SORTING PROGRAM
110 GOSUB 400
120 GOSUB 500
```

Complete the next subroutine by filling in the blanks.

```
500 REM***DATA ENTRY SUBROUTINE
510 FOR Z=_____ :LET X(Z)=INT(100*RND(1)+1):_____
520 _____
```

— — — — — — — — —

```
500 REM***DATA ENTRY SUBROUTINE
510 FOR Z=1 TO N : LET X(Z) = INT(100*RND(1)+1) : NEXT Z
520 RETURN
```

9.   Now write a subroutine to produce the printout below. You write a program segment to produce a similar RUN.

```
RUN
HOW MANY NUMBERS IN THE TEST TO BE SORTED? 8
UNSORTED RANDOM NUMBERS:     81          100          16
  63            4             44          22           55
```

Here is the main program so far.

```
100 REM***NUMBER SORTING PROGRAM
110 GOSUB 400
120 GOSUB 500
130 GOSUB 600
```

Complete the subroutine below.

```
600 REM***SUBROUTINE TO PRINT UNSORTED LIST

610 _____

620 _____

630 _____
```

— — — — — — — — — —

```
600 REM***SUBROUTINE TO PRINT UNSORTED LIST
610 PRINT "UNSORTED RANDOM NUMBERS:",
620 FOR Z=1 TO N : PRINT X(Z), : NEXT Z : PRINT
630 RETURN
```

10.   The subroutine at line 700 is the really big one. It arranges the numbers in the array into ascending order. We don't think you're ready to write this one yet so here it is. We'll go over it together.

```
700 REM***SUBROUTINE TO SORT NUMBERS IN ASCENDING ORDER
710 FOR K=1 TO N-1
720 FOR J=K+1 TO N
730 IF X(K) <= X(J) THEN 770
740 T = X(K)
750 X(K) = X(J)
760 X(J) = T
770 NEXT J
780 NEXT K
790 RETURN
```

Fill in the blanks here. This method of sorting eventually places the smallest value in position $X(1)$ of the array and the largest value in $X(\underline{})$. Between these two elements are the other numbers arranged in order. This is accomplished by comparing pairs of numbers located in contiguous array elements, one pair at a time and interchanging the two numbers wherever possible. In which statement(s) are the 2 numbers compared? _____

— — — — — — — — — —

_____ _____

X(N); 730

11. Referring to frame 10, answer the following question. If the first two array elements are compared, and if the content (value) of X(2) is less than that of X(1), then what happens? _____

— — — — — — — — — — —

X(2) and X(1) are interchanged so that X(1) will be less than X(2).

12. What variable temporarily holds the value of X(1) so that it can later be assigned to X(2), when X(1) is larger than X(2)? _____

— — — — — — — — — — —

T in line 740

13. Examine the two FOR-NEXT loops that begin in lines 710 and 720. Starting with the first element of the array, the computer will compare its value to all the remaining values in the array, and will exchange values where needed. The first time through the loops, the value of FOR-NEXT loop control variable K is 1. The value of control variable J = K + 1 = 1 + 1 = 2. So X(1) is compared to X(2) in line 730. If the value of X(1) is less than or equal to X(2), then by branching to line 770 NEXT J, the computer is ready to compare X(1) to X(3). If the comparison X(1) <= X(3) is false, then the values of X(1) and X(3) are exchanged, and the computer continues to compare the new value of X(1) to the rest of the values in the array to see if any smaller ones are encountered that should go into the X(1) position.

   Look again at line 730. How is the computer instructed to compare only the array elements with *subscripts* larger than X(K)? _____

_____

_____

— — — — — — — — — — —

The second FOR-NEXT loop's control variable always starts at K + 1, so that only the elements of the array with subscripts greater than X(K) are compared.

14. Eventually, the numbers are all arranged in ascending order in array X. It's time for you to write a subroutine at line 800 to print a report like the one on the following page.

```
SORTED RANDOM NUMBERS:        4              16           22
  44              55          63             81           100
```

```
800 REM***SUBROUTINE TO PRINT SORTED LIST

810 _____

820 _____

830 _____
```

— — — — — — — — — —

```
800 REM***SUBROUTINE TO PRINT SORTED LIST
810 PRINT "SORTED RANDOM NUMBERS:",
820 FOR Z=1 TO N : PRINT X(Z), : NEXT Z : PRINT
830 RETURN
```

15. Wait just a minute! Doesn't that subroutine at line 800 look *almost* exactly like the one at line 600? Why not change the program somehow so we just use the subroutine at line 600—twice. Brilliant idea. Let's look at it.

```
130 GOSUB 600

150 GOSUB 800

600 REM***SUBROUTINE TO PRINT UNSORTED LIST
610 PRINT "UNSORTED RANDOM NUMBERS:",
620 FOR Z=1 TO N : PRINT X(Z), : NEXT Z : PRINT
630 RETURN

800 REM***SUBROUTINE TO PRINT SORTED LIST
810 PRINT "SORTED RANDOM NUMBERS:",
820 FOR Z=1 TO N : PRINT X(Z), : NEXT Z : PRINT
830 RETURN
```

If we change line 130 to say

130 PRINT "UNSORTED ";: GOSUB 600

What would we do to line 150?

150 _____

— — — — — — — — — —

150 PRINT "SORTED ";: GOSUB 600

16. We can now delete the entire subroutine that starts at line 800. Show how line 610 may be changed so that the RUN will still print as shown in frames 9 and 14.

610 _____

— — — — — — — — — —

610 PRINT "RANDOM NUMBERS:",

17. You have just seen another excellent use of subroutines. Whenever you have to do the same thing more than once in a program, it can be handled in a subroutine and the RETURN will send the computer back to the statement following the GOSUB statement that called the subroutine. Here's the final program and RUN.

```
100 REM***NUMBER SORTING PROGRAM
110 GOSUB 400
120 GOSUB 500
130 PRINT "UNSORTED RANDOM NUMBERS:" : GOSUB 600
140 GOSUB 700
150 PRINT "SORTED RANDOM NUMBERS:" : GOSUB 600
160 END
400 REM***INITIALIZING SUBROUTINE
410 INPUT "HOW MANY NUMBERS IN THE TEST TO BE SORTED"; N
420 DIM X(N) : FOR Z=1 TO N : LET X(Z)=0 : NEXT Z
430 RETURN
500 REM***DATA ENTRY SUBROUTINE
510 FOR Z=1 TO N : LET X(Z)=INT(100*RND(1)+1) : NEXT Z
520 RETURN
600 REM***SUBROUTINE TO PRINT LIST
610 PRINT
620 FOR Z=1 TO N : PRINT X(Z), : NEXT Z : PRINT
630 RETURN
700 REM***SUBROUTINE TO SORT NUMBERS IN ASCENDING ORDER
710 FOR K=1 TO N-1
720 FOR J=K+1 TO N
730 IF X(K)<=X(J) THEN 770
740 T=X(K)
750 X(K)=X(J)
760 X(J)=T
770 NEXT J
780 NEXT K
790 RETURN

RUN
HOW MANY NUMBERS IN THE TEST TO BE SORTED? 50
UNSORTED RANDOM NUMBERS:
 37             4             88            77            21
 61             38            23            75            26
 94             46            4             89            1
 5              28            50            75            38
 74             13            38            88            3
 21             70            5             58            72
 90             23            13            31            12
 71             79            55            29            81
 49             100           14            87            13
 10             77            43            77            99
SORTED RANDOM NUMBERS:
 1              3             4             4             5
 5              10            12            13            13
 13             14            21            21            23
 23             26            28            29            31
 37             38            38            38            43
 46             49            50            55            58
 61             70            71            72            74
 75             75            77            77            77
 79             81            87            88            88
 89             90            94            99            100
```

Why did we add line 160 to the main program? _____

_____

— — — — — — — — — —

so that the computer would not attempt to execute the subroutine sections of the program after completing the main program

18.   The next section of this chapter will take you through the process of assembling a program from subroutine blocks that can perform a variety of common statistical computations. Using subroutines, the program is conveniently organized according to functions performed; that is, each subroutine does a particular part of the statistical computations.

The statistical measures to be discussed are: mean, variance, and standard deviation.

If you are familiar with these statistical measures and wish to sharpen your programming skills, continue on in this section of text. Otherwise turn to frame 22 on page 309.

In this section you will have the opportunity to develop the computational subroutines themselves. Perhaps more important, however, you will gain skill in using subroutines as prefabricated mini (or not so mini) programs by assembling previously written subroutine units into a complete program. (To learn or review statistics, we recommend Donald J. Koosis, *Statistics*, 2nd edition, from this same series of Self-Teaching Guides published by John Wiley & Sons.)

The statistical measure used in previous examples in this book is the *average* or *mean* of values or scores obtained through some method of measurement or observation. The mean (referred to in statistics as "one measure of central tendency" of the data) is calculated by adding all the values and dividing that sum by the total number of values. In common statistical notation, the formula for the mean is as follows.

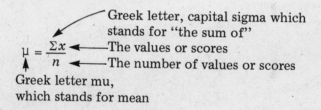

$$\mu = \frac{\Sigma x}{n}$$

Greek letter, capital sigma which stands for "the sum of"
The values or scores
The number of values or scores
Greek letter mu, which stands for mean

Each score in a set of scores lies some distance from the computed mean of the set; some scores may be just at the mean, some higher, some lower. The *variance* and its square root, the *standard deviation*, are measures of the "average" distance of all the scores in the set from the mean of the set. Statisticians call these "measures of variability (or dispersion)."

On the following page is a computational formula for finding the variance of a set of scores or values.

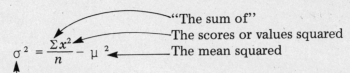

$$\sigma^2 = \frac{\Sigma x^2}{n} - \mu^2$$

"The sum of"

The scores or values squared

The mean squared

Greek letter sigma,
squared, stands for variance

The standard deviation is the square root of the variance, and in statistical notation looks like this.

$$\sigma = \sqrt{\sigma^2} = \sqrt{\frac{\Sigma x^2}{n} - \mu^2}$$

We will use the following BASIC variables in the program.

$N = n$ (number of scores or values)
$X = x$ (scores or values)
$M = \mu$ (mean)
$T = \Sigma x$ (sum or total of scores)
$D = \Sigma x^2$ (sum or total of each score squared)
$V = \sigma^2$ (variance)
$S = \sigma$ (standard deviation)

So let's get down to it. Write a subroutine to provide us with values for N, T, and D which are needed to calculate the mean and variance. The scores are provided in a DATA statement.

```
900 REMARK DATA FOLLOWS. DATA LIST ENDS WITH -1.
910 DATA 75,67,38,89,23,97,75,18,56,37,-1
```

Complete the subroutine below.

```
300 REMARK SUBROUTINE: COMPUTE N, SUM X, SUM X↑2
```

– – – – – – – – – –

```
300 REMARK SUBROUTINE: COMPUTE N, SUM X, SUM X↑2
310 LET N=0
320 LET T=0
330 LET D=0
340 READ X
350 IF X<0 THEN 399
360 LET T=T+X
370 LET D=D+X↑2
380 LET N=N+1
390 GOTO 340
399 RETURN
```

19. Circle the parts of the following formulas for which subroutine 300 calculates values.

$$\mu = \frac{\Sigma x}{n} \qquad\qquad \sigma^2 = \frac{\Sigma x^2}{n} - \mu^2$$

— — — — — — — — — —

$$\mu = \frac{\boxed{\Sigma x}}{\boxed{n}} \qquad \sigma^2 = \frac{\boxed{\Sigma x^2}}{\boxed{n}} - \mu^2$$

20. Now write a subroutine to finish the computations for the statistical measures.

```
500 REMARK SUBROUTINE: COMPUTE MEAN, VARIANCE, STD. DEV.
```

— — — — — — — — — —

```
500 REMARK SUBROUTINE: COMPUTE MEAN, VARIANCE, STD. DEV.
510 LET M=T/N
520 LET V=D/N-M↑2
530 LET S=SQR(V)
540 RETURN
```
(See pg. 330 for SQR function explanation)

21. We want a RUN of the program to look like this.

```
RUN
N = 10
MEAN = 57.5
VARIANCE = 680.85
STANDARD DEVIATION = 26.0931
```

Complete the subroutine to print the results.

```
600 REMARK SUBROUTINE: PRINT RESULTS
```

— — — — — — — — —

```
600 REMARK SUBROUTINE: PRINT RESULTS
610 PRINT "N =";N
620 PRINT "MEAN =";M
630 PRINT "VARIANCE =";V
640 PRINT "STANDARD DEVIATION =";S
650 RETURN
```

22. All you non-statisticians rejoin us here. We statisticians have written the following subroutines. A list of what the variables stand for is given in frame 18.

```
300 REMARK SUBROUTINE: COMPUTE N, SUM X, SUM X↑2
310 LET N=0
320 LET T=0
330 LET D=0
340 READ X
350 IF X<0 THEN 399
360 LET T=T+X
370 LET D=D+X↑2
380 LET N=N+1
390 GOTO 340
399 RETURN

500 REMARK SUBROUTINE: COMPUTE MEAN, VARIANCE, STD. DEV.
510 LET M=T/N
520 LET V=D/N-M↑2
530 LET S=SQR(V)
540 RETURN

600 REMARK SUBROUTINE: PRINT RESULTS
610 PRINT "N =";N
620 PRINT "MEAN =";M
630 PRINT "VARIANCE =";V
640 PRINT "STANDARD DEVIATION =";S
650 RETURN

900 REMARK DATA FOLLOWS. DATA LIST ENDS WITH -1.
910 DATA 75,67,38,89,23,97,75,18,56,37,-1

RUN
N = 10
MEAN = 57.5
VARIANCE = 680.85
STANDARD DEVIATION = 26.0931
```

Complete the main program so that the program will function as indicated in the preceding RUN.

```
100 REMARK MEAN, VARIANCE AND STANDARD DEVIATION
110 REMARK COMPUTE N, SUM OF X, SUM OF X↑2

120 _____
130 REMARK COMPUTE M, V, S

140 _____
150 REMARK PRINT RESULTS

160 _____

199 _____
```

— — — — — — — — — —

```
120 GOSUB 300
140 GOSUB 500
160 GOSUB 600
199 STOP
```

Or END (your choice).

23. Now a nice thing about subroutines is that they may easily be changed or interchanged. (Non-statisticians can skip to frame 24.) Suppose that our data contained only two values or kinds of score. For example, we could score a voter poll using the value 1 to represent an "aye" vote and the value 2 to represent "nay" or "no opinion." The scores can then be tabulated or *grouped* by listing each kind of score (X) opposite its frequency (F), the number of times that that kind of score occurred in the data. Suppose the following are the data of two kinds.

1,1,2,1,1,2,1,1,1,2,1,1,1,2,2,2,1,2,2,1

We can set up a table showing the "frequency of appearance" of each kind of data.

	X	F
Kind of data (only two possible values)	1	12
	2	8

Grouped data (two groups or kinds)

Here are the data for the computer.

```
900 REMARK GROUPED DATA FOLLOWS. DATA LIST ENDS WITH -1,-1.
910 DATA 1,12,2,8,-1,-1
```

There are 12 cases of value 1   There are 8 cases of value 2

The table below compares the formulas for mean, variance, and standard deviation for "ordinary" data versus grouped data.

Statistic	"Ordinary"	Grouped
Mean	$\mu = \dfrac{\Sigma x}{n}$	$\mu = \dfrac{\Sigma (f \cdot x)}{n}$ where $(n = \Sigma f)$
Variance	$\sigma^2 = \dfrac{\Sigma x^2}{n} - \mu^2$	$\sigma^2 = \dfrac{\Sigma (f \cdot x^2)}{n} - \mu^2$
S.D.	$\sigma = \sqrt{\sigma^2}$	$\sigma = \sqrt{\sigma^2}$

Translated into BASIC, we require values for 3 variables.

$T = \Sigma x$ or $\Sigma f \cdot x$
$D = \Sigma x^2$ or $\Sigma f \cdot x^2$
$N =$ the number of scores ($n = \Sigma f$ for grouped data)

In the DATA statement for grouped data, there are *pairs* of values: a score (X) followed by the frequency (F) of appearance of the score. There is also a double flag, which should be a programming clue for you that values are to be read in pairs. Below is a sample DATA statement.

```
900 REMARK GROUPED DATA FOLLOWS.  DATA LIST ENDS WITH -1,-1.
910 DATA 1,12,2,8,-1,-1
```

With careful reference to the formulas presented, you should be able to complete the subroutine, particularly if you worked through the earlier statistics subroutines for ordinary (ungrouped) data.

```
400 REMARK SUBROUTINE: COMPUTE N, SUM X, SUM X↑2 (GROUPED DATA)
```

```
400 REMARK SUBROUTINE: COMPUTE N, SUM X, SUM X↑2 (GROUPED DATA)
410 LET N=Ø
420 LET T=Ø
430 LET D=Ø
440 READ X,F
450 IF X<Ø THEN 499
460 LET T=T+F*X
470 LET D=D+F*X↑2
480 LET N=N+F
490 GOTO 440
499 RETURN
```

24.   Non-statisticians rejoin us here. Look at subroutine 400 in frame 23.
For which BASIC variables are values computed? _____

— — — — — — — — — — —

T, D, N (any order)

25.   Look at subroutine 500 below, from our program in frame 22.

```
500 REMARK SUBROUTINE: COMPUTE MEAN, VARIANCE, STD. DEV.
510 LET M=T/N
520 LET V=D/N−M↑2
530 LET S=SQR(V)
540 RETURN
```

What variables must have values computed previously in order for subroutine
500 to compute M, V, and S? _____

— — — — — — — — — — —

T, D, N (any order)

26.   Got the idea? Subroutine 400 for grouped data computes values for the
same variables that subroutine 300 (frame 22) computes for "ordinary"
(ungrouped) data. Therefore, merely by substituting subroutine 400 for subroutine 300 in the program you have a complete program for computing the
statistics for grouped data.

If the DATA statement for grouped data is provided, show what modification of the main program (frame 22) is needed to RUN the complete

program for grouped data. _____

— — — — — — — — — — —

Change one line in the main program: 120 GOSUB 400.

You have now finished this book. Try the Self-Test on the next page to test
your new skills. Then go on to evaluate your overall learning with the Final
Self-Test. As you use BASIC on your own computer, you may find the summary of BASIC functions provided in the Appendix useful for quick reference.

SELF-TEST

This Self-Test will consist of a single long problem. Write a program that
will give complete arithmetic drills to the user. You should offer the choice
of addition, subtraction, multiplication, or division problems. A complete
program will look something like the printed output shown below. You
should prepare the following subroutines for this program.

     Addition problem generator
     Subtraction problem generator
     Multiplication problem generator
     Division problem generator
     Random number generator
     Score-keeping routine

```
RUN
ENTER YOUR NAME? LEROY
WHICH KIND OF PROBLEMS:ADD, SUBTRACT, MULTIPLY OR DIVIDE? ADD
HOW MANY PROBLEMS? 4
HOW MANY DIGITS IN EACH NUMBER IN A PROBLEM? 1

  2 + 5 =? 7
RIGHT ON. GOOD

  4 + 6 =? 9
SORRY, WRONG ANSWER

  1 + 6 =? 7
RIGHT ON. GOOD

  8 + 2 =? 1Ø
RIGHT ON. GOOD
CONGRATULATIONS LEROY YOU HAVE COMPLETED 4 PROBLEMS
WITH A SCORE OF 3
DO YOU WANT TO DO SOME MORE? NO
```

We have allowed space for your program to be written below and on the
following page.

Answer to Self-Test

```
10 REMARK COMPLETE ARITHMETIC DRILL
20 INPUT"ENTER YOUR NAME";N$
30 INPUT"WHICH KIND OF PROBLEMS:ADD, SUBTRACT, MULTIPLY OR DIVIDE";C$
40 INPUT"HOW MANY PROBLEMS";N
50 INPUT"HOW MANY DIGITS IN EACH NUMBER IN A PROBLEM";D
60 LET R=0
100 REM SUBROUTINE SELECTION ROUTINE
110 IF MID$(C$,1,1)="A"THEN GOSUB 1000
120 IF MID$(C$,1,1)="S"THEN GOSUB 2000
130 IF MID$(C$,1,1)="M"THEN GOSUB 3000
140 IF MID$(C$,1,1)="D"THEN GOSUB 4000
200 REM PRINT RESULTS
210 PRINT"CONGRATULATIONS ";N$;" YOU HAVE COMPLETED";N;" PROBLEMS"
220 PRINT"WITH A SCORE OF ";R
230 INPUT"DO YOU WANT TO DO SOME MORE";C$
240 IF C$="YES"THEN 30
250 STOP
1000 REM SUBROUTINE FOR ADDITION
1025 FOR K=1 TO N
1010 GOSUB 5000
1020 REM PRINT PROBLEM AND REQUEST ANSWER
1030 PRINT : PRINT A;"+";B;"="
1040 INPUT C
1050 REM TEST ANSWER
1060 IF C<>A+B THEN PRINT"SORRY, WRONG ANSWER" : GOTO 1100
1070 GOSUB 6000
1080 PRINT"RIGHT ON. GOOD"
1100 NEXT K
1110 RETURN
2000 REM SUBROUTINE FOR SUBTRACTION PROBLEMS
2005 FOR K=1 TO N
2010 GOSUB 5000
2020 REM PRINT PROBLEM
2030 PRINT : PRINT A;"-";B;"=";
2040 INPUT C
2050 REM TEST ANSWER
2060 IF C<>A-B THEN PRINT"SORRY, WRONG ANSWER" : GOTO 2100
2070 GOSUB 6000
2080 PRINT"GOOD ANSWER"
2100 NEXT K
2110 RETURN
3000 REMARK SUBROUTINE FOR MULTIPLICATION
3005 FOR K=1 TO N
3010 GOSUB 5000
```

continued on the next page

```
3020 REM PRINT PROBLEM
3030 PRINT : PRINT A;"*";B;"=";
3040 INPUT C
3050 REM TEST ANSWER
3060 IF C<>A*B THEN PRINT"SORRY, WRONG ANSWER" : GOTO 3105
3070 GOSUB 6000
3080 PRINT"GOOD ANSWER"
3100 NEXT K
3110 RETURN
4000 REMARK SUBROUTINE FOR DIVISION
4005 FOR K=1 TO N
4010 GOSUB 5000
4020 REM PRINT PROBLEM
4030 PRINT : PRINT A;"/";B;"=";
4040 INPUT C
4050 REM TEST ANSWER
4060 IF C<>A/B THEN PRINT"NO GOOD" : GOTO 4100
4070 GOSUB 6000
4080 PRINT"NICE ANSWER"
4100 NEXT K
4110 RETURN
5000 REMARK SUBROUTINE TO GENERATE NUMBERS
5010 LET A=INT(10↑D*RND(1)) : IF A<10↑D/10-1 THEN 5010
5020 LET B=INT(10↑D*RND(1)) : IF B<10↑D/10-1 THEN 5020
5030 RETURN
6000 REM SUBROUTINE TO KEEP SCORE
6010 LET R=R+1
6020 RETURN
```

} See additional solutions pg. 181

Final Self-Test

Now that you're done with the book, try this final examination to test all your skills. The answers follow the test. Use separate paper for your programs and calculations.

1.   STARS is a number guessing game that was first published in *People's Computer Company* newspaper. It's fun to use with players of all ages and you should find it challenging to program as well.

Here are the rules typed by the computer. You don't have to include them in your program.

> "I will think of a whole number from 1 to 100. Try to guess my number. After you guess my number, I will type one or more stars (*). The closer you are to my number, the more stars I will type. One star (*) means you are far away from my number. Seven stars (*******) means you are very, very close to my number!!"

Logic: If the guess is 64 or more away, one star; 32-63 away, two stars; 16-31 away, 3 stars; 8-15 away; 4 stars; 4-7 away, 5 stars; 2-3 away, 6 stars; 1 away, 7 stars. You will need to use the absolute value function, something new to you but easy to use.

Clues: ABS(10) = 10
          ABS(−10) = 10
          IF ABS(X−Y) = 10 THEN 100

```
RUN
ENTER YOUR GUESS? 1Ø
**
ENTER YOUR GUESS? 25
***
ENTER YOUR GUESS? 5Ø
******
ENTER YOUR GUESS? 6Ø
****
ENTER YOUR GUESS? 45
******
ENTER YOUR GUESS? 42
*****
ENTER YOUR GUESS? 47
*******
ENTER YOUR GUESS? 48
WINNER!!!
```

2.   You may have used matrix commands on some other computer. (Matrix is just another name for array.) Versions of BASIC for home computers generally do not include matrix commands. However, they are easy to simulate. Try it.

You have two 5 by 3 arrays called A and B, filled with small numbers that are read into the elements or boxes in the array from DATA statements. Write a program to add the contents of each element in array A to the corresponding element in array B, and place the results in the proper place in a third array, C.

A

7	8	9
3	4	1
6	8	2
1	4	1
8	10	2

B

3	6	8
2	4	7
1	3	1
8	4	9
6	6	6

C

10	14	17
5	8	8
7	11	3
9	8	10
14	16	8

Example: A(1,1) + B(1,1) = C(1,1)
A(1,2) + B(1,2) = C(1,2) etc.

```
RUN
A ARRAY CONTENTS

   7              8              9
   3              4              1
   6              8              2
   1              4              1
   8             10              2


B ARRAY CONTENTS

   3              6              8
   2              4              7
   1              3              1
   8              4              9
   6              6              6


C ARRAY CONTENTS

  10             14             17
   5              8              8
   7             11              3
   9              8             10
  14             16              8
```

3.   Your child plans to set up a weekend sidewalk stand selling "junk" from around the house (also known as a garage sale). Your youngster has no trouble finding merchandise and no trouble pricing it. But he or she really doesn't understand the money system and is worried about making change when people buy these "goods."

Write a program to allow the child to enter the amount of the sale and the amount of money received, and have the computer then print exactly how much and what kind of change to give back. The RUN is shown below.

```
RUN
ENTER TOTAL SALES AMOUNT? .35
ENTER AMOUNT RECEIVED? 1.00
COIN CHANGE .65

1 HALF DOLLAR
 1 DIME
 1 NICKEL

ENTER TOTAL SALES AMOUNT? 3.45
ENTER AMOUNT RECEIVED? 20.00

BILL CHANGE IS 16
 1 $10 BILL
 1 $ 5 BILL
 1 $1 BILL

COIN CHANGE .55

1 HALF DOLLAR
 1 NICKEL
```

Warning: Some versions of BASIC will round off numbers in peculiar ways (deep inside the computer) because of the way the electronics performs arithmetic. So beware! 4.9999 pennies is no fair. Write your program to avoid this kind of problem by checking for integer values for change that includes pennies.

4.   Write a program to perform conversions from selected U. S. standard measures to their metric equivalents and vice versa. Set up your program so that the user can select conversions as shown in the RUN below.

```
RUN
DO YOU WANT CONVERSIONS FOR
(1) METRIC TO U.S. STANDARD MEASURES
(2) U.S. STANDARD MEASURES TO METRIC
TYPE 1 OR 2? 1
DO YOU WANT THE LIST OF CONVERSIONS (Y OR N)? Y
SELECT CONVERSION DESIRED FROM THIS LIST:
(1) CENTIMETERS TO INCHES
(2) METERS TO FEET
(3) KILOMETERS TO MILES
(4) KILOGRAMS TO POUNDS
(5) GRAMS TO OUNCES
(6) LITERS TO QUARTS
(7) DEGREES CELSIUS TO DEGREES FAHRENHEIT
ENTER THE NUMBER OF THE CONVERSION DESIRED? 5

HOW MANY GRAMS? 10
 10 GRAMS = .35 OUNCES

DO YOU WANT CONVERSIONS FOR
(1) METRIC TO U.S. STANDARD MEASURES
(2) U.S. STANDARD MEASURES TO METRIC
TYPE 1 OR 2? 2
DO YOU WANT THE LIST OF CONVERSIONS (Y OR N)? Y
SELECT CONVERSION DESIRED FROM THIS LIST:
(1) INCHES TO CENTIMETERS
(2) FEET TO METERS
(3) MILES TO KILOMETERS
(4) POUNDS TO KILOGRAMS
(5) OUNCES TO GRAMS
(6) QUARTS TO LITERS
(7) DEGREES FAHRENHEIT TO DEGREES CELSIUS
ENTER THE NUMBER OF THE CONVERSION DESIRED? 3

HOW MANY MILES? 2
 2 MILES = 3.218 KILOMETERS

DO YOU WANT CONVERSIONS FOR
(1) METRIC TO U.S. STANDARD MEASURES
(2) U.S. STANDARD MEASURES TO METRIC
TYPE 1 OR 2? 1
DO YOU WANT THE LIST OF CONVERSIONS (Y OR N)? N
ENTER THE NUMBER OF THE CONVERSION DESIRED? 1

HOW MANY CENTIMETERS? 50
 50 CENTIMETERS = 19.5 INCHES

DO YOU WANT CONVERSIONS FOR
```

Since the list was printed above, no need to repeat it again.

And so on.

We suggest the following manner of organizing the program, making extensive use of subroutines. The main program is shown at the top; here the user selects which type of conversion is to be made. The program then branches to subroutines which list the specific conversions. From these subroutines, the program GOSUBs again, to one of fourteen sub-subroutines (seven for each "direction" of conversion).

```
DO YOU WANT CONVERSIONS FOR
(1) METRIC TO U.S. STANDARD MEASURES
(2) U.S. STANDARD MEASURES TO METRIC
TYPE 1 OR 2? 2
```

```
DO YOU WANT THE LIST OF CONVERSIONS (Y OR N)? Y
SELECT CONVERSION DESIRED FROM THIS LIST:
(1) CENTIMETERS TO INCHES
(2) METERS TO FEET
(3) KILOMETERS TO MILES
(4) KILOGRAMS TO POUNDS
(5) GRAMS TO OUNCES
(6) LITERS TO QUARTS
(7) DEGREES CELSIUS TO DEGREES FARENHEIT
ENTER THE NUMBER OF THE CONVERSION DESIRED? 5
```

```
DO YOU WANT THE LIST OF CONVERSIONS (Y OR N)? Y
SELECT CONVERSION DESIRED FROM THIS LIST:
(1) INCHES TO CENTIMETERS
(2) FEET TO METERS
(3) MILES TO KILOMETERS
(4) POUNDS TO KILOGRAMS
(5) OUNCES TO GRAMS
(6) QUARTS TO LITERS
(7) DEGREES FARENHEIT TO DEGREES CELSIUS
ENTER THE NUMBER OF THE CONVERSION DESIRED? 3
```

From any one of these subroutines, return to the subroutine that sent it, and from there, return immediately to the main program to start over again.

Here are the conversion values to include in the program.

Metric to U.S. Standard
1 centimeter = .39 inches
1 meter = 3.28 feet
1 kilometer = .62 miles
1 kilogram = 2.2 pounds
1 gram = .035 ounces
1 liter = 1.0567 quarts
$C° = 5/9(F° - 32)$

U.S. Standard to Metric
1 inch = 2.54 cm
1 ft. = .3048 meters
1 mile = 1.609 kilometers
1 pound = .45 kilograms
1 ounce = 28.35 grams
1 quart = .946 liters
$F° = 9/5C° + 32$

ANSWERS TO FINAL SELF-TEST

1.
```
10 REMARK***STARS GAME
20 LET N=INT(100*RND(1))+1
30 INPUT "ENTER YOUR GUESS"; G
35 IF G=N THEN PRINT "WINNER!!!" : GOTO 20
40 LET D=ABS(G-N)
50 IF D>=64 THEN 170
60 IF D>=32 THEN 160
70 IF D>=16 THEN 150
80 IF D>=8 THEN 140
90 IF D>=4 THEN 130
100 IF D>=2 THEN 120
110 PRINT "*";
120 PRINT "*";
130 PRINT "*";
140 PRINT "*";
150 PRINT "*";
160 PRINT "*";
170 PRINT "*" : GOTO 30
```

2.
```
10 REMARK***SIMULATION OF MATRIX ADDITION
15 REMARK INITIALIZE
20 DIM A(5,3), B(5,3), C(5,3)
25 REM LOAD A AND B ARRAY FROM DATA STATEMENTS. PRINT ARRAYS
27 PRINT "A ARRAY CONTENTS" : PRINT
30 FOR X=1 TO 5
35 FOR Y=1 TO 3
40 READ A(X,Y) : PRINT A(X,Y),
45 NEXT Y
50 PRINT
55 NEXT X : PRINT : PRINT
57 PRINT "B ARRAY CONTENTS" : PRINT
60 FOR X=1 TO 5
65 FOR Y=1 TO 3
70 READ B(X,Y) : PRINT B(X,Y),
75 NEXT Y
80 PRINT
85 NEXT X : PRINT : PRINT
90 REM ADD A + B INTO C
92 PRINT "C ARRAY CONTENTS" : PRINT
95 FOR X=1 TO 5
100 FOR Y=1 TO 3
105 LET C(X,Y)=A(X,Y)+B(X,Y) : PRINT C(X,Y),
110 NEXT Y
115 PRINT
120 NEXT X
130 REM DATA FOR A ARRAY
135 DATA 7,8,9,3,4,1,6,8,2,1,4,1,8,10,2
140 REM DATA FOR B ARRAY
145 DATA 3,6,8,2,4,7,1,3,1,8,4,9,6,6,6
```

3.

```
10 REMARK***COIN CHANGER
20 INPUT "ENTER TOTAL SALES AMOUNT"; T
30 INPUT "ENTER AMOUNT RECEIVED"; M
40 IF M<T THEN PRINT "NOT ENOUGH MONEY RECEIVED":GOTO 20
50 IF M=T THEN PRINT "EXACT CHANGE, NO CHANGE REQUIRED":PRINT:GOTO 20
60 LET C=M-T:IF C<1.00 THEN 150
65 PRINT
70 LET B=C-(C-INT(C)):PRINT "BILL CHANGE IS"; B
75 LET C=C-B
80 LET B1=INT(B/20):IF B1=0 THEN 100
85 PRINT B1; "$20 BILL"
90 LET B=B-(B1*20)
100 LET B2=INT(B/10):IF B2=0 THEN 120
105 PRINT B2; "$10 BILL"
110 LET B=B-(B2*10)
120 LET B3=INT(B/5):IF B3=0 THEN 140
125 PRINT B3; "$ 5 BILL"
130 LET B=B-(B3*5)
140 IF B<1 THEN 150
145 PRINT B; "$1 BILL":PRINT
150 LET C=INT((C+.005)*100)
152 LET C=INT(C)
155 PRINT "COIN CHANGE"; C/100:PRINT
160 IF C<50 THEN 180
170 PRINT "1 HALF DOLLAR":LET C=C-50
180 IF C<25 THEN 200
190 PRINT "1 QUARTER":LET C=C-25
200 LET D=INT(C/10):IF D=0 THEN 220
210 PRINT D; "DIME":LET C=C-(D*10)
220 LET N=INT(C/5):IF N=0 THEN 240
230 PRINT N; "NICKEL":LET C=C-(N*5)
240 IF C<1 THEN PRINT:GOTO 20
250 PRINT INT(C); "PENNY":PRINT:GOTO 20
```

4.

```
100 REM***SELECTED MEASUREMENT CONVERSIONS
110 PRINT "DO YOU WANT CONVERSIONS FOR"
120 PRINT "(1) METRIC TO U.S. STANDARD MEASURES"
130 PRINT "(2) U.S. STANDARD MEASURES TO METRIC"
140 INPUT "TYPE 1 OR 2"; N
150 ON N GOSUB 1000, 1100
160 GOTO 110

1000 REM***USER SELECTS DESIRED METRIC TO U.S. CONVERSION
1010 INPUT "DO YOU WANT THE LIST OF CONVERSIONS (Y OR N)"; A$
1020 IF A$="N" THEN 1040
1030 PRINT "SELECT CONVERSION DESIRED FROM THIS LIST:"
1031 PRINT "(1) CENTIMETERS TO INCHES"
1032 PRINT "(2) METERS TO FEET"
1033 PRINT "(3) KILOMETERS TO MILES"
1034 PRINT "(4) KILOGRAMS TO POUNDS"
1035 PRINT "(5) GRAMS TO OUNCES"
1036 PRINT "(6) LITERS TO QUARTS"
1037 PRINT "(7) DEGREES CELSIUS TO DEGREES FARENHEIT"
1040 INPUT "ENTER THE NUMBER OF THE CONVERSION DESIRED"; M : PRINT
1050 ON M GOSUB 2100,2200,2300,2400,2500,2600,2700
1060 RETURN

1100 REM***USER SELECTS DESIRED U.S. TO METRIC CONVERSION
1110 INPUT "DO YOU WANT THE LIST OF CONVERSIONS (Y OR N)"; A$
1120 IF A$="N" THEN 1140
1130 PRINT "SELECT CONVERSION DESIRED FROM THIS LIST:"
1131 PRINT "(1) INCHES TO CENTIMETERS"
1132 PRINT "(2) FEET TO METERS"
1133 PRINT "(3) MILES TO KILOMETERS"
1134 PRINT "(4) POUNDS TO KILOGRAMS"
1135 PRINT "(5) OUNCES TO GRAMS"
1136 PRINT "(6) QUARTS TO LITERS"
1137 PRINT "(7) DEGREES FARENHEIT TO DEGREES CELSIUS"
1140 INPUT "ENTER THE NUMBER OF THE CONVERSION DESIRED"; S : PRINT
1150 ON S GOSUB 3100,3200,3300,3400,3500,3600,3700
1160 RETURN

2100 REM***CM TO INCHES
2110 INPUT "HOW MANY CENTIMETERS"; C
2120 PRINT C; "CENTIMETERS ="; C*.39; "INCHES"
2130 PRINT : RETURN

2200 REM***METERS TO FEET
2210 INPUT "HOW MANY METERS"; M
2220 PRINT M; "METERS ="; M*3.28; "FEET"
2230 PRINT : RETURN

2300 REM***KM TO MILES
2310 INPUT "HOW MANY KILOMETERS"; K
2320 PRINT K; "KILOMETERS ="; K*.62; "MILES"
2330 PRINT : RETURN

2400 REM***KG TO POUNDS
2410 INPUT "HOW MANY KILOGRAMS"; K
2420 PRINT K; "KILOGRAMS ="; K*2.2; "POUNDS"
2430 PRINT : RETURN

2500 REM***GRAMS TO OUNCES
2510 INPUT "HOW MANY GRAMS"; G
2520 PRINT G; "GRAMS ="; G*.035; "OUNCES"
2530 PRINT : RETURN
```

continued on the next page

```
2600 REM***LITERS TO QUARTS
2610 INPUT "HOW MANY LITERS"; L
2620 PRINT L; "LITERS ="; L*1.0567; "QUARTS"
2630 PRINT : RETURN

2700 REM***DEGREES C TO DEGREES F
2710 INPUT "HOW MANY DEGREES CELSIUS"; D
2720 PRINT D; "DEGREES CELSIUS ="; 9*D/5+32; "DEGREES FARENHEIT"
2730 PRINT : RETURN

3100 REM***INCHES TO CM
3110 INPUT "HOW MANY INCHES"; I
3120 PRINT I; "INCHES ="; I*2.54; "CENTIMETERS"
3130 PRINT : RETURN

3200 REM***FEET TO METERS
3210 INPUT "HOW MANY FEET"; F
3220 PRINT F; "FEET ="; F*.3048; "METERS"
3230 PRINT : RETURN

3300 REM***MILES TO KM
3310 INPUT "HOW MANY MILES"; M
3320 PRINT M; "MILES ="; M*1.609; "KILOMETERS"
3330 PRINT : RETURN

3400 REM***POUNDS TO KG
3410 INPUT "HOW MANY POUNDS"; P
3420 PRINT P; "POUNDS ="; P*.45; "KILOGRAMS"
3430 PRINT : RETURN

3500 REM***OUNCES TO GRAMS
3510 INPUT "HOW MANY OUNCES"; O
3520 PRINT O; "OUNCES ="; O*28.35; "GRAMS"
3530 PRINT : RETURN

3600 REM***QUARTS TO LITERS
3610 INPUT "HOW MANY QUARTS"; Q
3620 PRINT Q; "QUARTS ="; Q*.946; "LITERS"
3630 PRINT : RETURN

3700 REM***DEGREES F TO DEGREES C
3710 INPUT "HOW MANY DEGREES FARENHEIT"; D
3720 PRINT D; "DEGREES FARENHEIT ="; 5/9*(D-32); "DEGREES CELSIUS"
3730 PRINT : RETURN
```

Appendixes

PERSONAL COMPUTING PERIODICALS

Personal Computing
Benwill Publishing Corp.
167 Corey Rd.
Brookline, MA 02146

Popular Computing
Box 272
Calabasas, CA 91302

On-Line
D.H. Beetle
24695 Santa Cruz Hwy.
Los Gatos, CA 95030

BYTE
70 Main St.
Peterborough, NH

Computers & People
815 Washington St.
Newtonville, MA 02160

PET User Notes
P.O. Box 371
Montgomeryville, PA 18936

Creative Computing
P.O. Box 789-M
Morristown, NJ 07960

Calculators/computers
P.O. Box 310
Menlo Park, CA 94025

People's Computers
P.O. Box E
Menlo Park, CA 94025

Dr. Dobb's Journal of Computer
  Calisthenics & Orthodontia
P.O. Box E
Menlo Park, CA 94025

Computer Notes
MITS
2450 Alamo SE
Albuquerque, NM 87108

COMPUTE
National Semiconductor
2900 Semiconductor Dr.
Santa Clara, CA 95051

Data General Education News
Data General Corp.
Southboro, MA

Kilobaud
The Small Computer Magazine
Peterboro, NH 03458

TRS-80 Users Group Newsletter
7554 Southgate Road
Fayetteville, NC 28304

EDU
Education Products Group
Digital Equipment Corp.
146 Main St.
Maynard, MA 01754

HP Educational Newsletter
Hewlett Packard
5303 Stevens Creek Blvd.
Santa Clara, CA 95053

Microcomputer News
Intel Corporation
3065 Bowers Ave.
Santa Clara, CA 95051

BASIC FUNCTIONS

This Appendix describes some of the more common and useful functions included in most versions of BASIC used on personal computers. It is by no means an exhaustive list, and the functions may perform differently on the computer you use. Check the reference manual for your computer system for the complete list of functions available in your version of BASIC.

Arithmetic Functions

(In the following, "exp" stands for any BASIC expression, variable, or number.)

ABS(exp): Gives the absolute value of the expression, i.e., ABS(A) = A if
A >= 0, ABS(A) = −A if A < 0.
Example: IF ABS(X−G) >= 64 THEN PRINT "*"

EXP(exp): Computes the exponential function, base e, where e =
2.71828 . . . . Usually there is an upper limit on the value of the variable. In MICROSOFT™ BASIC, the value in the parentheses must be
less than 87.3365.
Examples: B = EXP(X)
             Y = C*EXP(−A*T)

FRE(0): Used to determine how much space is left in the computer's memory that is not being used by BASIC or the program stored in memory.
Enter it in a print statement, with zero in the parentheses, and the
number of unused bytes is given.
Example: PRINT FRE(0)
See also FRE(string variable) under String Functions.

INT(exp): Computes the greatest integer less than or equal to exp. Notice
that INT(3.14) = 3, but INT(−3.14) = −4. You may wish to check the
reference manual for your version of BASIC for the similar function
FIX.

LOG(exp): Gives the natural logarithm, base e, of exp.
Example: D = LOG(1 + X↑2)

RND(parameter): Generates a random number between 0 and 1 with control by the parameter value. For example, in MICROSOFT™ BASIC,
any positive value in the parentheses gives a new random number each
time. A zero in the parentheses gives the same random number as was
last generated by a RND function. Each different negative number (including fractions) gives a different random number, but the same random number is always given for the same negative value in the

parentheses. The RND function may not work as described above for other versions of BASIC, so check your reference manual for details.

SGN(exp): Gives a 1 if the expression evaluates to a positive value (>0); gives a 0 if the expression evaluates to zero (= 0); gives a −1 if the expression evaluates to a negative value (<0).
Example: ON SGN(X) + 2 GOTO 100, 200, 300
If X is negative, the above statement will branch to line 100; If X = 0, it will branch to line 200; if X is positive, it will branch to line 300.

SQR(exp): Gives the positive square root of exp. Expression in parentheses must be zero or a positive value (no negative values).

Trigonometric Functions

SIN(exp), COS(exp), TAN(exp), ATN(exp): The SIN, COS, and TAN functions give the sine, cosine, or tangent of exp, where exp is assumed to be given in radians. ATN computes the principal value of the arctangent, in radians. The value of ATN(exp) will be in the range:
$-\pi/2 < ATN(exp) < \pi/2$.

Output Positioning Functions

TAB(exp): Spaces to the character position indicated by the evaluated expression, variable, or value in the parentheses. Only used in PRINT statements. If the print head or CRT cursor is already past the character position indicated in the parentheses, TAB has no effect. No negative values allowed. Remember, the leftmost space in a line is character position 0 (zero), then 1, 2, and so on up to 71 on a teletypewriter standard line. (This may vary for CRT's and other hard copy printers.)

SPC(exp): Used in print statements to space over the number of spaces indicated by the expression, variable, or value in the parentheses.
Example: PRINT X; SPC(5); Y; SPC(5); 2

String Functions

ASC(string): Gives the ASCII code numeric value for the first character in a string.
Example: PRINT ASC(B$)

CHR$(exp): Converts a number to the corresponding ASCII character.
Example: The ASCII code number 7 rings the bell on a teletypewriter

or causes a beep on many CRT's. To ring the bell, use CHR$(7) in a PRINT statement, like this: PRINT CHR$(7)

FRE(string variable): Gives the number of free (unused) bytes in the memory's reserved string space. See also FRE function under Arithmetic Functions.

INSTR(string variable, substring variable),

INSTR(start search point, string variable, substring variable): Gives the character position where first occurrence of the substring is found in the main string. INSTR stands for In String, and it searches through the main string until it finds the substring. If the substring is not found, or if the main string is a "null string" (a string containing no characters), INSTR gives a zero. If the substring is a null string, it gives a 1. The second form above allows the user to indicate where in the main string to start the search for the substring, by indicating the character position for starting the search.

    Examples: PRINT INSTR(X$,Y$)
                  PRINT INSTR(X$,"THE")
                  PRINT INSTR(8,A$+B$,Y$)

Notice that the main string or the substring can be indicated by string variables, string expressions (strings that are "strung together" or connected with "+"), or string literals (characters enclosed by quotation marks).

LEFT$(string, length): Gives the leftmost characters in a string, including the number of characters indicated by the value given for length.

    Example: B$ = LEFT$(X$,3)

RIGHT$(string, length): Gives the rightmost characters in a string, including the number of characters indicated by the value given for the length.

    Example: C$ = RIGHT$(Y$,4)

MID$(string, start position),

MID$(string, start position, length): First form gives the portion of the string from the character at the start position to the right end of the string. Second form gives the portion of the string from the character at the start position and including as many more characters toward the right end of the string as indicated by the length value.

    Examples: PRINT MID$ (X$,3)
                  PRINT MID$ (X$,3,5)

LEN(string): Gives the number of characters included in the string; spaces are always counted as characters.

    Examples: FOR K – 1 TO LEN(X$)

STR$(exp): Converts a numeric expression to a string. The minus sign in a negative value is included in the string, and the leading space for the assumed "+" in a positive value is included in the string.

Example: B$ = STR$(X*Y)

VAL(string): Converts a string representation of a number to a numeric value. String must be numeric character.

Example: X$ = "33.3"

X = VAL(X$)

ASCII CHARACTER CODES

Decimal	Character	Decimal	Character	Decimal	Character
000	NUL	043	+	086	V
001	SOH	044	'	087	W
002	STX	045	–	088	X
003	ETX	046	.	089	Y
004	EOT	047	/	090	Z
005	ENQ	048	0	091	[
006	ACK	049	1	092	\
007	BEL	050	2	093	]
008	BS	051	3	094	↑
009	HT	052	4	095	←
010	LF	053	5	096	`
011	VT	054	6	097	a
012	FF	055	7	098	b
013	CR	056	8	099	c
014	SO	057	9	100	d
015	SI	058	:	101	e
016	DLE	059	;	102	f
017	DC1	060	<	103	g
018	DC2	061	=	104	h
019	DC3	062	>	105	i
020	DC4	063	?	106	j
021	NAK	064	@	107	k
022	SYN	065	A	108	l
023	ETB	066	B	109	m
024	CAN	067	C	110	n
025	EM	068	D	111	o
026	SUB	069	E	112	p
027	ESCAPE	070	F	113	q
028	FS	071	G	114	r
029	GS	072	H	115	s
030	RS	073	I	116	t
031	US	074	J	117	u
032	SPACE	075	K	118	v
033	!	076	L	119	w
034	"	077	M	120	x
035	#	078	N	121	y
036	$	079	O	122	z
037	%	080	P	123	{
038	&	081	Q	124		
039	'	082	R	125	}
040	(	083	S	126	~
041	)	084	T	127	DEL
042	*	085	U		

LF = Line Feed   FF = Form Feed   CR = Carriage Return   DEL = Delete

Index